THE BOOK OF ACTS
A SOCIAL JUSTICE DEVOTIONAL COMMENTARY

Jim Reiher

© Jim Reiher, 2014

Published 2014 by UNOH Publishing

2/6–12 Airlie Avenue, Dandenong
Victoria 3175, Australia
www.unoh.org/publishing

National Library of Australia Cataloguing-in-Publication entry : (paperback)

Creator:	Reiher, Jim, author.
Title:	The book of Acts : a social justice devotional commentary / Jim Reiher.
ISBN:	9780994202307 (paperback)
Subjects:	Bible. Acts--Commentaries. Bible. Acts--Theology. Social justice--Religious aspects. Political theology.

Dewey Number: 226.6

Author: Jim Reiher
Design: Les Colston at Urban Zeal
Editor: Darren Cronshaw

The first Christians gave a blueprint for the church to follow. It is more radical than many of us have thought. Jim Reiher, in his typically engaging manner, shows us just how radical the early church really was. This series of studies will not only challenge you; they will make you want to keep going back to the Book of Acts to emulate the early Christians in following our Lord.

Tim Costello, CEO of World Vision Australia

Courage to change is a virtue Micah promotes within our network. This begins with recovering a missionary understanding of God and requires us to set time aside to re read the Bible through a missional lens. As we do this we will begin perceiving our role in the world as Disciples of Christ.
Jim Reiher's devotional commentary on the Book of Acts provides us with an inspiring and challenging guide to provoke us to reflect and act on issues such as a simple lifestyle, being present with marginalised people and seeing the future of God in them, identifying with those who are oppressed, growing in our awareness of injustice and how to respond to it.
I encourage you to personally, within your family, within your church and amongst your friends and colleagues to set time aside and work through the 60 studies contained in this book. But be aware – it will take courage to think, to hope and to act on what you learn.

Sheryl Haw, International Director, Micah Network

The devotional commentary presents a thread line of Jim's insights weaving a mosaic of personal and skillful conviction. We are left considering what it means to live justice beyond a revolutionary tactic of self determination. The book is a tapestry of justice and character in harmonious colours of selected intention. We find ourselves heading into our own missionary journeys wanting to live right while righting wrongs.

Christine MacMillan, World Evangelical Alliance Chair, WEA Global Human Trafficking Taskforce

Straightforward, honest, insightful and engaging' — these words not only describe Jim Reiher the man, but are also clearly reflected in the writing of this wonderful devotional commentary of the Book of Acts. Jim has a unique ability to make the pages of the ancient text come to life. He not only provides outstanding scholarly research on the Book of Acts, but also takes the reader past mere head knowledge to a heart-to-heart engagement with the men and women of the early church, and the Holy Spirit who was so active amongst them. This commentary will not fail to challenge and inspire.

Lynn Moresi, Bible teacher on the teaching Team at CityLife Church, and Theology Lecturer for Tabor Victoria

This series of studies on the Book of Acts by my friend, Jim Reiher, is excellent in every way. They are well written, well informed, accessible and practical. They provide resource material that would enrich and aid any group seeking to discover how the Book of Acts speaks to the world in which we find ourselves.

Kevin Giles (ThD), pastor, theologian, author and long time student of the writings of St Luke

Jim Reiher is not afraid of asking hard questions. Be prepared to be challenged as you read this book. But Jim's primary concern is not to correct our beliefs. His desire is that the reader's life may be transformed by the stories in Acts, resulting in a fresh orientation towards the heart of God. One may not agree with every detail of Jim's interpretation of Acts. Yet it would be unwise to reject the call to authentic discipleship advocated in this valuable devotional commentary. So, enjoy Jim's many provocative challenges, and argue with him if you like. But importantly, reflect on what it means to follow Jesus, and put it into practice.

Dr. Siu Fung Wu, Theologian, lecturer, PhD in Paul and the Book of Romans

Home Bible Study/fellowship groups are very important in the life of the Church and the growth of individuals. Finding good study material is always a challenge. Jim Reiher's studies on Acts will fill a real need and be enjoyed by many.

Lynley Giles, President of CBE, Victoria. Marriage Educator/Marriage Counsellor

Jim Reiher brings a scholar's mind, a passion for the Holy Spirit, and a social activist's experiences, to the study of Acts. Few people are more gifted to help us understand what was first happening in Acts and then find dynamic ways to respond to our contexts today. In many ways Jim is doing for Acts what Ched Myers did for Mark's Gospel and Wes Howard Brooks did for John's Gospel. If you want to engage God's world as a Spirit-filled follower of Jesus in deeper ways, then this book is well worth your prayerful and thoughtful reading, reflection and action.

Ash Barker, Convener, International Society for Urban Mission (newurbanworld.org) and author of 'Slum Life Rising' and 'Make Poverty Personal'

Contents

Acknowledgements	9
Foreword	11
Introduction	13

Part 1: From the Ascension of Christ to the death of Stephen

Acts 1 — 19
1) Acts 1:1. Theophilus who? — 19
2) Acts 1:6-9. Not what Jesus wants us to talk about — 21
Getting a handle on how the Book of Acts will proceed — 23
3) Acts 1:12-26. Making major decisions in life — 23

Acts 2 — 27
4) Acts 2. Baptism in the Spirit — 27
5) Acts 2:41-47 and Acts 4:32-37. Radical living for radical people — 30
6) Acts 2:42. Devoted to the apostles' teaching — 33

Acts 3 — 37
7) Acts 3:6. Penniless apostles — 37
8) Acts 3:12. The wrong focus — 41
9) Acts 3:19. Repentance *then* refreshing — 43

Acts 4 — 47
10) Acts 4:12. Is Jesus the *only* way to God? — 47

Acts 5 — 67
11) Acts 5:1-11. Ananias and Sapphira were dead wrong! — 67
12) Acts 5:29. Civil disobedience — 71
13) Acts 5:34. Advocacy — 75

Acts 6 — 79
14) Acts 6:1. Dealing with complaints — 79
15) Acts 6:1-4. Caring for the poor versus preaching — 81

Acts 7 — 83
16) Acts 7:48-49. God does not dwell in houses built by people — 85
17) Acts 7:60. I'm just human — 87

Acts 8 — 89
18) Acts 8:2. It is okay to mourn — 89
19) Acts 8:17-23. The origin of the sin of 'Simony' — 91

Part 2: The conversion of Paul to the council of Jerusalem

Acts 9 — 95
The Conversion of the Apostle Paul — 95
20) Acts 9:10-17. Does God sometimes miss the latest news? — 97
21) Acts 9:43. Peter stays with Simon the Tanner — 98

Acts 10 — 101
22) Acts 10:28. No longer call anyone 'unholy or unclean' — 101
23) Acts 10:34-43. Peter's other words to Cornelius — 104

Acts 11 — 109
24) Acts 11:22-26. Barnabas the encourager — 109

Acts 12 — 113
25) Acts 12:1-12. God does not treat us all the same — 113
26) Acts 12:12-16. The home of Mary — 115
27) Acts 12:15. Faith and Prayer — 118
28) Acts 12:17. Report these things to James — 121

Acts 13 — 125
The start of Paul's missionary journeys — 125
29) Acts 13:13. Handling people who disappoint us — 125
30) Acts 13:43. Continue in the grace of God — 129

Acts 14 — 133
31) Acts 14: 8-20. Cross cultural blunders — 133

Acts 15 — 137
32) Acts 15:1-29. When the church has to solve a contentious problem — 137
33) Acts 15:36-40. A friendship is severed — 140

Part 3: The 2nd and 3rd Missionary Journeys of Paul

Acts 16 — 147

34) Acts 16:1-3. Paul has Timothy circumcised. What is going on? — 147
35) Acts 16:10. Luke becomes a character in the story — 151
36) Acts 16:16-18. A demon-possessed fortune-telling slave girl — 155
37) Acts 16:16-18. Paul's laid back attitude to demons — 159
38) Acts 16:25. Rejoicing in troubles — 160
39) Acts 16:35-39. Paul uses the legal system — 163

Acts 17 — 167

40) Acts 17:10-12. What makes us 'noble minded' — 167
41) Acts 17:18-34. How to live in a multicultural/multi-faith community — 169

Acts 18 — 175

42) Acts 18:1-3. Meet Priscilla and Aquila — 175
Women in the Book of Acts — *179*
43) Acts 18:3. Paul was a 'tradie' — 180
44) Acts 18:17. Persecution that backfired — 181

Acts 19 — 187

The 3rd missionary journey that does not end well — 187
45) Acts 19:19. Is book burning ever a good idea? — 188
46) Acts 19:37. Living side by side with other faiths — 191

Acts 20 — 197

47) Acts 20:2-3. Paul writes the book of Romans — 197
48) Acts 20:17,28-31. Church leaders can be the problem! — 202
49) Acts 20:33-34. Money is not our focus — 207
50) Acts 20:35. A quote from Jesus — 211

Acts 21 — 217

51) Acts 21:4,10-12. *Not* listening to the Holy Spirit — 217

Part 4: Paul in prison

Paul's jail time — *221*

Acts 22 — **223**
52) Acts 22. Roman soldiers and governors in Acts — 223

Acts 23 — **229**
53) Acts 23:12,13. An oath to commit murder — 229

Acts 24 — **233**
54) Acts 24:27. Paul in prison in Caesarea — 233

Acts 25 — **237**
55) Acts 25:13ff. A King meets an Apostle — 237

Acts 26 — **241**
56) Acts 26:28. Agrippa's famous words — 241

Acts 27 — **245**
57) Acts 27. Shipwreck and great danger — 245

Acts 28 — **249**
58) Acts 28:1-5. Do bad things only happen to bad people? — 249
59) Acts 28:1-9. Miraculous healings and/or medicinal aid? — 251
60) Acts 28:30-31. Paul in Rome — 254

Acts has ended, but what did happen to Paul? — *257*

Index of characters in Acts — 260

Acknowledgements

You can't be the person you are, or do the things you do, without the accumulated impact of everyone who crosses your path. Some lives that touch ours cause us pain and some cause us joy (and usually all lives give us a bit of both), but the sum total of it all is *who we are now*. So, thanks for all the joyful and painful moments that each and every one of my friends have been a part of over my lifetime.

I couldn't have done this book without you!

This book has been a long time coming. It is something I have wanted to do for many years. Thanks to all who have inputted into my life in ways that helped me grow to love the Book of Acts and its stories.

Thanks to the Christians I met when I was first interested in the faith: the ones who helped me catch a deep love for the New Testament stories. It goes right back over 50 years to my 'Sunday School' days when Mrs Pearce taught me at the Collaroy Plateau Methodist Sunday School. She was the first person I remember who opened up some of those incredible stories and events to me.

Like most kids of that generation, I stopped going to church when I was old enough to 'decide for myself'. But in my mid-teens I did get interested in a 'fellowship group'. That particular group loved the Bible. We would meet one evening a week to read some of the stories and talk about them. I still remember Alan and Pam, Gary, John and Susie, Sue, and others I have lost contact with over the decades. Their love for the Bible was infectious, and our eagerness to hear the stories and weigh how they applied to our lives has stayed with me.

Then there were the people I met as a young adult in my 20s and 30s: those who became my friends and 'fellow travellers' as we sought to read the New Testament and apply the principles and lessons to our own daily situations. There was Merridie and Luke; Glen and Penny; Brian and Sue-Ellen; and others. They were some of my closest friends at the time.

As life moves on, the realities of life change. People move on. Some of my dearest friends back then no longer have any interest in the Christian faith or the Bible. Others still do. But that is how it is: we are all on our own journeys. Someone's current state does not change how much I feel privileged to have shared a decade of my life with each and every one of them all those years ago.

In more recent decades, others have impacted my personal Christian journey. My wife Julie; my four children Pete, Daniel, Timothy and Gabi; my friends from Tabor College while I was there: John Capper, Wynand de Kock, Cheryl McCallum, Les Henson and others. My students likewise, some of whom have well and truly surpassed me in their academic achievements, others of whom will do just that, in the years ahead: Siu Fung Wu, Lynn, Michelle, Vikki, and others.

Then there are my friends I met through my political activity for a decade: Rob, Dave, and Colleen especially – people who showed me that faith and working for justice are most compatible companions!

Of course there are also my friends from Urban Neighbours of Hope (UNOH), an amazing bunch of people, all on a journey together. Ash and Anji (formerly with UNOH), Jon, Lisa, Dave, Denise … there are too many to name individually, but all of them have been a contributing part, in big or small ways, in my own story.

There are also the associated friends of UNOH who support and engage with UNOH activities. The 'Companions' and other UNOH workers or friends that I was more a part of: Sharon; Phill and Jacquie; Russell, Liz, Rachel and Reuben; James and Bec - Bec: thanks for being one of the proof readers of this volume! Likewise to the other proof readers: David Gallus, Gabriel Hingley, Nils von Kalm, Lynette Leach and Angela Weekes, and Les Colston for the design and layout of the book – thanks heaps.

Thanks everyone. You are all a part of the mosaic that makes up my life.

Foreword

This book is a sign of a healthy and encouraging development that has been taking place in evangelical circles in the West and beyond during the last few decades. I refer to the development that the subtitle of the book clearly reflects: *Social Justice Devotional Commentary*. A devotional commentary based on a New Testament book, yet dealing with themes such as advocacy, justice, civil disobedience, multiculturalism, and identifying with the marginalized? Are not these themes traditionally related to subversive movements? How can a "devotion" that takes Scripture as its starting point be related to activities that perturb the social order?

Quite likely, these are the kinds of questions that the subtitle of this book will raise in the minds of many prospective readers. From their viewpoint, subversion of the status quo does not seem to fit into a program of activities to bring about the kind of social change that is desirable from a Christian perspective!

The biblical reflections that Jim Reiher presents here, however, go a long way to show the importance that subversion of the dominant powers for the sake of social justice had for the church in the first century as portrayed in Acts. Beyond that, his reflections help us to see the importance that subversion for the sake of social justice has for the life and mission of the church today. His line of thinking is very much in line with Paul's exhortation: "Do not conform any longer to the pattern of this world, but be transformed by the renewing of your mind" (Rom. 12:2). What does nonconformity to "the pattern of this world" mean today, in a world ruled by Mammon, obsessed with the faith-ideology of consumerism, and deeply affected by greed? What does it mean in a world where the distance between the rich and the poor continues to increase, where millions and millions of people are unable to cover their basic needs, where racial discrimination is taken for granted, and where law and order are placed at the service of injustice?

Under the influence of secular thinking, and especially of the Enlightenment, the church of modern times in the West (and elsewhere, largely by dissemination from the West) made a divorce between the Christian faith and socioeconomic and political life. As a result, Christianity, especially in Protestant circles, retreated into the religious sphere - the sphere of moral and spiritual values that were regarded as relevant to the believer's individual life but set apart from social realities. From this perspective, it made no sense to talk about "a social justice devotional commentary" based on the book of Acts!

The 1974 *Lausanne Covenant* was a sign of the change of perspective that took place in evangelical circles during the second half of the twentieth century - a change that opened the door to the recovery of the wider dimensions of the Gospel and of the Christian mission. Paragraph 5 of the Lausanne Covenant points to that change in the following terms: "We affirm that God is both the Creator and the Judge of all men. We therefore should share his concern for justice and reconciliation throughout human society and for the liberation of men and women from every kind of oppression. Because men and women are made in the image of God, every person, regardless of race, religion, colour, culture, class, sex or age, has an intrinsic dignity because of which he or she should be respected and served, not exploited. Here too we express penitence both for our neglect and for having sometimes regarded evangelism and social concern as mutually exclusive. . . . The message of salvation implies also a message of judgment upon every form of alienation, oppression and discrimination, and should not be afraid to denounce evil and injustice wherever they exist. When people receive Christ they are born again into his kingdom and must seek not only to exhibit but also to spread righteousness [better: justice] in the midst of an unrighteous [better: unjust] world. The salvation we claim should be transforming us in the totality of our personal and social responsibilities. Faith without works is dead."

Thank you, Jim, for writing this devotional commentary! I warmly welcome its publication as a very valuable incentive for the people of God to implement in practical life the kind of subversion that the wonderful historical statement that I have quoted represents.

C. René Padilla
President Emeritus
Kairos Foundation

Introduction

The Book of Acts has always been one of my favourite books in the New Testament. It is right up there in my favourite three with Luke and James.

Acts is a long and detailed story. It was written (most historians and theologians agree) by Luke – the same writer who wrote the Gospel named after him. He wrote Acts as the sequel. The Gospel of Luke was about the life and work and teachings of Jesus. Acts picks up after Jesus has been crucified and raised from the dead: it is about what happened after that. The book covers the first 30 or so years of the church, from the resurrection in c. 30 A.D. to about 62 A.D.

Acts starts with Jesus saying goodbye to his followers and 'ascending into heaven' (1:9-12). It then describes the life and work of the disciples of Jesus. That is initially the 11 who were left (remembering that Judas was dead by then) and the wider group of over 100 followers in Jerusalem. That group expands quite quickly into the thousands as the story unfolds.

The reasons for that growth are seen in the Book of Acts itself. The early Christians have a strange encounter in chapter 2 where they become empowered by God's Spirit to be able to speak and act with great boldness and miraculous activity. When a cripple is healed, it causes a lot of interest in the apostles and their message. They always talk about 'this Jesus who you crucified', and more and more people embrace their message for themselves.

As the book continues, there is persecution by those who killed Jesus. They don't like being talked about negatively, and they sure don't like the disciples' message about Jesus being the Messiah. But persecution caused more zeal, and more zeal saw more people join the church!

Soon an important character is introduced into the story. At the end of chapter 7 we meet Saul, a man who would later be known as the Apostle Paul. He is initially a persecutor of Christians and a good religious Jew. He is introduced to us as a part of the execution squad for the first murder of a Christian in Jerusalem: Stephen. But Saul would soon have a personal encounter with the risen Christ (chapter 9) that changed him forever. He then joined the group he was previously persecuting!

Much of the rest of the Book of Acts is about Paul's travels, teachings and exploits. From chapter 15 onwards it is pretty well all about Paul. He does a number of so called 'missionary journeys', starting churches in numerous cities around the Roman Empire.

During the 3rd journey, Paul is arrested in Jerusalem. From Chapter 20/21 to the end of the book (in chapter 28) Paul is in a series of jails and has a number of trials. He is hauled in front of governors and a king, and the story ends with him in a kind of 'open imprisonment' in Rome. There he is awaiting trial before the Emperor Nero.

The book ends without telling us what the outcome of that trial was. The most logical reason for that is that this must have been the time when Luke finished writing the book. Luke was a historian and storyteller, not a prophet who could predict the future. He could only tell us the story up to where it was at, 'at the time of writing'.

Luke, the author of Acts, appears in the story in places, from chapter 16 onwards, but not by name. He becomes a travelling companion of Paul's, and so we see Luke in third person plural moments when he says, 'we went here... and we went there'. He is with Paul right at the end of the book as well, in Rome - probably serving him in his open imprisonment.

Acts has some wonderful dialogues, stories and lessons for us to benefit from. This ancient piece of literature is bubbling with life application and relevance for today. I hope in this series of studies on Acts, to share some of those gems with you.

This book can be used by an individual alone, in their quiet moments with God, or it can be used in group Bible studies, or sharing times. There are questions at the end of each devotion for reflection (if alone) or discussion (if in a group). Often the questions assume you are in a group, and will at times ask you to share your thoughts on a particular question with others, if you so wish to. The questions at the end of each devotion begin with a different verse or verses from scripture, that relate to the theme being discussed. They are there to look up and consider, and weigh along with the devotion itself. They will often come from the letters of Paul – partly because he is such a prominent figure in the Book of Acts, and partly because so many of his letters were written during the events described in the Book of Acts. And at other times there will be references to Christ and occasionally to the Old Testament.

To make the most of each devotion, it would be helpful to have read the relevant chapter from Acts, beforehand. Sometimes the devotions are about a whole story, and at other times about a single statement made (in the middle of a story). That is why it is helpful to re-read the whole chapter the devotion relates to, first, before doing the study. (That is called keeping things in 'context').

This book will be quoting from either the TNIV 2004, or its next revision, the NIV Church Bible 2011, unless otherwise stated. (Both are gender inclusive translations).

Part One:
From the Ascension of Christ to the death of Stephen

ACTS 1

Read Acts 1 before reflecting on the first three studies

1) Acts 1:1. Theophilus who?

Acts is written to a man called Theophilus. Verse 1: 'In my former book, Theophilus, I wrote about all that Jesus began to do and teach…' Well now, here is my second account. Luke is of course, here referring to his first book: the Gospel of Luke.

The Gospel of Luke starts with a reference to the same person: in Luke 1:3 and 4, we see that the book is addressed by Luke to Theophilus. He wrote the original gospel to him, '… since I myself have carefully investigated everything from the beginning, I too decided to write an orderly account for you, most excellent Theophilus, so that you might know the certainty of the things you have been taught.'

So, both books were written to the same guy: a friend of Luke's. But what do we know about him? Nothing, other than what we have here in these two short passages.

Some scholars will say that Theophilus was not an actual person but is anyone who is 'loved of God'. After all, that is the literal meaning of the name, Theophilus. While that is possible, and Luke might be writing to all who see themselves as God's beloved, the curious thing is that in one reference he is 'most excellent Theophilus', and in the other he is just 'Theophilus'. Using 'most excellent' in the gospel seems to add to the likelihood that it is a real individual being addressed. (It was a real name for individuals, after all).

It is curious that in the gospel of Luke the addressee is called 'most excellent Theophilus' whereas in Acts he is just called 'Theophilus'. Why the change? Is he no longer 'most excellent'? Why did Luke drop the fancy title in the second book?

Besides the possibility that Luke had simply got to know the gentleman better over time, and so dropped the formalities, there are two other main theories.

1) Perhaps Theophilus was originally a prominent member of the community; or held

a high post in the public service; or was of the nobility: 'most excellent' is quite an honourable title. (It will appear three more times in the writings of Luke: Acts 23:26; 24:3; and 26:25 – in all three cases being used of the Roman Governor.)

This theory suggests that when Luke first knew him, Theophilus was not a Christian, and Luke was addressing him in a manner he would have expected. That is how the *gospel* addresses him but not the book of Acts.

Perhaps in-between receiving the gospel and receiving the book of Acts, the gospel itself helped to convert him. When he converted, he either felt a call to abandon his high office, or perhaps lost his job or position because of his faith. For one reason or another he was no longer in that high role. Therefore in the second book, Luke just calls him 'Theophilus'.

2) Alternatively, he was indeed originally a prominent member of the community, or held a high post in the public service. He then became a Christian in-between the Gospel of Luke and the Book of Acts. But in this theory he does not lose his job. He is now a brother in Christ. In the church, people did not concern themselves with titles and status that the world holds as important. In the church everyone is equal and no one is 'more excellent' than anyone else.

So we don't have to speculate that he lost his job or felt compelled to give it up. He may still have had it! But now, as far as other Christians are concerned, he is a brother and a friend. Not an 'upper class' member, a cut above the rest, to be addressed accordingly.

I prefer the second theory. It sounds a lot more like Paul (Galatians 3:28; 1 Timothy 2:9-10 where he exhorts rich women not to show off their wealth in their jewelry, clothing and hair styles) and James (James 2:1-6), and even more importantly, it is consistent with Jesus:

> Jesus called them together and said, 'You know that those who are regarded as rulers of the Gentiles lord it over them, and their high officials exercise authority over them. Not so with you. Instead whoever wants to be great among you must be your servant, and whoever wants to be first must be the slave of all. For even the Son of Man did not come to be served but to serve, and to give his life as a ransom for many (Mark 10:42-45).

'Most excellent Theophilus' found faith, and became a brother. After that, he is just 'Theophilus'.

None of us should be worried about titles and worldly honours. They are distractions and undermine humility. They can foster pride and feelings of entitlement. We might achieve some things that would give us worldly titles and honours, but we should not be using those titles and reminding folk of those honours in the church. We would do well to follow the teaching of Jesus and the example of Theophilus and Luke.

Reading:
Consider Jesus' words in Matthew 23:1-12.

Asking the hard questions:
How do these words of Jesus affect you? Is it possible that we have fallen into the snare of the world around us by copying their practices and traditions? How might we be a bit too proud of our titles and achievements?

2) Acts 1:6-9. Not what Jesus wants to talk about

The Book of Acts begins with Jesus talking to his disciples after his resurrection. He is about to ascend into heaven (1:9). Before he leaves them, a small fragment of their final conversation is captured by Luke. It is a strange dialogue.

> So when they met together, they asked him, 'Lord, are you at this time going to restore the kingdom to Israel?' He said to them: 'It is not for you to know times or dates the Father has set by his own authority, but you will receive power when the Holy Spirit comes upon you; and you will be my witnesses in Jerusalem, and in all Judea and Samaria, and to the ends of the earth.' And after he had said this, he was taken up before their very eyes, and a cloud hid him from their sight (1:6-9).

The disciples wanted Jesus to talk to them about 'the end times'. They wanted to know if now was the time when he would 'restore the kingdom to Israel'. That seems to be a reference to some kind of political Jewish empire, dominated by the Messiah and running the world. They were clearly programmed by their upbringing and teaching to think that was to be expected or somehow desired.

But Jesus was not interested in that. He deflects their comments, focusing on what he wants to emphasise.

The disciples had been with Jesus for over three years. They had been with him 24/7 much of that time. They had heard him teach. They had seen him do his miracles. They had gone out two by two spreading the message of Jesus. They had cast out demons and been used by God to do miracles themselves. They would have sat at the feet of Jesus when he gave the Sermon on the Mount. They would have heard his parables when they were first taught. They were there when he first said 'the greatest commandment is to love God and love your neighbour'. They should have known him better than anyone else in the world!

Yet here, just as he is about to leave them, they want to talk about something that is of no interest to Jesus at all.

You know what that says to us today? It says that we need to be careful not to pretend to know Jesus really well. We might have been going to church for years, reading the Bible for ages, and praying regularly. We might think we have it all worked out; but the simple reality is that we often get it wrong. We don't speak with absolute clarity and certainty for Jesus, or know his priorities perfectly. We are flawed and we have been influenced by our upbringing and teachings from our religious traditions just as much as Jesus' disciples were from theirs.

We can think we know what the most important topics are, and we might think that Jesus is just as concerned about them as we are. However, the truth is that if we really *listen to Jesus* we might just find out that he is interested in other things.

The message of Acts 1:6-9 is a message of humility. Let's not be overconfident that we speak the very words and thoughts of Jesus, or know what his priorities are. Let's be prepared to be surprised by Jesus. Just maybe the things we want to talk about all the time are not the things he wants us to talk about!

Reading:
Read Mark 10:13-16.

Asking the hard questions:
Think about how the disciples assumed that they knew Jesus so well here. They had been with him for years; they knew what he needed. They knew what he was thinking. Didn't they? Clearly not all the time!

Think about the possibility that there might just have been times in our lives when we presumed to be speaking for Jesus when really we were just reflecting something about ourselves. How can we avoid doing that?

Getting a handle on how the Book of Acts proceeds

In Acts 1, Luke uses a statement of Jesus to serve as almost a kind of 'index' to the Book of Acts. Note what Jesus said to his followers in 1:8: '...you will receive power when the Holy Spirit comes upon you; and you will be my witnesses in Jerusalem, and in all Judea and Samaria, and to the ends of the earth.'

That really sums up the following 27 chapters in the order that they travel in:

Chapter 2 – 'You will receive power when the Holy Spirit comes upon you'

Chapters 3-7 – 'and you will be my witnesses in Jerusalem'

Chapter 8-12 – 'and in all Judea and Samaria'

Chapters 13-28 – 'and to the ends of the earth.'

The book more or less follows that short summary. As it unfolds, we read some of the incredible stories that have great life application for us still to this day.

3) Acts 1:12-26. Making major decisions in life

If you read the rest of Acts 1, you get the story of the replacement of Judas. This is a fascinating story that is hardly ever used by Bible teachers and preachers today. The reason it is not used is that it ends with the disciples drawing lots to decide a major decision, and we don't really want to encourage people today to 'not think, not pray, just draw lots and let God tell you how to make your decisions from day to day'!

Sadly, that should NOT be the message one draws from the story if they do read it, for pretty glaring reasons. But first things first, it is a great story! It actually has some really good advice in it for us today when we grapple with big decisions. It shows us how Jesus' first disciples made a big decision, and as such, it models some terrific principles for us as we make important decisions.

Some might call this, 'How to discern the will of God'. Others might simply call it, 'How to make a big decision'.

If you read from Acts 1:12 to the end of the chapter, you will see the whole story. The disciples were spending time together (v. 13); they were praying together (v. 14); Peter was reading the scriptures (vs. 15-20) and was inspired by what he read; they reasoned together about replacing Judas (vs. 21-22); they developed a criteria for the applicant to have to fulfil by their reasoning together (v. 22); they reduced the list of applicants to two excellent candidates (v. 23); they prayed some more (vs. 24-25), and then they drew lots between the two of them (v. 26).

That is pretty solid (at least up to the point where they draw lots. Right?) Think about the things they did when making a big decision, *before any drawing of lots*:

- They talked together and discussed things.
- They listened to each other and they considered the wise thoughts of mature, like-minded people.
- They read the scriptures and let them inspire them.
- They prayed.
- They used their God-given reasoning capacity to develop an intelligent and sensible grid to follow.

At the end of the day, when they had done all that, after all the above, they just were not 100% sure, so they 'stepped out in faith'. The expression of that stepping out in faith was to draw lots. For us today it might be a different prayer and a different stepping out in faith. It might be, 'God, I have put in for two jobs. If either comes back to me with a firm offer, I will take it. Please intervene so as to stop either or both if it is not a wise move.' If and when one comes back with an offer, we interpret that as an answer to our prayer and we step out in faith by doing it. True?

Acts 1 reminds us that before we make big decisions, we should talk to the people in our life who matter. Talk to wise people who know about life. Read the scripture and let it inspire you. Pray. Talk more. Reason together. At the end of all that you still won't have certainty. You will almost never have 100% certainty. If you had that, you would not need to live by faith. You would never need to step out and pray and trust and go on what seems to be God's direction.

So be encouraged: we are not meant to have absolute certainty as we journey through life. It is no failure to be uncertain. It is the way things are. But what we do have, what we have got, is the encouragement to be in community, and to share our lives with others, and to be people who relate and talk and think and reason and read and pray - *and* who step out in faith so long as we do all that other stuff too.

Reading:
Read Paul's words in Romans 12:1-2.

Asking the hard questions:
How important is it to 'know the will of God' in all things? I mean, seriously: how 'paranoid' do we become trying to work out the will of God for all the small decisions of everyday life? We might for the big decisions, but where do we draw the line? Could it be that as we grow in Christ, 'knowing the will of God' happens more naturally?

ACTS 2

Read Acts 2 before reflecting on studies 4, 5 and 6

4) Acts 2. Baptism in the Spirit

This famous 'Pentecostal' chapter is well known to most Christians. It is the moment not long after the resurrection, when the disciples were filled with the Spirit of God. It was a deeply experiential and very tangible moment for them. It was something that empowered them to a new level of confidence and boldness. It was something they would never forget.

For those who are Pentecostal by denomination or tradition, they will take great comfort in this chapter. It seems to be the biblical foundation and justification needed to affirm their denominational emphasis.

For those not Pentecostal it can be downplayed or even ignored. Or it can be honestly read and weighed, and the lessons learnt here can still be taken on board.

There are so many lessons to be learnt from this chapter! They include the following:

1) *It is a good and wonderful thing to allow the Spirit of God to fill us and empower us.*

When Jesus was crucified, the disciples were hiding behind closed doors for fear of their lives. They ran from Jesus at his arrest, and hid during his ordeal. They were scared and cowardly. But in the Book of Acts, we suddenly see them boldly preaching on the streets and not fearing persecution! Something changed them! I had always been told that the answer for what changed them was *the resurrection!* The amazing reality of the risen Christ was so overwhelming that they lost their timidity and were now empowered and emboldened to face whatever came their way!

Well, as important as the resurrection was (and it was and is critical to the Christian tradition), that was *not* the key thing that empowered the disciples. The key that made them bold, fearless and unshakable was actually the experience of being filled with the Spirit of the living God. Jesus had said as much just before his ascension in 1:8:

'you will receive power when the Holy Spirit comes upon you, and you will be my witnesses...'

2) *The filling experience was accompanied by some unusual physical manifestations: physical experiences are not wrong or bad or poor theology.*

Even though I am not a Pentecostal by adherence or tradition, I can't deny the teaching and example of this passage. It was not 'just for the apostles' or 'just for the early church until the canon was complete'. Peter unpacks what happened here in the rest of the chapter. He says in v. 39, 'The promise is for you and your children and for all who are far off, for all whom the Lord our God will call.' Jesus had referred to the filling of the Spirit as that which the Father had promised (1:4). Of course the context of 2:39 is glaringly clear in that it refers to the filling of the Spirit that had just happened. It is for 'all whom the Lord our God will call'. It is for every single one of his followers!

Now the real question then, is not, 'is this still relevant?' Of course it is (read again v.39 – it is for 'all' – even those 'who are far off' in space and time). The real question is, 'Does the filling with the Spirit of God have to take the same form and be witnessed the same way, when it happens?' On that question, it seems to me that the answer has to be 'no'. We can't box God in like that. He is in charge and he can do as he pleases. We don't create formulas and then expect God to operate by them.

If we really wanted to believe that it has to be the same every time, then most Pentecostals have already denied that because their version of tongues is not intelligible languages from other nations (as in Acts 2), but rather a non-intelligible babble that is not a human language. So the pattern is not being copied exactly even by those who embrace this message the strongest. God can and does fill us with his Spirit in many and various different ways. (Consider also 1 Corinthians 12:4-11, 28-31.)

The focus should not be on the mechanics of *how* it will happen. The focus should be on *allowing it* to happen, and then embracing it, *however* it manifests. If you want real evidence that it really has happened to you, then note points (3) and (4) here.

3) *The merging of the Spirit of God into our lives leads to a radical equality that defies social distinctions.*

When Peter does unpack the experience that happened to them that day, he quotes from the prophet Joel in the Old Testament. He says,

In the last days I will pour out my Spirit upon all flesh, and your sons and your daughters will prophesy, and your young men shall see visions and your old men shall dream dreams. Even upon my bond-slaves, both men and women, I will in those days pour out my Spirit (vs. 17, 18).

If we are not operating in an environment where men and women can equally minister and participate, if we are not living in a context where those from all levels of the social strata are equally embraced and able to minister, then we are not allowing the Spirit of the living God to empower and change us!

4) *Life in the Spirit of God leads to radical expressions of community and selflessness.*

It is amazing that the very next thing that happens after this radical experience of God is that the disciples begin to live radically. They begin to live communally, discarding many of their own possessions to care for the poor and the needy. Acts 2:41-47 should not be left out of any discussion about the 'empowering of the Holy Spirit'! It is the natural outworking of the experience!

If we are not living more simply, if we are not living more generous lives, if we are still focused on making lots of money and collecting lots of personal stuff in this ridiculously materialistic world, then we have not had a life-changing encounter with the Holy Spirit.

But I will say more on 2:41-47 in the next reflection.

Reading:
Consider Paul's words (one of his prayers for the church) in Ephesians 3:14-19.

Asking the hard questions:
Think about what it actually means to allow the Holy Spirit to empower us. How might our denominational bias *hinder us* from ever venturing down that path? If you are from a tradition that does pursue the empowering of the Spirit, what kind of risks do you face in understanding this passage? Is it possible that you could have so boxed the process into a 'formula' that you don't actually seek evidence of the Spirit's presence by a changed and radical lifestyle?

5) Acts 2:41-47 and 4:32-37. Radical living for radical people

These two similar passages in Acts describe the 'life of the early church in Jerusalem'. It is radical! It is so radical in fact that many Christians throughout the Church's history have been embarrassed by the accounts. It smacks of socialism, or even worse, communism! Does the Bible really tell us here to sell our homes and land and give the money to the poor?

The people who don't like the radical message of this part of the story say things like, 'Of course, Acts can't be used to tell us how to live with any degree of definitiveness. It is historical narrative, after all. It is not clear doctrinal teaching or universal teaching about how to live, as you tend to get in the epistles.'

There is some truth in that, of course. Acts is historical narrative. But does that mean we can't take lessons from it? Does it mean that we can't apply to our daily lives the stories we are reading? After all, the gospels are largely historical narrative too. We get doctrine and lifestyle teaching from them! Can't we get doctrine and lifestyle examples and principles from this book too?

Of course we can. Luke did not just write to tell us irrelevant old stories that are nothing more than nice historical curiosity pieces. He wrote to convey great truths and to show people – Christ-followers in particular – how to live.

So here we see a radical and challenging story – mentioned twice mind you (it must have been important to the author to make him do that) – about communal living and sharing of possessions. Actually, when you think about it, it also sounds just like Jesus who said to one wealthy man, 'Sell all that you have and give to the poor and you shall have treasure in heaven' (Luke 18:22); and to all his followers, 'Sell your possessions and give to the poor. Provide purses for yourself that will not wear out, a treasure in heaven that will not fail, where no thief comes near and no moth destroys' (Luke 12:33). There is a very strong and unambiguous anti-materialism message that runs right through the New Testament.

If we list the things that Luke mentions in these two summary stories of the life of the Jerusalem church, they include other things besides selling possessions and providing for the poor. Nevertheless, that radical communalism is the major point made and elaborated on.

All of the various points made are:

- New believers were water baptised (2:41)
- They learnt the 'apostles' teaching' (2:42)
- They spent time in 'fellowship' (2:42, 46)
- They 'broke bread' together (2:42, 46) – shared meals, which would have included the recently introduced practice of 'communion' (only introduced by Jesus a couple of months earlier).
- They continued to visit the temple (2:46) – Christian Jews would do that until it was destroyed.
- They shared their possessions (2:44, 45; and 4:32-37) – to such an extent that if they had houses or land, these were sold and the money given to those more needy!

All the above could be elaborated on, but in this short reflection we are highlighting their communal living.

Now there are those who still reject this example of living by the first Christians. They go to great lengths to explain these passages away. Some will say, 'Acts shows us how the first followers lived, but it does not say we have to do it that way too.'

Now that *is* partly true. But, ironically, the very people who say that do draw other lessons from this book that *they* say should apply to all. Let me give you some quick examples:

- Some Pentecostals take the speaking in tongues passages at face value and want to apply it to everyone.
- Baptists draw a lot from the water baptisms that happen in this book *after conversion*, and they want others to embrace that teaching and example.
- Presbyterians who baptise infants draw from this book the stories of whole households (Cornelius, Lydia, and the jailer at Philippi) being baptised and want us to accept infant baptism as well.

- Missiologists draw a lot of teaching and example from Paul's activities in other lands where he mixes with people from other ethnicities and religions. They want us to embrace the examples provided.

I think it is still fair to say that the stories in Acts often show us *A* model of how to live. They do not always show us *THE* only model of how to live. *A* model, not *THE* model. That is probably true here. We don't all *have* to sell our homes and lands and give the money to the leaders of the church to give to the poor.

If that much is true, what is the value of a story like this? I mean, if we say some examples in the Book of Acts are *a* model that is optional, but not necessarily compulsory to follow to the letter – what else do we usually add? Don't we say something like this: 'Even though it is not compulsory to do exactly what we are reading here, it is sensible to ask what the *principle* is that we can take from it. What is the *lesson* and how can that be applied to our context, even if we don't follow the actual example?'

Don't we say something like that?

It is good to see the *principle* being taught here, and it is wise to follow that *principle* in our lives. We might express it differently, but it is the principle that matters, not so much the optional ways of expressing that principle (selling our land and houses and living communally).

I suspect you might think that is a good way to handle stories like these too.

If that is so then it begs the question, 'What is the principle being taught here in these two stories that tell us about the communal living of the Jerusalem church?' Think about that for a bit before reading my suggestion. What timeless principle is being conveyed in these stories about the communal living of the early disciples?

It seems to me that the principle behind both accounts is that *we radically look after those in need, even if it costs us personally!*

If that is the case, *do we live that way?* Do we radically share our stuff with others in need? Do we hold onto material things *lightly*? Do we give stuff away, money and/or possessions, when others worse off than ourselves are in need?

Challenging stuff hey! *That* is why hardly anyone ever preaches from these stories in a modern, western, individualistic, capitalist nation like ours.

Reading:
Hebrews 13:16.

Asking the hard questions:
If sharing your possessions is a 'sacrifice' that pleases God, shouldn't we be more actively sharing our possessions? What holds us back? How do we overcome the ingrained cultural bias that makes us so materialistic?

6) Acts 2:42. Devoted to the apostles' teaching

Our last reflection spent some time focused on the sharing of possessions that happened in the early church. I want to revisit the Acts 2 account and highlight one more thing mentioned there. New followers of Christ were baptised, and then they 'were continually devoting themselves to the apostles' teaching...'

It is interesting that the text does not say they 'studied the Scriptures with the apostles'. If it had said that, it would be emphasising that part of the Bible we call the Old Testament. None of the New Testament had been written at this early point in the story of the young church. So the term 'scripture' for now, is a reference to the material we know as the Old Testament. That would change over time, but certainly not at that stage (just a couple of months after the resurrection of Christ).

So it is worth noting that this passage does *not* say the new believers were saturated with the Old Testament 'scripture'. What it does say is that they were devoted to the 'apostles' teaching'.

Think about that term: 'the apostles' teaching'. What would that have consisted of? What would they have talked about?

Also think about the way the New Testament would come together in the decades and centuries ahead. It would be written during the next 60 years. It would circulate as separate scrolls or small clusters of scrolls and be copied by different churches in different locations over the next few hundred years.

But it was all written (most agree) by the end of the first century. It was written by *the apostles or the immediate first generation disciples of the apostles.* The New Testament documents contain the apostles' teaching.

The first converts wanted to be saturated in the 'apostles' teaching' (Acts 2:42). They were devoted to it. As we imitate that emphasis, it will mean that the New Testament material is much more important for the Christian than the Old Testament material. The New Testament material, or the apostles' teaching, is for you and me.

I am not arguing that the new disciples were not trained in the Old Testament, or that the Old Testament is not valuable. We have already seen in Acts 1 that Peter was inspired by his reading of the scriptures to replace Judas. Their scriptures (our Old Testament) were loved and read. The first disciples were Jews by ethnicity. They automatically valued those scriptures. But the apostles thought it necessary to emphasise and teach the things that had happened recently! The life and teaching of Jesus! *His* stories. *His* teachings. *His* life, death, and resurrection, and all that that meant to them.

So new Christians were students of the teaching and life of Jesus, even more than of the Old Testament scriptures. That is the emphasis we should still continue to have. We are, after all, Christ-followers. We are not under the Old Covenant – we are under the New Covenant! We are not under law. We are under grace. We are not followers of Moses. We are followers of Jesus. Moses had some revelation from God. Jesus was the ultimate expression of God's self-revelation: Immanuel – God with us! All we live and apply and do, if we call ourselves 'Christian', should be based squarely on Christ.

The New Testament is our foundation for living. The Old Testament is seen by us in the light of Christ. We don't re-explain the New to fit into an understanding of the Old. No. If need be, we re-explain the Old to fit into our understanding of the New!

Pre-Christ revelation bows to the ultimate revelation of God, Christ himself. As Jesus said in Matthew 5:17, he did not come to abolish the Old, *but to fulfil it*. In his explanation of how he fulfils the Old (the rest of Matthew 5) Jesus gave example after example where he took the Old teaching further ('you have heard that it was said… but I say to you….'), demanded more of his followers ('don't murder' became 'don't hate'; 'don't commit adultery' became 'don't think lustfully'), and he even declared some parts of the Old to have had their shelf life and that they were no longer relevant ('hate your enemies' was replaced with 'love your enemies'; 'an eye for an eye' was replaced with 'turn the other cheek').

Christ is our focus (Hebrews 12:1-2) and he is the foundation we base everything else on. All this emphasis is summed up in the phrase 'the apostles' teaching' – the stuff about Christ! The first believers were 'devoted to the apostles' teaching'.

We should be devoted to 'the apostles' teaching' too.

Reading:
Re-read Matthew 5:17-20 (and note the 6 examples that follow, especially verses 21-22, 27-28, 31-32, 33-34, 38-39, and 43-44).

Asking the hard questions:
If Jesus means what he said here, and he has come to fulfil the Old Testament scriptures, should we just bite the bullet and admit that the New Testament is more important than the Old? Is it more fully the revelation and teaching of God for us? How do you hold the Old Testament and the New Testament together?

ACTS 3

Read Acts 3 before reflecting on studies 7, 8 and 9

7) Acts 3:6. Penniless apostles

Acts 3:1-11 records a wonderful miracle. It was amazing! A man born lame, who was now over 40 years old (4:22), was instantly able to walk! Incredible!

A small detail that often goes unnoticed in the bigger story is that when the apostles were passing by the lame man, he begged for money. He was a full-time beggar. That is not such a surprise: there were no social services back in those days, no Centrelink, no welfare. If you had a major problem or were poor, you survived any way you could. This crippled man begged for a living.

What is not often thought about much in the retelling of the story is that the disciples – Peter and John in particular (the two key leaders of the early church, the two most prominent of the apostles) – had to tell the poor beggar that they had no money! 'Peter said, 'I do not possess silver and gold, but what I do have I give to you: in the name of Jesus Christ the Nazarene – walk!"' (Acts 3:6).

I used to know an old Sunday School song that was about this miracle. That song included the line, 'silver and gold have I none, but such as I have give I thee.' But other than singing that song as a child, I have never heard a single sermon or a single talk reflect on the fact that the two key leaders of the early church at this point in time *were broke*.

Think about it. In the chapter just before this one we saw that many of the new believers 'sold property and possessions to give to anyone who had need' (2:45), and in the repeat of that story the extra details included: 'there was no needy person among them. For from time to time those who owned land or houses sold them, brought the money from the sales and put it at the apostles' feet, and it was distributed to anyone who had need' (4:34,35).

So what does all that mean? Is there enough information in these stories to draw any solid conclusions?

When I have mentioned to some Christians the comment by Peter that he had no money to give to a beggar, they try to get around the comment. They have suggested things like, 'Perhaps he just left his wallet – or its first century Palestinian equivalent – home for the day.' Or, 'It doesn't mean he had no money, he just did not have the very valuable silver or gold coins! But he would have had the normal coins of the day made from other metals.'

Both those attempts to make the first apostles – well…. more like us - are a bit weak.

First: you did not forget to take your first century wallet to the Temple. These church leaders were going to that building that day (3:1). There were opportunities to give to poor beggars as you went there (a pious thing to do), and there were opportunities to give to the Temple treasury (a bit like the modern day offering, without it being organised - another pious thing to do). The story of a poor widow giving the smallest of coins to the Temple treasury in the sight of Jesus and his disciples is recorded in the gospels (Luke 21:1-4) for example. To suggest the church leaders would purposely leave their money at home, so as to avoid having to give to beggars is to reduce these passionate disciples of Jesus, to be like some wishy-washy modern Western materialistic Christians!

Secondly: if Peter had some coins on him 'of other metals' but told the beggar that he had nothing to give him and 'got around it by saying 'silver and gold have I none' - then he was a bit deceitful. That does not fit the character of Peter the apostle. Do we really want to conclude he was a bit crafty with his words so as to be able to avoid giving something to a beggar? Do we really believe he played a 'technically I did not say that,' word game with the poor man?

Now we all know that Peter had something more valuable than silver or gold to give to this man. We will unpack that more in the next devotion, but for now let's just remember that *he lived extremely simply*. He did not even have loose change on him! We might have that experience today, not from living simply, but simply by having credit and debit cards in our wallet instead. To my shame I have not been able to give to beggars in the streets of Melbourne on occasion, because of our 'cashless society'. But Peter? It actually seems like he really was broke.

But here is the thing: it did not seem to bother him. It was not something to be sad about. It was not something to be distressed over. In fact, it was inconsequential, partly because such great things were happening in his life. He might not have had money, but he had the power of God living in him. He might not have had cash to splash around, but he was close to the Spirit of God. He might not have had a lot of stuff, but he was being used by God to do miracles, to share the gospel, and to radically impact thousands of lives!

Isn't it also interesting that despite being the recipient of a lot of money (the proceeds of house and land sales from other church members, specifically), Peter had no money personally. Didn't he 'draw a wage'? Keep most of it and give 10% to the poor? Get a percentage of the profits? Cover his time and work costs?

He had *nothing*?

I suspect the disciples did allow themselves to eat and continue to have some type of cover over their heads. Jesus had given some pretty solid teaching on how to survive as a disciple, including, 'Freely you have received, freely give. Do not get any gold or silver or copper to take with you in your belts [oh, there it is: the first century equivalent to the modern wallet!] – no bag for the journey, or extra shirt or sandals or a staff – for workers are worth their keep' (Matthew 10:8-10). But after being provided for in the essentials of sustaining life, it seems that they did not have anything else. It was not their focus. They did not get distracted chasing temporal 'stuff'.

Money could come into their hands – large sums of it, in fact – and it went straight out again to care for others in need. It is an impressive example of how to live. It seems so totally different to everything we do in life.

In a country like my own (Australia) it is the national pastime to acquire more things. We stroll through shopping malls looking for more unnecessary objects to add to the insane collection already in our possession. We have so much, in fact, that we have to have our local councils organise 'council clean ups.' These are special days devoted to collecting the excess, or the out of date, or the slightly broken items, from our cluttered homes. We have some of the largest homes on average per head of population in the world, and yet they hardly have any people in them. Room after room is full of furniture and other material possessions. Less and less people live in bigger and bigger spaces and yet the homes are full and overflowing. Sheds and garages are full of excess furniture and things we can no longer fit into our larger homes. Even storage units are permanently owned when more space is needed to house the things we are collecting but hardly ever use.

Most Christians live just like everyone else regarding all this. Gone is any emphasis on Jesus when he said, 'Do not store up for yourselves treasures on earth that moth and rust consume and thieves break in and steal' (Matt 6:19). Or his other teaching, 'Watch out! Be on your guard against all forms of greed; life does not consist in an abundance of possessions' (Luke 12:15). Gone is any application of the words of Paul when he wrote that godliness should be linked to contentment: 'For we brought nothing into the world, and we can take nothing out of it. But if we have food and clothing, we will be content with that. Those who want to get rich fall into temptation and a trap and into many foolish and harmful desires that plunge people into ruin and destruction' (I Timothy 6:6-9).[1]

A small comment in the Book of Acts: 'silver and gold have I none...' has a lot more in it than might first appear!

Reading:
I Timothy 6:6-11.

Asking the hard questions:
We often hear 1 Timothy 6:10 quoted in comments like this: 'It is not *money* that is the problem, it is the *love* of money, like it says in 1 Timothy 6:10. So I don't *love* money, I just have lots of it and can tithe and use it responsibly.' But if you actually take the time to read that verse in its context, you see in verse 9, just before the famous sentence, a definition of 'the love of money': it is 'the desire to be rich'. Suddenly our motives are brought into question. How does verse 9 challenge us?

---

[1] There is a lot of debate about the authorship of I and II Timothy and Titus, and many scholars reject Pauline authorship of all three letters. Other scholars are not convinced to ditch Paul as the author. And some have even concluded that if any of the three really is Paul's, then it is probably II Timothy. (That little letter has no real doctrinal barrow being pushed, and is intensely personal.) I am happy to talk about them as if all of them are Paul's, even if followers of Paul wrote them later and attributed Paul's name to them. Some documents were written like that in ancient times. It was not considered 'cheating' or 'lying' if the teaching and words were indeed consistent with the teaching and words of the one they attributed it to.

8) Acts 3:12. The wrong focus

The healing of the man born lame is a well-loved story in the Book of Acts. Peter and John (the two key leaders of the young church) went up to the Temple to pray, and they passed the cripple. He begged for money but they give him a miraculous healing instead!

It is interesting that Peter did not actually pray to God to heal the man. Peter just sort of *declared* him healed in the name of Jesus Christ of Nazareth.

Now there are scriptures that tell us to pray for those who are sick (e.g. James 5:14) but it is worth noting that for many of the healing and deliverance stories in Acts, a *declarative statement* takes place more often than a prayer (see Acts 9:33-34; 9:40; 14:10; 16:18).

Here we see this lame man healed, and the crowd goes nuts! '…They were filled with wonder and amazement at what had happened…' (3:10) and, 'All the people were astonished and came running to them in the place called Solomon's Colonnade' (3:11).

Something huge had just happened, and the crowd (predictably) ran to check it out.

Nothing much changes over the centuries, does it? The wonder workers are still 'run to' today. We lined up to sit in audiences where John Edward said he could talk to dead people. We clambered to watch Uri Geller bend spoons.

Even some Christians race to this meeting and that meeting when they hear of possible real miracles happening. They want to see it! Even though they won't usually admit it, they actually are in awe of the miracle workers! They will be so entertained and amazed that they will splash big notes into the offering that goes around.

Well this crowd was no different. Peter could have worked the crowd. He could have told big stories and made himself look amazing. He could have told them of all the stories he was a part of when Jesus was doing his thing. He could have embellished the role he played in some of those stories. He could have talked about when they went out two by two and came back with stories of demon deliverances! He could have even begun 'Simon-Peter Ministries' and given out flyers and announced the launch of his new ministry. He could have got his own ministry web site: www.apostlepetermiracleworker.org (okay, we know that wasn't an option – but you know what I mean). He could have taken up an offering and brought in a big pay load that day.

But he did none of that.

Perhaps he remembered the words of Jesus when he taught them, 'Freely you have received, freely give' (Matthew 10:8). Perhaps he remembered all the times he failed Jesus – it was not all that long ago, in fact, when he was denying he even knew him.

When the crowd raced to him to marvel at his power and talents, he spoke out these incredible words: *'People of Israel, why does this surprise you? Why do you stare at us, as if by our own power or godliness we had made this man walk?'* (3:12).

Peter goes on to explain that it is *all about Jesus*. It was Jesus and faith in Jesus that did the miracle. Certainly not Peter!

The crowd was focusing on the wrong person. They were focusing on the channel of God's power rather than on Jesus. They were directing their fascination at the wrong guy! Peter sets them straight. If I could paraphrase Peter's words (the two key words being 'power' and 'godliness'), then Peter is talking like this:

> What are you looking at *me* for? You think I did this? You think that this fisherman from Galilee has the *power* to do miracles? You think this clumsy man who makes so many mistakes and has so many faults – you think I am so religiously devout, so righteous, so pure and holy, so *godly*, that I can command a lame man to be healed? *Are you kidding?* It wasn't me. I was just the vehicle used by God on this occasion, a flawed and powerless, sinful man. No. It was not my power or godliness that did this. It was God himself! It was Jesus!'

For us today: If we do not deflect personal adoration and praise away from ourselves and back to God and Jesus, we are being seduced by pride and personal ambition. If we allow praise to be dumped on us, or if we allow people to put us up on a pedestal that belongs to Christ, we are failing God and falling into sin. If we pretend that the ministry we do is ours, and any money or praise that comes in because of it is somehow ours as well, then we are not following the pattern and example of the Apostle Peter here in the Book of Acts. We have compromised and failed an integrity test.

The truth is that we, like Peter, do NOT have the power or the godliness to receive such misplaced accolades. Give credit where credit is due: to Jesus.

Reading:
Proverbs 11:2 and James 4:6.

Asking the hard questions:
Humility seems to be an under-emphasised and even unimportant quality in our community today. We are constantly being encouraged to excel in all we do, and it is kind of okay to revel in the glory that comes from that. This can even infect the church. How should we put into practice the teaching of humility in our lives? How can I live differently from how I live right now, today, as I seek to implement this?

9) Acts 3:19. Repentance *then* refreshing

After the wonderful healing happened that day (3:1-11), Peter gave a talk to the crowd that had run to him and John. Peter's speech is no doubt a summary of the full talk given. Indeed, the Book of Acts has many speeches recorded in it by a whole host of people, and they are all summaries or shortened versions. Some are more shortened than others. Most Christians would say that they believe the summaries to be accurate, even if they are not the whole speech.

Speeches can sometimes be read quickly and skipped over because we want more exciting stories. But to be fair to the author, speeches contain a lot of information in them for the readers' benefit. These words are packed with significance.

Here we get one of Peter's talks. He says a lot of important things. He has a wonderful collage of 'names' or 'titles' or 'descriptions' for Jesus that keep surfacing throughout the speech (God's servant; the Holy and Righteous one; the Prince of life; the one God raised from the dead; the suffering Christ; the appointed Christ; the prophet like Moses; and the seed of Abraham).

But there is one statement in the talk that stands out to me. It is a statement that we sometimes would do well to meditate on. In 3:19 Peter says to the crowd, *'Repent then and turn to God, so that your sins may be wiped out, that times of refreshing may come from the Lord.'*

I know too many church-going folk who are keen to be *blessed* in a particular way. They just love being 'touched' by God. They are conference junkies and they go from one fix to the next, trying to find another spiritual high to revel in. Over the last couple of decades I have seen the 'laughing phase', the 'gold dust' phase, the 'slaying in the Spirit' conferences, the 'being hit by so-and-so's coat' meetings, and more. You name it and there are church goers who will chase it. They want to be blessed. They want the times of refreshing. They want to be able to tell others that they were knocked off their feet by the wind of the Spirit, or they were overwhelmed with a laughter that they could not control nor stop. Oh, if only it could last forever!

But you know what? It is all putting the cart before the horse. In this passage, Peter reminds us that if you want refreshing from the presence of the Lord, then you need to repent first. If you want to taste the experiential side of the Holy Spirit's indwelling in your life, you need firstly to be sincere about wanting to get your life right before God.

The word 'repent' captures the idea of 'turning around because you are going the wrong way'. It is doing a 180! It is acknowledging that things in your life are not what they should be and it is resolving to change that.

Interestingly, 'repenting' does not guarantee 'doing it all right forever and a day afterwards'. Repenting is admitting the wrong and determining to try harder to do the right thing. That's it. It is a change of attitude, a new resolve with an honest appraisal about our life to date. As far as actually getting everything right in our lives? Well, that takes a lifetime and even then we still won't have got it *all* right. When we repent, we aim afresh for the bulls-eye, even if the truth is that we hardly ever hit it. As we practise more (live each day with that renewed focus) we will hit that bulls-eye more often, just not every time.

There are way too many people who want the blessing without the repentance. There are too many preachers who feed to that erroneous idea. Instead of 'repent and be refreshed' the message is all too often turned into, 'Come forward to the front and be refreshed!' Repentance has been dropped.

I guess it is not all that politically correct to talk about faults and failings and areas we know we need to do better in! Indeed, it may be that we have here a key reason why some folk are *not* actually getting blessed at all – in a way that is empowering and lasting.

Reading:
Read Matthew's account of John the Baptist's ministry in Matthew 3:1-12. Note the way he calls for repentance before he mentions how Jesus will then come and offer the Holy Spirit.

Asking the hard questions:
How do modern churches treat the topic of 'conversion'? Is it oversimplified and too non-demanding? Should we be emphasising *repentance* more? Why might some churches dodge the whole repentance emphasis?

ACTS 4

Read Acts 4 before reflecting on study 10

10) Acts 4:12. Is Jesus the *only* way to God?

A quick question to help start us off: What happens to people who have never heard about Jesus? What happens to them after they die? The infant who dies as a baby or toddler (too young to ever comprehend faith or embrace Jesus Christ)? The person in a far off land who never hears the Christian message?

Most Christians would probably *not* say 'they go straight to hell because they never invited Jesus into their heart'. Most Christians would *usually* say something like: 'We are not 100% sure, because the Bible shows us the *sure way of salvation* (faith in Jesus Christ) but it does not go into detail about what happens to others who don't ever get a chance to respond to Jesus personally. We know that God is a just and loving God of mercy and grace. He probably has some other option that we are not privy to the details of. For example, with a baby, if one of the parents is a believer, then maybe the faith of that parent is enough to cover the infant till they are at an age where they can decide for themselves or not'.

Would that be a reasonable answer to the original question?

If you accept that answer, or something similar, then you are actually acknowledging something that we don't usually say out loud. That is: God might have other ways of 'saving' some people apart from personal faith in Jesus Christ. We kind of intuitively realise that is probably the case, but we find it hard to really explore it.

Okay... with that sitting on the back burner, being allowed to bubble away as we proceed, let's do just that. Let's proceed. We shall find ourselves coming back to that question in this chapter.

Acts 4:12 sees Peter proclaim, 'Salvation is found in no-one else, for there is no other name given under heaven by which we must be saved.'

This is a profound statement that causes much anxiety in our world today. Is Jesus *really* the only way to reach God? This is one of the most important questions we can ask.

I live in a very multicultural city. Melbourne, Australia, is the most multicultural city in the southern hemisphere. Where I work, in Dandenong, there are over 100 religions practised. Dandenong has the oldest 'interfaith network' in Australia. In this wonderfully diverse city, we have a strong culture of 'live and let live', of 'celebrate diversity and tolerate those who are different to you'. Dandenong is, in fact, a wonderful (yet still imperfect) role model for the rest of the world.

Living in such a multi-faith community raises all kinds of theological questions for the reflective mind. When I rub shoulders with Muslims, Hindus, Jews, Sikhs, Baha'i, and Buddhists, it obviously makes me wonder about their faith, their belief systems, and their lifestyles. It can't help but make me compare, contrast, consider and weigh other religions.

The question that must be addressed is this: Christians claim that Jesus is the key to 'salvation' or 'peace with God' or 'eternal life' – but is Jesus the *only* way people can find God?

We cannot escape consideration of this. Are other religions equally real paths to God as well? Do all belief systems end up at the same place? Are we all different plants in the earth, reaching and growing up towards the same sun (as one of my Sikh friends once described it to me)?

This question is so big and so important – and so fraught with strong feelings and emotions - that this devotion is going to be considerably longer than the others. I make no apologies for it: it is a really important issue to grapple with.

Jesus is essential for salvation

Evangelical Christians say dogmatically that there is only one way to God, and that is through Jesus. They are dogmatic, to be sure. But many of them are also kind. They might reluctantly say their position if pressed, but they are gentle about it. Loving. Wanting others to find the joy they have found in Jesus, the peace, the forgiveness and reconciliation with God. So yes, Jesus is the only way, but we are not saying that to hit you over the head and damn you to hell. No, we are saying that because the Bible teaches it, and we love you and want you to enjoy eternal life too.

Sometimes analogies are used. It is like we have been fortunate enough to come across the cure for an incurable disease that we are all slowly dying from. Imagine if that was cancer and all of us had it. Amazingly we have been given the cure! We did not invent it or create it, but we have been blessed to receive it. Therefore, imagine how unloving it would be for me not to share it with others who are also dying from this cancer? It is not pride or judgmentalism that drives me to share the cure with my neighbour: it is love. My neighbours might believe other things about the cancer. They might have their own local remedies that they apply. But sadly they just don't work. They are not the cure. So we seek to share the cure with others.

In a nutshell, the evangelical, fundamentalist position is based on two things:

1) Belief that the Bible is the perfect word of God and must be taken literally and believed absolutely, and

2) The Bible says in a number of places that without Jesus, you cannot be saved. Note especially: This passage in Acts 4:12 (Peter's words, recorded by Luke)

'I am the Way, and the Truth, and the Life. No-one comes to the Father except through me' (Jesus recorded by the Apostle John, in John 14:6).

'There is one God and one mediator between God and human beings, Christ Jesus, himself human.' (The Apostle Paul in his letter to a friend: 1 Timothy 2:5).

The three verses stated above do make it clear that Christians see Jesus as essential to salvation. If you want to connect to God, you need Jesus, according to Jesus, Paul, Peter, John and Luke.

But just what does it mean when we say Jesus is necessary for salvation? I mean, the evangelical position says, 'You have to invite Jesus into your heart. You need to give your life to him. You need to consciously follow him. You need to know him personally by name.'

Of course, what I never really noticed before was that none of those verses says anything quite like that. None of those verses says anything about inviting Jesus into your heart and knowing him personally by name.

It is all about the cross

Here is a thought. Since Christians believe that Jesus died on the cross for the sins of the world (1 John 2:2) then could it possibly be that Jesus *is* essential for salvation because of the work he did on the cross? His death on that cross all those years ago is accepted by God as the sufficient sacrifice for all humankind's sin. There is, therefore, no-one on earth who is left out now: every one of us is able to access the love of God in Christ Jesus. There is nothing stopping us from being accepted by God anymore!

Jesus' death paid the price of sin and opened the way for everyone to have forgiveness and acceptance by God. In the cosmic order of things, that one death (Jesus') was declared by God to be the sufficient sacrifice for human failings and sin. It is done! It is paid for. Nothing can separate us now from the love of God in Christ Jesus (Romans 8:38-39).

But if that is so, then why do some add, 'And you have to invite him into your heart and know him personally?'

Where is that extra more personal and individual bit coming from?

Could it be that the death of Jesus opened the door for us to be able to relate to God and be acceptable to God – *and that is enough*? It is a wonderful bonus when people embrace Jesus personally and live their lives for God here and now by following the teaching and example of Jesus. But is that really a prerequisite to salvation?

Surely the work of Christ on the cross is the critical thing. The price has been paid. There is no other name under heaven by which we must be saved. If you want to connect to the Father you need the work of that one mediator between God and humankind. You are tapping into the wonderful truth that Jesus is the Way, the Truth and the Life and no one can possibly get to the Father except by him (*because* of his work on the cross).

If that might just be the emphasis we need to focus on, then could it be that some people are indeed 'saved' even if they do not know the name of Jesus personally? Maybe everyone is? Hmm… maybe not everyone. I mean, seriously? Hitler? Stalin? Pol Pot? Attila the Hun? Genghis Khan? Oh dear. Well, if not everyone, then how is a distinction made by God? But maybe everyone who loves God and seeks to live for him, whatever his 'label', is acceptable to God (because sin is paid for by Christ's sacrifice on the cross)?

Many Muslims, Jews and more: people who love God and seek to live for him. They have not personally invited Jesus into their hearts, and their upbringing and experiences makes them suspicious of Christians and the Christian message, but if their hearts are for God, and they are seeking to live a life on earth that reflects that priority – could it be that they are indeed just as 'saved' as the evangelical Christian who calls Jesus by name?

This suggestion is a hard pill for some to swallow. All I am actually asking here is for us to *explore that possibility*.

William P. Young and C.S. Lewis

There have been two best-selling stories that have been written over my lifetime that both grapple with this issue in a fictional way. The most recent one is the book called *The Shack*[2].

In this story, a father loses his beloved little daughter. She is kidnapped and brutally murdered. It sends him into despair and it weakens his faith in a loving God. He simply exists from day to day and his life is empty and miserable. As the story unfolds and a few years have passed, the father gets a bizarre invitation to go to the Shack (the place where his daughter was murdered) to meet God, and to be able to talk with God personally. His suspicions and fears about that invitation are eventually overcome and he ends up at the Shack. In the story, he does indeed meet God and is able to explore the many questions he has.

Most of the book is dialogue between the dad and either God the Father (who appears more often as a Mother), Jesus the Son, or the Holy Spirit. In a late chapter when he is talking to Jesus, Jesus makes a most provocative statement that relates to our discussion here about other faiths and religions, and knowing him personally by name. Let me quote here from the book:

'I am not a Christian' [said Jesus]. 'The idea struck Mac [the dad] as odd and unexpected, and he could not stop himself from grinning. 'No, I suppose you aren't'.

---

[2] William P. Young, *The Shack*, Windblown Media Los Angeles, California, 2007.

They arrived at the door of the workshop and again Jesus stopped. 'Those who love me come from every system that exists. They were Buddhists, or Mormons, Baptists or Muslims, Democrats, Republicans, and many who don't vote or who are not part of any Sunday morning or religious institutions. I have followers who were murderers and some who were self-righteous. Some were bankers and bookies, Americans and Iraqis, Jews and Palestinians. I have no desire to make them Christians, but I do want to join them in their transformation into Sons and Daughters of Papa [God], into my brothers and sisters, into my Beloved!'

It is at this point in the story that the dad asks Jesus the question we have been asking all through this chapter. 'Does that mean,' asked Mac, 'that all roads will lead to you?'

At this critical moment in the dialogue, the writer has Jesus say the following reply: 'Not at all… most roads don't lead anywhere. What it does mean is that I will travel any road to find you.'[3]

When I first read that dialogue, it resonated with my spirit. Most roads are human efforts to 'touch the invisible', to 'connect to God', or to 'feel like you are doing something that demonstrates your desire for God or truth'. Most roads have good and not so good aspects to them, and they are often trod by sincere people seeking God, or Truth, or reality, or just 'that which is'. But they are in the end, human constructs.

Even though, as the story said, 'they don't actually get there' – the reality is that God finds sincere seekers. Jesus, when on earth, said many wonderful things and one of the great statements he made was, 'Seek and you will find' (Luke 11:10).

As I read that part of *The Shack*, I recalled an older story that I had also read some years earlier: C.S. Lewis' more well-known 'Narnia' books. The final book in the series was called 'The Last Battle'[4] and it is an analogy about how the world will climax, just before God brings all things to completion. It is about the Bible prophecies that talk about the future: the 'end times'.

In the pretend world of the story, there are people who follow Aslan (the true God – the Christ figure), and there are people who follow Tash (the God of the warring neighbour country: a cruel God who encourages ruthlessness, deceit, cruelty and

---

3   *The Shack*, p. 182.

4   C.S. Lewis, *The Last Battle*, Fontana Lions, London, 1980 (original 1956).

savagery). The story has the two nations at war, and the enemy nation is winning. As the children and the talking animals are being overwhelmed, they are watching the enemy soldiers and they see the cruelty and the savagery. But they notice one soldier who is more 'noble' than the rest. During the times of parley, he demonstrated principles of integrity and honesty that his colleagues seemed to be lacking. He talked of his love for his god Tash, and how he wanted nothing more than to serve and please his god. But his concept of Tash seemed to be something different to the concept his fellow countrymen had. This noble soldier's concept of Tash was such that it led him to live to higher ideals, more honest ethical principles, and a nobler way of life.

In the end, as the battle resumes and continues, all the Narnians are defeated, killed, or rounded up and driven into the death trap, 'the barn', that seems to have some evil killing force inside it (the enemy says that Tash himself was in the barn). At one point in the story, the more noble enemy soldier ended up in the barn and was never seen again.

When the children are finally driven into the small barn, the strangest thing happens. They are no longer on the battlefield. They are no longer in a dingy farm barn. They are in Aslan's country! They have been transported to the very land of Aslan himself. They meet all their comrades and friends who had been killed on the battlefield. They are all alive and well and happy. They are in the 'new heaven and new earth' that the Bible predicts.

But here is the twist: they meet the Tash-worshipping enemy soldier there too. Not the rest of the enemy army, just this one soldier who boasted of his love for Tash. The children are confused, and an intriguing dialogue takes place between the soldier and the children. The soldier begins to tell how he entered the barn expecting to find his god Tash, whom he worshipped and adored, but instead found Aslan.

But Aslan accepted him!

> '... there came to meet me a great Lion. ... Then I fell at his feet and thought, Surely this is the hour of my death, for the Lion (who is clearly worthy of all honour) will know that I have served Tash all my days and not him. Nevertheless it is better to see the Lion and die, than to rule the world and not to have seen him. But the glorious one bent down his golden head and

touched my forehead with his tongue and said, 'Son, thou are welcome'. But I said, 'Alas Lord, I am not a son of thine but the servant of Tash'. He answered, 'Child, all thy service thou has done to Tash, I account as service done to me'. Then by reason of my great desire for wisdom and understanding, I overcame my fear and questioned the Glorious One and said, 'Lord, is it then true, as the Ape [the false prophet] said, that thou and Tash are one?' The Lion growled so that the earth shook, (but his wrath was not against me), and said 'It is false. Not because he and I are one, but because we are opposites, I take to me the service which thou has done for him. For he and I are so different that no service which is vile can be done for me, and no service which is not vile can be done for him. Therefore if any man swear by Tash and keep his oath for the oath's sake, it is by me that he has truly sworn, though he know it not, and it is I who reward him. And if any man do a cruelty in my name, then though he says the name Aslan, it is Tash who he serves, and by Tash his deed is accepted. Do you understand child?' ... I said 'Yet I have been seeking Tash all my days.' 'Beloved', said the Glorious One, 'unless thy desire had been for me, you would not have sought for so long, or so truly. For all find, when they truly seek."[5]

Both of the above fictitious stories attempt to grapple with the reality of sincere people in other world religions. They end with the thought, 'Those who seek will find'.

Whatever you do with those reflections, my own thoughts on this are that God accepts the sincere heart that seeks after him; that seeks for Truth, awakening, awareness, and that which is. Call it what you want, but if people are really seeking, God finds them – *even if they don't know that they are being blessed because of Christ's work on the cross.*

But why did the early apostles have such commitment to preaching and evangelism?

Let me offer a counter argument to the above that evangelicals will be glad to hear.

As nice as it might sound (that all the sincere of any religion are saved), there is a New Testament problem with that. It is not any one of the three favourite verses cited

---

[5] *The Last Battle*, pp. 155-156.

earlier. We have had to admit that they do not quite say what evangelicals want them to say. But there are two more things that we need to address about the New Testament.

1) There are other passages of scripture that seem to imply that people need to embrace Jesus consciously to be saved.

Consider Paul in Romans 10:9-15:

> If you declare with your mouth 'Jesus is Lord' and believe in your heart that God has raised him from the dead, you will be saved. For it is with your heart that you believe and are justified, and it is with your mouth that you profess your faith and are saved. As Scripture says, 'Anyone who believes in Him will never be put to shame'. For there is no difference between Jew and Gentile - the same Lord is Lord of all and richly blesses all who call upon him, for, 'Everyone who calls on the name of the Lord will be saved'. How, then, can they call on the one they have not believed in? And how can they believe in the one of whom they have not heard? And how can they hear without someone preaching to them? And how can anyone preach unless they are sent? As it is written: 'How beautiful are the feet of those who bring good news!'

And of course there is the famous John 3:16. 'For God so loved the world that he gave his one and only Son, that whoever believes in him shall not perish but have eternal life.' Doesn't that tell us that people have to personally believe in Jesus to be saved?

I will return to these passages shortly, but for now let me say that it leads straight into the second consideration:

2) The early apostles had an incredible passion to share Jesus with other people. They were enthusiastic to make disciples of all nations.

The first apostles were utterly dedicated (after about Acts chapter 8) to getting the message of Jesus 'out'. The Apostle Paul travelled around the then known world for years and years, trying to convince people to embrace Jesus and live renewed lives in Christ. The Book of Acts covers about 30 years in total, and the second half of the book is devoted to the activity of Paul and his colleagues. They were so enthusiastic to share Jesus with others: others of different cultures and different religions. They did not sit back and say, 'Hey, no worries what you believe, so long as you are sincere'. They did not rest and say, 'No need to disrupt their thinking and their culture and worldview by telling them about Jesus. After all, his death on the cross has opened up a way for them to be accepted now by God, and so they are fine. No need to evangelise.' They actually went out of their way to tell others about Jesus.

They wanted people to embrace Jesus here and now, and know him by name. They suffered persecution, ridicule, physical harassment, and finally a violent death, telling people (a lot of whom did not want to listen) about Jesus. They confronted people of other cultures and worldviews, and even offended them at times (though not intentionally). They were usually sensitive to others as they shared the gospel message (Paul in Athens in Acts 17 is probably the best example of that). But of course, all the sensitivity in the world still won't stop some personality types being offended if you actually try to tell them that they should change something in their worldview!

So this is a pretty telling point. The first apostles did not relax and sit back. They had a passionate drive to convert and disciple people. They were quite enthusiastic and devoted about it. They risked everything (even their own lives) to get people to find out about Jesus.

What the apostles did seems to be directly linked to the words of Jesus recorded at the end of the Gospel of Matthew. Jesus was instructing his disciples on what they were to do now that he had risen from the dead. He was giving them some final direction before his ascension into heaven and his physical departure from them. 'Therefore go and make disciples of all nations, baptising them in the name of the Father and the Son and the Holy Spirit, and teaching them to obey everything that I have commanded you. And surely I am with you always, to the very end of the age' (Matthew 28:19-20).

That is pretty specific and quite 'full on'. Jesus wants his disciples to go and make new disciples and to actually tell them about Jesus and his teachings. He wants new disciples in every nation to learn about his teachings, and to be baptised in the name of the Father, Son, and Holy Spirit. That is certainly not sitting back and saying 'all paths seem to be the same'. It is not saying, 'Well, there you go – the atoning sacrifice has happened – all humanity is able to be accepted by God now, so the sincere of any faith or religion or world view are now acceptable to God.'

What do we do with that?

Passion for evangelism could be a passion to see people's lives empowered and transformed as they become part of the Kingdom of God here and now

One possible explanation that explains both enthusiasm for missionary activity and a belief that people from other faiths are still saved, even if they don't embrace Jesus personally, is as follows.

It is compelling and worthwhile getting the gospel message out there and teaching about Jesus to others, for *various* reasons. For starters: those who *do* embrace Jesus and his way will have their lives lifted to a whole different level! By getting the message out and seeing lives changed, that activity is a contributing part of bringing the Kingdom of God to earth, *now*.

The person who embraces Christ will be conscious of their relationship with God in a new way. They will be enthusiastic to live for God in a fresh and vital way. So, awakening them to Jesus and his significance and his teaching does not necessarily only affect a person's eternal destination. It also makes a great difference to their life *here and now*! It makes a great difference to how they live in the world for the rest of their life. By awakening to the gospel and becoming conscious of the call of God on their life, they will change their life in the *present*. And as people live better lives for God in this world – as they love their neighbour in practical and caring ways – as they love their enemies and do good to those who hate them; and as that impacts their neighbours and friends; as they share their possessions and care for the poor; as they share the love of God to all around them - *that work gives glory to God, and it is a contribution to bringing the Kingdom of God into the world*. The effects in this world today are worth having!

'Salvation' to the first Christians was not just 'where you end up after you die'. No! It was a whole life experience – now and later. Salvation meant a changed life here and now. And as it affects more and more people, it means a changed world here and now (not just later, in the future).

So evangelism and missionary activity are still necessary and important, but not just 'to win souls for eternity'. No, it is rather to awaken those souls to their call, their potential, and to see them live better lives in the world. It helps change the world and make it a better place. It gives glory to God here and now as that happens.

But what about the Romans 10 passage quoted above? That still has to be considered. Paul wanted preachers to go out and share the good news of Christ, so that people could confess with their mouths and believe in their hearts, personally. Think about that: perhaps Paul is making it clear that a personal commitment to Jesus Christ *is* a *certain* way of salvation. But he does not actually add the following: 'Oh by the way, no one else anywhere in the world can ever be saved outside of what I have just said even if they have never heard the name of Jesus or ever had the opportunity to follow him personally.'

There is a difference between telling us that Jesus should be embraced personally and that will lead to salvation, and telling us that *only* embracing Jesus personally will lead to salvation. The 'only' is not there in Romans 10. Likewise John 3:16. Could it be a bit like this analogy: 'The *sure* way to drive from Melbourne to Sydney is on the major highway between the two cities. If you drive on that highway you will get there.' But that statement does not say, 'Oh, and no other road gets there.' There is a difference between sharing the truth of a *certain* clear way to attain something, and declaring that it is the *only* way to attain something.

Can some kind of solution be found in this discussion?

How were people saved *before* Jesus came into the world?

Question: How were people saved, before Jesus came into the world? People could not believe in him personally. No-one could not express faith in Christ yet. So how was anyone saved before Christ, before God's ultimate self-revelation in the person of Jesus?

Answer: The same way as they are saved since Jesus came into the world: by responding in faith to *whatever revelation they had been blessed to receive – revelation given to us by the grace of God.*

That question (how were people saved before Jesus came into the world?) is not all that different to another question that also gets asked: How are people judged by God if they have never heard of the name of Jesus, *since* Jesus came into the world? Keep that in the back of your thoughts as you read on.

In God's dealings with us humans, he has always had the same plan: he wants us to be reconciled to him – he wants us to be 'saved' – and he has always done it *by revelation that needs to be responded to by faith*. Abraham was saved by faith, not by circumcision or works of the law, and not by inviting Jesus into his heart. Everyone who has ever been saved has been saved *by faith*: faith in whatever revelation God has graciously provided.

Sometimes we hear preachers say that God used to save the people before Jesus by their law-keeping – by their good works, their avoidance of sin, their acts of charity. If they kept the laws they were saved. But that is not the case. They were, and we still are, saved by faith. Faith in whatever revelation we have. Faith in the revelation that God provides.

For some people, the revelation that they had shown to them was not a lot of specifics. It might be the creation itself. (We might call this 'natural revelation' or 'general revelation'). For others it might be a personal encounter with God ('special revelation'). Abraham, for example, heard something. He knew that there was just the one God and that God called him to leave the land of Ur and move to a different place. He had some kind of specific revelation. *And he responded to that specific revelation in faith*. He stepped out and obeyed. So faith, if it is real, leads us to obedience – but obedience is not what 'saved' Abraham – it was the faith in that revelation. Obedience demonstrated his faith (as it should ours). But faith saves. Obedience follows.

As I mentioned above, for some people the only revelation they have is the creation itself. The very beauty and complexity and enormity of the creation causes people to realise there is a God. To have the creation without a creator is to have a Mona Lisa without a Leonardo. The beauty and complexity of life in the cosmos demands an artistic designer behind it. And so it is no surprise that the overwhelming majority of people on the face of the earth have always believed in some kind of God. Paul talks about the world revealing God to humankind. Listen to his words in Romans 1:20: 'For since the creation of the world, God's invisible qualities – his eternal power and divine nature - have been clearly seen, being understood from what has been made, so that people are without excuse.' People intuitively know that there is a God. They sense him simply through observing nature, the world, and the stars in the sky.

Some people get more revelation than just natural revelation. They actually connect to God. And it is not just the Hebrew people in the Bible who are privy to special revelation. Non-Hebrews are sometimes seen to be 'hearing' more from God than even some of the Hebrews did. Melchizedek was the 'king of Salem' during the time of Abraham, and from the small amount of material we have on him in Genesis, he seems to be a priest of the one true God (See Genesis 14:18-21). Melchizedek seems to have had a 'good' connection with the one true God, and is seen as one of the godly people in the Old Testament story – yet he was not a Hebrew.

There was another non-Hebrew who also has a special connection with God: Balaam. He does not get such a good wrap as Melchizedek, but there is no denying that he seems to communicate with God and God speaks to him in clear ways (Numbers 22:5-21). So God can and has gone beyond general or natural revelation – and he sometimes communicates more specifically to some people. And they are saved, or not, depending on how they respond to that revelation: if they have faith in it – faith that leads to obedience.[6]

There are a number of ways in which God speaks to some people that are more specific than general revelation. Sometimes he might give people a dream or vision. The God-fearing young man, Joseph, received dreams from God (Genesis 37). But not only descendants of Abraham experienced such occurrences. The Pharaoh of Egypt received a dream from God (Gen 41) and Joseph interpreted it for him. Later, the pagan King of Babylon, Nebuchadnezzar, received dreams and visions from the one true God. The prophet Daniel interpreted them for him (Daniel 2).

People sometimes heard direct words from God as well. Moses seemed to have a direct line to God. The Bible tells us that Moses talked with God often. He received the law from God. The law was an example of very specific revelation from God. It was much more specific than general revelation. People were 'saved' or not, by responding in faith to whatever revelation they received. Believing it was from God, and believing that it informed them about God and his ways. That faith was seen in obedience to the revelation given.

Later in the Old Testament story, there are a number of prophets who seem to hear God speak to them. They received messages from God and communicated them

---

6   I would add that all this is possible because of the work of Christ on the cross. The cross applies to all humanity, before, during and after the time that Jesus was actually here. Since God is the creator of all things, including time, God sits outside of time. The death of Christ has always been the sufficient sacrifice for humanity's sin.

directly to the target group the message was for. Usually the majority of Old Testament prophets were speaking to the descendants of Abraham, the Hebrew people. But occasionally some of the prophets spoke to non-Hebrew people. Jonah spoke to the people of Assyria. Obadiah spoke to the Edomites. Daniel spoke to the Babylonian King. Prophets might have heard audible messages, or had such clarity of inner conviction that they 'sensed' God's specific words. Usually their message consisted of telling the hearers where they were going wrong, and calling them back to serve God faithfully in obedience.

Finally, God's self-revelation climaxed in the coming of Jesus Christ into the world. There had been dreams and visions, prophets and seers. There had been general revelation and certain kinds of specific revelation. But finally, at last, God came into the world and lived amongst us (John 1:14)! He revealed himself in a most radical and clear way: he became one of us and walked among us. Jesus, Immanuel – 'God with us' (Matthew 1:23). The writer of the New Testament Book of Hebrews talks about the ways God communicated to people over time. In his opening words to this rather complex book, he states, 'In the past God spoke to our ancestors through the prophets at many times and in various ways. But in these last days he has spoken to us by his Son…' (Hebrews 1:1-2).

What a wonderful gift of love! What clarity! What an amazing way to understand God better.

Just as all people all over the world, all through time, are 'saved' by responding in faith to the revelation they have been given, so too those who encounter Christ are 'saved' on the basis of faith. Faith in the revelation they have received, faith in Christ himself, faith that will be evidenced by a changed life and a life of good works.

But it does beg that other question alluded to briefly above: What happens to people who have never encountered Christ? Who know nothing of Jesus?

I would suggest that they too are also saved by the grace of God, through faith. Faith in whatever revelation they have. Faith in the small or large amount of understanding they have been given.

It seems that Paul realises *both* of these things. He sees the reality that people are saved by responding in faith to whatever revelation they have. But he also sees the reality that God visited the world in Christ - and embracing Christ in faith *is the most sure and most wonderful way of responding to God in faith*. Paul appreciates God's natural revelation, but he also seems to think that for many people, natural revelation has not been all that successful in drawing people to God (Romans 1:18-32). He knows that the sure way of salvation is because of the grace of God, through faith in Jesus Christ, and he sees that as an immeasurably more powerful and certain way of salvation than just relying on natural revelation.[7]

Consider how Paul sees both things happening. Read Romans 2, especially verses 12-16 and 25-26. Paul says that people who have sinned without law [without specific, special revelation] will also perish without law. But people who do not have the law, but do by nature the things in the law, show the work of the law written in their hearts. Paul says that their conscience bears witness, and either accuses or excuses them on judgment day. Paul then goes on to speak specifically to Jews who are proud to have the law and circumcision. He reminds them that circumcision is only profitable if they keep the law. He adds that if an uncircumcised man [someone without that specific revelation] keeps the righteous requirements of the law, then his un-circumcision will be counted as circumcision.

In Romans 5 Paul reflects on how sin was in the world since Adam, and how all humans have sinned. He notes that even before the law was given to Moses, sin was already in the world. But he then adds the incredible statement, 'But sin is not charged against anyone's account where there is no law' (Romans 5:13). That is a telling aside! Sin is not counted against the person where there was no special revelation to inform the person on the details of how God wanted them to live.

Paul does not deny that people without the law were still sinners – they still died (the punishment for sin since the Garden of Eden) (Romans 5:14). But his aside still stands: before special revelation comes to someone, they are not 'weighed' in the same way as someone who has special revelation from God. They are saved or not, by how they respond to *whatever* revelation they have.

Paul said something similar on another occasion, to people who had no specific revelation from God (Athenians). Read Acts 17:24-30. After talking about people caught up in idol worshipping ignorance, Paul makes the rather amazing statement

---

[7] Hence one of the reasons for his passion in wanting to get the message out, I would add.

that 'in the past God overlooked such ignorance, but now he commands all people everywhere to repent' (v. 30).

God overlooks ignorance? That is not the evangelical message. They just jump to the next bit: 'now he commands all people everywhere to repent'. But before he said that evangelical-sounding line, he first said that *God overlooks such ignorance*. If people have only general revelation, it might be that they respond in faith, and in their hearts they sense something true and wonderful. They might not be able to put it into words, and they certainly won't know the name of Jesus without special revelation – but they are still 'saved'. Of course having said that, Paul does go on to call on people to embrace Jesus, because Jesus is the *sure* way of salvation. Faith in Christ is a certain way of reconciliation with God. It eliminates any ambiguity or uncertainty about the 'general revelation' pathway, and offers a new way of living to the person who accepts Christ.

So Paul sees general revelation as significant: the uncircumcised person can be seen by God as someone *who is right with him*, if his or her heart leads them to live life accordingly, because they are responding to whatever level of faith and awareness they have.

So we come back to Romans 10:9-15. Can you see now, that this does not mean that those who have never heard of Jesus are automatically damned for eternity? They are not destined to burn forever in some kind of hell-fire. No, they will be saved, or not, on the basis of how they have responded to whatever level of revelation they have been privy to. It has always been about faith in God's self-revelation – whether general or specific. It continues to be that. Like Paul, we might catch the vision of sharing Christ with as many as we can – because of the certain path that it is for reconciliation with God.

Paul has yet another reason for wanting to get people to embrace Christ personally: because it awakens them to a life of discipleship and holiness. *They can receive the Holy Spirit of God himself* (Romans 5:5), and live a life here and now that honours him. He wants to make *disciples* of all nations – not just converts. He wants people to become dead to sin and alive to righteousness in Christ. Romans 6 is written with an excitement and joy that is hard to miss. 'Count yourselves dead to sin, but alive to God in Christ Jesus' (Romans 6:11). By becoming a conscious follower of Jesus we change our lives and live a life that glorifies God and demonstrates holiness and righteousness in this world.

Conclusion

To limit 'personal faith in Jesus' as the *only* way people can connect to God is to ignore some important scriptures, and, for many Christians, it limits our wonderful God from moving in the hearts of others who might never have personally heard the name of Jesus.

But to not inform others about Jesus is withholding the certain and most wonderful gift of salvation to others. It is like *not* giving water to a person dying of thirst. Yes, God probably does deal with others who have never heard the name of Jesus, by weighing them on their response to the revelation they have received. But when we have such a wonderful answer to sin and brokenness – when we have awareness of a gift that can empower people to live lives that honour God and love others to higher levels – how can we not share that?

You know, when the cosmos is wrapped up, and when the 'new heaven and new earth' are humming along, we will be surprised I think, when we see just who is there with us. I have a feeling that it won't just be a narrow band of people who fit a particular definition!

Reading:
Turn ahead in the Book of Acts to chapter 10:34-35.

Asking the hard questions:
'Embracing Jesus is clearly the *sure* way of salvation in the New Testament, but it may not be the *only* way (even if scripture does not completely explain the other ways that are possible).'

When you read a statement like that, what thoughts and feelings does it raise up in you? Does it intimidate you, or your theology? Or, alternatively, is a view such as has been outlined in this study, simply mistaken? Are there other things that still need to be said?

Despite this chapter being very long, it did not address one other related area of consideration: What happens to people who have *heard* of Jesus, but who *reject* him? Discuss that briefly.

After a short time of reflection, consider the main positions different Christians have taken over the centuries in answer to that question, and discuss it again. The main views are:

(1) they are damned to hell – they have rejected the ultimate self-expression of God and his love for us;

(2) they are judged by a *just* and *loving* God who sees into the complexities of their life experiences (the sum total of their life experiences might make them balk at the name of Jesus or the religion of Christianity, and they are 'behind the 8-ball' so to speak, even before they start);

(3) they are weighed by God on the basis of a different criteria – one that we don't get sufficient detail about to be able to explain;

(4) they go to purgatory after they die, but after a lengthy period of time of cleansing determined by God, they eventually get accepted into heaven; or

(5) it doesn't matter: a God of love accepts everyone eventually and so everyone is saved.

ACTS 5

Read Acts 5 before reflecting on studies 11, 12 and 13

11) Acts 5:1-11. Ananias and Sapphira were dead wrong!

Here we have a pretty unpleasant story. It is a story that implies that God strikes dead a husband and wife for the sin of lying, and big-noting themselves. This story is quite ugly. It leaves a bad taste in my mouth. It sits most *uncomfortably* with my belief that God is patient and gracious, longsuffering and full of loving kindness. My belief in that is so strong, because of other scriptures, as well as personal experience, that if one has to be 'sacrificed' for the other, well: I would let this story go. But it is here, staring us in the face, and demanding some kind of discussion.

This unpleasant, harsh, and possibly unjust story comes just after the amazing and wonderful description of the early church community that we looked at in an earlier study (Acts 4:32-37):

> All the believers were one in heart and mind. No one claimed that any of his possessions was his own, but they shared everything they had. With great power the apostles continued to testify to the resurrection of the Lord Jesus. And God's grace was so powerfully at work in them all that there were no needy persons among them. For from time to time, those who owned lands or houses sold them, brought the money from the sales and put it at the apostles' feet, and it was distributed to anyone who had need. Joseph, a Levite from Cyprus, whom the apostles called Barnabas (which means Son of Encouragement) sold a field he owned and brought the money and put it at the apostles' feet. Now a man named Ananias…..

Really, the passage just before the death of this couple should go in the same chapter as this ugly story, and be the prelude to it. Clearly they are about the same thing. What an amazing testimony the chapter 4 material is to a community of Christ followers getting it right! They were caring for the poor even if it meant sacrificing some of their own security and material belongings. Talk about incredible. Then this unpleasant story happens in the midst of it all.

Some have likened the sin of Ananias and Sapphira here with the sin of Achan and his family in the Old Testament (Joshua 7). In both cases, it was the first real sin of a family in the new community of God. Achan committed a sin of greed and lying, just after entering the Promised Land – just after crossing the Jordan and seeing Jericho fall. This couple here, Ananias and Sapphira, committed the sin of greed and lying, just after entering the new covenant community of the church – just after Pentecost and the outpouring of the Spirit.

Such a cross reference reflection might be thought-provoking and interesting… but it still does not really soften what we are reading here. The story in Acts 5 is harsh! It seems the punishment is too great for the actual crime.

A lot of qualifications get made and discussed when reading the harsh story about the death of Ananias and Sapphira.

For example it is rightly pointed out that Peter did not kill anyone. According to the story, God kind of does that – sort of. Well, that is not even said either. It is just *implied*.

It is also pointed out that this was not an enforced and compulsory giving up your possessions to the church. It was always voluntary. See how Peter says, 'Didn't it belong to you *before* it was sold?' No one made them give up the land. And even after they had sold it, it was still theirs to do with as they pleased. Peter also said, 'And after it was sold, wasn't the money *at your disposal*?' So the sin of this couple was not in failing to give everything to the cult leaders at the commune base! It was not a sin of failing to obey orders, nothing like that. No, it was, rather, the sin of spiritual pride that caused them to lie and big-note themselves before the congregation.

Spiritual pride and big-noting themselves in front of others. Trying hard to look like impressive holy Christ-followers! Mr and Mrs Generous.

Okay, but even then, it is still a harsh punishment for spiritual pride. Thank God he does not strike us all down all the time, every time someone commits that sin. There would not be many of us left standing, I would think.

So our problems with this story are not really over.

And of course it *is* important to note that Peter did not kill anyone.

Hmm… so even though Peter is kind-of 'off the hook', it sure makes God look harsh. But maybe there are ways to explain this.

Every now and again unusual deaths happen, don't they? I mean, for example, an older couple might die very close to each other after the first one dies. The loss of the one so close to them is too much for the second person, and their heart gives out as well. Some have testified to their elderly parents even dying on the same day.

What if something like that happened here? What if this couple were an older couple (by Palestinian standards of the 1st century)? What if they were feeling tension and stress because of their scheme to lie to the church and to hide some of their money? What if that was weighing heavily on them? And when Peter confronted the husband, is it possible that a combination of factors came together, and his heart failed? And then, 3 hours later, when the wife hears of her husband's death – that news on top of the stress of all they were carrying, caused her to die as well? Is it possible? Maybe. Maybe not.

If something like that happened, you would imagine that the religious folk of the day would have tried to put it into some kind of framework that made sense to them. Since they were good Jews as well as Christ followers, then it would be very easy to see God as the one striking them dead. And so the story got told as it did.

Maybe? Possible? Yes. Probable? Perhaps not. This explanation might be really just a desperate attempt to 'makes sense of this passage in my own current framework of a good God who is gracious, patient, and just'. Perhaps I should heed the advice of other Christian thinkers whom I respect and simply accept the hard passages of scripture without trying to explain them. Let them just sit. It is okay to be confused over them. Over time confusion leads to more growth.

Maybe God did strike one or both of them dead for spiritual pride and lying.

Clearly if he did, *he has not continued to do so.* There are a lot of folk who commit that same offence every day somewhere in the church, and they live on and grow old. There are people who commit far more horrid offences in the church, who also continue to live on for decades (That really is my problem with this story).

Is there anything positive that we can take from this horrible story?

I think there is. Besides the very obvious 'It is wrong to tell lies!' moral, there are other things here too.

Regarding the full equality of women and men: note that the wife was just as guilty as her husband. She was responsible for her own sin, just as he was for his. The husband did not 'cover' the wife and she did not get 'let off' or receive a 'lesser punishment' because she was obeying her husband's commands. No, men and women both have the same standing before God. What we have here is a back-handed reminder that women and men are fully equal in the sight of God!

This story can also remind us that God wants us to care for the poor and the needy, sincerely from the heart. We don't care for the poor to be seen by others. We don't give to worthwhile causes for our own pride or ego-pampering. Rather, we do it genuinely and compassionately. We should learn from this story that we are not meant to big-note ourselves and seek accolades from others in the church. Such spiritual pride is the cause of many a downfall.

In the picture painted here of the death of Ananias and Sapphira we are reminded that pride and greed will kill us– if not now, then spiritually and eternally.

So some good lessons can be gleaned from a tough story (Even if it does not take away the problems some of us still have with the actual story itself).

Reading:

Read Genesis 1:28-30; 2:16,17; 3:1-24. The Genesis 1 passage was written before sin came into the world; these are the first spoken words of God to humankind. God tells man and woman to fill the earth and rule it together. It seems that it was not God's intent to have men 'rule' over women, but rather men and women to 'rule over the creation together.' If this was God's original intent before sin spoiled the world, then what happened to change that? Should we support structures that make women *less* equal than men?

In Genesis 2:17 we note that the punishment for sin is death. Nothing else is mentioned. Just death. Paul says the same thing in Romans ('the wages of sin is death,' Romans 6:23). Note too, in Genesis 3, that God punishes both the man and the woman for their sins. The woman's sin was not that she did not listen to her husband and obey all he said, *it was disobedience to God*. Man and woman are both individually responsible for their sin, individually answerable to God.

Finally, consider the long list of bad things that are going to happen in the world as a result of sin coming into the world (Genesis 3:14-19). Some people see these as 'God's will for the world', but that can't be true. It is actually a list of tragic repercussions that have entered the world because of sin. They are not God's wish list! They are a list of tragic outcomes because of evil in the world.

Asking the hard questions:
If all that is so, then how should we be living in the church as far as our relationship between men and women is concerned? Is it right to forbid women from being priests? Or from preaching and teaching?

12) Acts 5:29. Civil disobedience

Recall the context of growing persecution as we think about what else happens in chapter 5. The healing of the man born lame was wonderful and incredible. It was also the catalyst for trouble. The authorities began to take notice of the apostles. During Peter's speech to the people, 'The priests and the captain of the temple guard and the Sadducees, came up to Peter and John' (Acts 4:1) and arrested them. They were imprisoned overnight, and the next day brought before the leaders of Jerusalem.

This was not a nice time to live in! A wonderful miracle happened, the disciples drew a crowd, they spoke to the crowd, and then they got arrested. This is so different to our modern western democracies. Today, you would draw the media and get on the news. You would probably be invited to speak all over the place. Our governments would certainly not arrest you for talking about religion to a crowd that was interested in what you were saying. Even more so if it was peaceful!

The world was very different back then. The Jewish authorities arrested Peter and John. Those authorities actually did not like *what* the disciples were teaching. The apostles were teaching about a future 'resurrection from the dead in Christ' (Acts 4:2) – and Sadducees were quite adamant that that was a fantasy.[8] So Peter and John were

---

[8] See their encounter with Jesus, in Matthew 22:23-33

'theological rivals' to the Sadducees, and yet it was the Sadducees who held 'earthly power'. They used that power to try to put down their religious opponents.

The apostles were grilled at the meeting. You can read it in 4:7-22. Eventually they were threatened (4:21) and released. However, the disciples did not obey their commands, nor did they feel intimidated by their threats. Their statement to those with power (vs. 19-20) is quite confrontational. 'Which is right in God's eyes: to listen to you, or to him? You be the judges! As for us, we cannot help speaking about what we have seen and heard'.

Wow, talk about strong stuff! These uneducated fishermen from Galilee are boldly telling those who have the power to punish them (jail, torture, even death) that they are not going to obey them. They are standing up to an unjust command by their governing authorities and saying, 'Sorry, but what you want of us is wrong. We can't do that. We will continue to do the right thing.' In fact, in their case, they claim that they will continue to do what God wants them to do.

Now think about that. They are talking to a group of leading people who believe they are God's chosen leadership, ruling over God's people (at the time, the Jews). The disciples are saying to those authorities that God is actually directing them (the apostles) personally, and that any contrary commands from God's so-called leadership in Jerusalem are wrong!

Pride and power and jealousy and all sorts of nasty things would be bubbling up in the hearts and minds of the ruling elite. How dare these fishermen tell them what God wants and does not want! Who do these men think they are?

The apostles were then threatened and bullied (but not physically hurt - yet). They went home and prayed (4:23-30) and were further emboldened to continue doing what they were doing (4:31).

Okay… all that by way of reminder and context. Now, in chapter 5 we see the apostles disobeying the rulers of Jerusalem again. There is more preaching and healings and miracles. It must have been an incredible time for the residents of Jerusalem. If these words accurately capture what went on, well… can you imagine witnessing it? 'The apostles performed many signs and wonders among the people. ... people brought the sick into the streets and laid them on bed and mats so that at least Peter's shadow might fall on some of them as he passed by ... the sick and those tormented by impure spirits were all being healed' (5:12-16).

The authorities acted again. This time they would not be so easy going! The rulers (essentially the Sadducees – that rich elite group that ran Jerusalem) 'arrested the apostles and put them in a public jail' (5:17, 18). They would try them and punish them the next day.

The interrogation is summarised by Luke. The council leaders accused the disciples, 'We gave you strict orders not to teach in this name (Jesus)...' (5:28).

The next verse is our key for this reflection: 'Peter and the other apostles replied: "We must obey God rather than human beings"' (5:29).

This one sentence captures the dilemma of civil disobedience. Sometimes we have to obey God, not governments. Sometimes we have to march to a different drumbeat than the authorities on this earth. Sometimes we have to accept the consequences of our decisions and take a stand. Sometimes our governments are wrong.

It might not be an issue of being allowed to speak about your faith freely in a community (though sometimes it is about religious oppression). It might be all sorts of other issues. It may be that a minority group is being unjustly treated. It may be that the rich are being allowed to destroy critical parts of the environment that are essential to many others. It may be that unjust laws need to be highlighted and confronted. During World War II, when people were told to hand over Jewish neighbours and not hide them or help them escape, some people, like Corrie Ten Boon's family, disobeyed (and if caught, suffered the consequences).

Those with earthly power can hurt us. But they cannot *make* us do anything we don't agree to do. They might frighten us or intimidate us, but when we go along with an unjust order or command, we are *choosing* to do so. We might say, 'They made me', but that is technically not true. They made it hard for us not to, but we still choose. We can choose the easy, painless path. Or we can choose the hard path that might cost us much.

There comes a time for civil disobedience. Christians here in this story committed an act of disobedience – it is appropriate and even necessary for Christians to commit other acts of civil disobedience at times.

A few very quick things to add:

- Some Christians are so keen to take Romans 13:1-7 literally that they never countenance civil disobedience. However, Romans 13 says that Christians must 'be subject' to governing authorities. It does not say they must 'obey' governing authorities. In the original Greek, there are different words for 'submit', 'be subject to', and 'obey'. These are distinct. They are different words with different meanings. When the apostles *disobeyed* their governing authorities in Acts 4 and 5, they still *submitted* to them, by accepting the consequences of their actions.

- This Romans passage has itself been understood in different ways. An obsessive focus on verse 1 might make us compliant servants to a cruel regime, but as you read the rest of the paragraph, more material surfaces: Oh! Governments are supposed to do that which is right, that which is consistent with justice and a holy God. So if they are not? What then? The passage does not seem to be addressing that scenario. It is less clear on that point.

- The disciples remained peaceful at all times. Their civil disobedience was always expressed in pacifism. They were not passive! But they *were* pacifist. They never suggested or entertained the idea of violence in response to the violence they experienced.

However the disciples did suffer consequences for their civil disobedience. If you read the rest of chapter 5, you will see that they were beaten this time. Indeed some of the Sanhedrin wanted to kill them (5:33). Wiser council swayed the group, however, so they were 'only' whipped, and then released.

The apostles left the council and continued in their civil disobedience, and 'day after day, in the temple courts and from house to house, they never stopped teaching and proclaiming the good news that Jesus is the Messiah' (5:42).

A final warning: Don't use this passage to justify disobedience for anything and everything you happen to dislike. That is not what civil disobedience is about. But if the cause is just; if the issue is really consistent with a merciful and loving God, then Christians should be inspired by these words of Peter, 'We must obey God, not human beings'.

Reading:
Read the prophet Micah 6:8, then Matthew 5:9, and James 3:17-18.

Asking the hard questions:
How do we *do* justice in this world? And what does it mean to be a peacemaker in the world while we do that?

13) Acts 5:34. Advocacy

Gamaliel is not the most famous name in the Book of Acts. He is one of the many characters that Luke introduces to us. This one story is his main appearance.

We have already seen that the early church was persecuted. In Acts 4 and 5 it really intensified and that continues until in Acts 7 we see the murder of Stephen and the unleashing of a huge persecution that began in earnest.

Before the death of Stephen, however, some of the apostles were nearly killed when they had a tense encounter with the religious leaders of the day. In chapter 5, Peter is recorded as speaking really boldly to the Sanhedrin. The religious leaders of the Jews were not impressed. It says after Peter's brazen words, 'When they heard this, they were furious and wanted to put them to death' (v.33).

But they were not murdered that day. They were saved, in fact, by one of the religious leaders sitting on that very council. A man named Gamaliel.

'But a Pharisee named Gamaliel, a teacher of the Law, who was honoured by all the people, stood up in the Sanhedrin and ordered that the men be put outside for a little while' (v.34). He then spoke to the council, and his arguments and wisdom won the day. After his reasoned defence of the apostles, they took his advice and had them flogged but not killed (5:40).

What do we know about this man who saved Peter's life (and the lives of the other apostles) that day? Not a lot. But some Jewish writings do refer to him. What they say lines up with the brief comments we have about him here. He was a well-regarded teacher of the law and respected by all. The Mishnah (*Sotah* 9.15) refers to him with high regard, and that probably means that he did not convert to Christianity, even though some church traditions try to say that he did. Some Jewish traditions say that he was even the son of Hillel, the famous teacher who founded a 'school of theology'.

Paul also mentions Gamaliel briefly by name in Acts 22:3 as someone who had taught him when he was younger.

Clearly he was a wise and respected elder of the community.

This Jew saved the early Christian apostles' lives that day. A Jewish rabbi, a Pharisee (probably a more liberal one who belonged to the school of Hillel) and an elder of the people, saved the early Christians.

That rings with something wonderful don't you think? Sadly, it would not be the way of Jewish/Christian relations in the centuries to come. Christians would treat the Jews appallingly over the next 2,000 years, particularly during the Middle Ages, but also during the Reformation and afterwards. Catholics and Protestants both would persecute and harass the Jews. One of Martin Luther's worst moments was when his anti-Semitism surfaced on occasion – not least of all in one of his last main published books[9] (a book that would be used by the Nazi Party to add another layer of justification to what they would do to the Jews).

But way back at the beginning of the church, a practicing Jew saved Christians from being lynched.

What a great lesson for us today. Are we prepared to do similarly? Will we use our wisdom, our arguments, our standing in the community, to defend those who are a despised minority? Are we prepared to be a voice to speak for the voiceless? If you are a Christian, would you stand up and save the life of a Muslim? Would you stick your neck out? Would you 'be seen to be defending *them*'?

Gamaliel offers us a wonderful example of a good man, a wise person, and a noble individual. He is a person who can inspire us in a similar way. Let's not be afraid of those of other religions who are not exactly the same as us. Rather let us show mercy, compassion, and grace, just like Gamaliel did back in his day. And let us be advocates for those who struggle to be heard by others in our community.

---

9   Von den Juden und Ihren Lügen, *On the Jews and Their Lies*, published in 1543.

Reading:
Proverbs 31:8-9.

Asking the hard questions:
How do we speak up for the voiceless? How do we advocate *for* them and *with* them? How do we help empower others to speak up for themselves? And how do we seek to help their voices be heard? *Do we even do that?* What is our attitude towards asylum seekers? What is our attitude towards the handicapped? What about Muslims living in our Western culture? Who are the voiceless in our day and age and in our community?

ACTS 6

Read Acts 6 before reflecting on studies 14 and 15

14) Acts 6:1. Dealing with complaints

By Acts 6 there was a growing persecution that seemed to only embolden the disciples. There was radical communal living. There was so much generosity and sacrifice! More and more people were finding faith and embracing Christ.

But it was not all a walk in the park. While the disciples were increasing in number, 'the Hellenistic Jews among them complained against the Hebraic Jews...' in the church (Acts 6:1).

Even though that sounds a bit sad, and a bit of a 'defeat' in some ways, nevertheless it can be *reassuring* that these first Christians were still very human as well. They were not perfect at administration. They were not perfect in making sure people did not drop through the net they had created to care for those in need. They still made mistakes. And some of them complained about it.

The complaints being made were registered with the apostles. The essential concern boiled down to some of the widows in the church missing out on the daily distribution of food to the poor. But not just that, it actually looked like ethnic discrimination. 'The Hellenistic Jews among them complained against the Hebraic Jews because their widows were being overlooked in the daily distribution of food' (6:1b).

Ouch! Were the Hebrew Christians (the native Hebrew Christians – those who spoke Hebrew) deliberately leaving the *Hellenistic* Jewish widows on the bottom of the food distribution list? Were they 'looking after their own' and not all that interested in the Greek speaking Jews who were often deemed to be 'a bit second class' by orthodox Jews of the day? Was that old Jewish discrimination a part of the church as well?

How could that be?

Well, fortunately, it was not that at all. It might have looked like it to some, but looks can be deceptive. Such was the case here. As soon as the apostles realised the problem, they sought to remedy it. They gathered all the church together and directed the group to choose seven good men to oversee the daily distribution of the food to widows. All seven chosen were – wait for it – all seven were Hellenistic Jews! Not one token Hellenistic Jewish Christian on the panel to have their say, but with no overall influence. Not even three of the seven. Not even four of the seven! No, the whole job was given to the complaining minority group. We know this from the names. All seven are Greek names: Stephen, Philip, Prochorus, Nicanor, Timon, Parmenas and Nicolas (v. 5). And Nicolas was not even a Jew. He was rather 'a proselyte from Antioch' – someone who had converted to Judaism first and then found faith in Christ.

So the group that was being overlooked, who thought they were being discriminated against, got the job of doing the distribution to *all* the recipients! They could now distribute the daily food to *all* the widows, both Hebrew and Greek speaking!

It is almost a visual apology, a very clear statement that there were no hard feelings, and no discrimination intended. To prove it, the disciples simply said, 'Here, have the job! Now you can decide how to distribute the food to even the Hebrew widows who are not a part of your particular sub-group!'

What generosity and what a clever solution! It was a brave and trusting move. It made the previous authorities in that area (the apostles who were in charge) vulnerable and powerless. It was a sign of trust, and a concrete act of empowering others around them.

Are we that brave today? Or would we recoil from such a radical act of empowering others, because we fear that just maybe we might be discriminated against, or ignored, or marginalised?

Reading:
John 13:1-16.

Asking the hard questions:
If *serving* is really the 'mark' of a Christ follower, did the disciples here

in the Acts story start to lose the plot? Did they see serving as a second rate option? They were too busy serving – they needed to give up on that time-wasting activity and do the real ministry stuff: preaching! Is that the way to understand this passage? What might be missing when we draw that kind of conclusion? (We will revisit this *preaching versus serving* question in the next reflection).

Whatever you decide about that question, notice how the apostles gave over the full job to the group that were complaining. What are your impressions of that decision? How could that principle be applied in our context today? Should it be applied?

Discuss the tension between something being *the* model to copy versus it being *a* model that is optional to copy or not. Even if you decide it is *a* model, how and when might it be applied in our lives and in our context today?

15) Acts 6:1-4. Caring for the poor versus preaching

The Hellenistic Jewish widows were being overlooked in the daily serving of food. In response to that, 'the twelve gathered all the disciples together and said, "It would not be right for us to neglect the ministry of the Word of God in order to wait on tables. Brothers and sisters, choose seven men from among you who are known to be full of the Spirit and of wisdom. We will turn this responsibility over to them and will give our attention to prayer and the ministry of the word"' (Acts 6:1-4).

When I first read this passage many years ago, I thought, 'These early apostles were a bit "up themselves" with self-importance! They don't have the time to serve food to the poor? They have the "more important work" of ministering the Word, preaching the Gospel!? It all sounds a bit arrogant to me, and a drift away from the heart of Jesus who loved the poor and wanted us to love and care for the poor as well! Didn't Jesus wash his disciples' feet and tell them to do likewise to others?'

As it turns out, over time one sometimes sees things differently. I have done a 180-degree turn on how I see this passage. The apostles were not putting down the importance of caring for the poor. Not at all! It was so important in fact, that they knew they were not doing a good enough job of it. They were divided. They were busy preaching about Jesus, and they felt compelled to continue that. After all, there were not all that many people who were first-hand witnesses of Jesus' life and teachings and resurrection, so they knew that was their primary responsibility.

But at the same time, feeding the poor was very important. So important in fact, that seven really good people needed to be chosen to do it better than it was being done. The seven chosen were not new converts or theological dummies who could do nothing else. They were not chair shufflers. They had to be 'full of the Spirit, and full of wisdom.' The qualifications list for a potential candidate was actually quite rigorous!

Not only that, there is a wonderful thing to note in the Greek language here that is not made clear by the English translation. The word for 'distribution' (some translations say '*serving*') of food in verse 1, and the word for 'ministering' of the Word, in verses 2 and 4 – *are the same word*! They are both able to be translated as 'ministering'. They both could equally be translated as 'serving'.

To serve food to the poor is on the same level as serving people the Gospel. To tell people about God and Jesus is the same kind of work as feeding the poor! Both activities are called *service*. Both activities are called *ministry*.

There is nothing elitist about preaching over serving the poor. There is nothing super special about the one who specialises in one but not the other. They are both critical ministries for the church to maintain. They are both so important in fact that we need to find specialists in both areas who can get on with their emphasis. We also need to remember that all of us should do both, to one degree or the other, as we can!

Reading:
1 Corinthians 12:1-27.

Asking the hard questions:
1 Corinthians 12 is that famous chapter with comments by Paul on 'The Body of Christ' being made up of lots of different parts. If it is really true that greater honour should be given to the more insignificant parts (vs.23-24), how does that actually *look* in the church today? Do we really do that? How?

ACTS 7

Read Acts 7 before reflecting on studies 16 and 17

There was a need for seven good men of repute
to handle arising financial disputes.
'The twelve' summoned all the disciples together
and it was soon decided who would handle the matter.
Chosen were Philip, Timon, and Prochorus,
Nicanor, Parmenas, and Nicolaus,
and Stephen.

Now Stephen was full of grace and power
and was led by the Spirit each day and each hour.
Among the people he accomplished great wonders and signs,
and when challenged and accused, his enemies could not find
any wrong in his words. The Spirit guided his tongue.
His enemies then paid liars to accuse him of wrong.
'He's blasphemed!' they cried.

'Stephen's spoken blasphemy against Moses and God!'
He was seized and dragged by an angry mob
to the council where false witnesses spoke out against him.
They accused him of rejecting the law – a serious sin.
Gazing at him now were the eyes of all the council
but Stephen's face appeared then as one like an angel.
He replied to the charges.

He spoke of Abraham, Isaac, Jacob and Joseph,
and reflected as well, on the life of Moses.
He explained how their ancestors continually disobeyed
the law of God even up that their day!
He spoke also of David, and then he accused the council:

'You're just like your fathers – they killed those who announced
the coming of Christ!'

He accused them of murdering God's only Son.
They became enraged and they vented and fumed at this one
who then saw and explained a Spirit revealed sight
of God in His glory and Jesus on His right!
The council cried out, not wanting to hear
any more of this Stephen, who to them, it was clear
was a blasphemer!

They rushed upon Stephen and cast him out of the city.
They pounded his body with stones, lacking all pity.
As he was dying, Stephen called out to God above
to forgive those who were killing him – how great was his love!
With this he fell down and died as a martyr,
but his life had not really ended: he was beginning the 'life-after'
through faith.

During the murder, one man watching it all
had given his consent to it – he was known as Saul.
And on that day a great persecution began
against the members of the church in Jerusalem.
Many Christians were scattered throughout nearby regions,
but not the apostles or some devout men
who buried Stephen.

Stephen had lived a life of faith.
He had walked each day in God's incredible grace.
Neither authority nor pressure could destroy his love
for Christ and for others, or for his calling from above.
Stephen died for his God – he must have been sure
that he would never be abandoned, and that the heavenly door
was open to all believers.

16) Acts 7:48-49. God does not dwell in houses built by people

When Luke introduced us to the seven deacons, one of them was named Stephen. The Book of Acts now turns to that man and gives us a key story about him: his martyrdom.

Stephen is described in glowing terms: 'a man full of faith, and of the Holy Spirit' (6:5); 'full of God's grace and power' (6:8); 'performing great wonders and signs' (6:8); a person who spoke 'with the wisdom of the Spirit'; who won any debate he got into (6:10); and having the 'face of an angel' (6:15).

He was accused with false charges, arrested and taken to the Sanhedrin. He was then invited to answer the accusations against him. His reply is one of the longest speeches in the Book of Acts and fills most of chapter 7, from verse 2 to verse 53 in fact. It is an interesting speech in that it sums up much of the Old Testament story from Abraham (Genesis 12 onwards) to Kings David and Solomon (1 and 2 Samuel and 1 Kings). A number of prophets are also quoted in-between.

Towards the end of his speech he comes out with the clanger that got him killed. He dared to remind the Jewish religious leaders that God himself had said that no house built by any person is big enough to contain him! '... The most high does not live in houses made by human hands. As the prophet says: "Heaven is my throne, and the earth is my footstool. What kind of house will you build for me?" says the Lord. "Or where will my resting place be?"' (Acts 7:48, 49, quoting Isaiah 66:1).

Well, that was the turning point for his listeners. He dug himself deeper with his following comments as well, no doubt ('You stiff necked people! Your hearts and ears are still uncircumcised. ... you always resist the Holy Spirit!' etc). But to tell the Jewish religious leaders - who put so much emphasis on the Temple, their wonderful incredible lavish Temple, the place where there was the so called 'holy of holies' where God himself dwelt - that their emphasis was wrong? To tell people whose whole religious experience rotated around *that* building, that it was not really a satisfactory 'home' for God? That was to court disaster. How could this Greek-speaking Jew, now also a despised Christian, dare to teach the religious leaders of the day such a foreign thought! He was a blasphemer. He was theologically mistaken. He was a dangerous heretic!

And so they murdered him.

But the point Stephen made at the end of his speech and at the end of his life was something that has resonated throughout time. God *is* much bigger than any person's ability to 'capture' him. God is *not* to be 'boxed in' to my clever descriptions or your clever understanding, or some famous theologian's brilliant writings. God can't be contained. No human construct (physical or philosophical) can contain and 'tame' the God of all things. No physical building captures him fully or properly. None. Not a Jewish Temple, or a Muslim Mosque or a Christian Cathedral. Not the Vatican in Rome or a grass church hut in Fiji. Not the greatest Hindu temple or the most humble fibro church. Not the most wonderful Buddhist shrine or the most ornate Orthodox Church.

We will always limit and restrict God. God is, after all, the one who says 'Heaven is my throne and the earth is my footstool. What kind of house will you build for me?' (Isaiah 66:1).

A little humility seems to be suggested in all this, a recognition that all our best efforts to describe and contain God are, in the end, destined to be imperfect and flawed.

That, of course, should not stop us from grappling and growing and learning and applying what we learn. But let's do all that in a spirit of awe, humility, tolerance and grace towards others.

Reading:
Consider Jesus' words in Matthew 18:20.

Asking the hard questions:
If Jesus really said that, what does it mean for our obsession with church buildings? Seriously, we put so much emphasis on the church building, on the Sunday service, on the special time we meet together in the actual building. Maybe it is a distraction? Could it be that we are falling into a state of, well, almost *idolatry*, in the way we focus so much on bricks and mortar? The amount of time and money and energy that goes into building, maintaining, and even boasting about 'the size of our building; the number of people it seats, the number of people who come'? Have we used something that should be functional and incidental, and turned it into the most important thing? Have we taken the packaging and accidentally turned that into the gift? Discuss.

17) Acts 7:60. I'm just human

There was a time when I heard this quite a bit. Jesus lived very simply, but surely we are not really expected to. Jesus loved his enemies. Sure he did, but he was perfect. It is not as if mere humans can actually do that like he did! He was the Son of God after all. Surely we can't be expected to. Jesus died on the cross forgiving his torturers and executioners. Again, he was Immanuel, God with us! Surely that means he did stuff that is impossible for us frail humans to do.

Well, the attempt to impose that kind of logic and reasoning onto Jesus and his incredible life would be all very well and good *if it held up to observation*. But the actual reality is that real human beings have done exactly the same things as mentioned in the first paragraph. In the early church and in the early centuries after the end of the Book of Acts, and all throughout the last 2,000 years in fact, people *have* lived like Jesus.

In Acts 7:60 we see the end of the story of Stephen. Stephen, one of the seven deacons, was also a very gifted speaker. He could run rings around those who tried to argue against what he said. Indeed, that was what got him killed. His enemies stoned him to death (Acts 7:58-60). Not a nice way to die. Large rocks, the size of house bricks, were thrown at him while he was in a kind of pit or lower area to the stone-throwers. Being stoned to death was a cruel, painful and slow way to die.

The story in Acts tells us that as Stephen was dying, one of his last comments was, 'Lord! Do not hold this sin against them!' (7:60). Saying that phrase, he echoed Jesus himself who, as he died on the cross prayed, 'Father forgive them, for they do not know what they are doing' (Luke 23:34).

Stephen was a 'mere mortal'. He was not God incarnate. He was not the Son of God – perfect in every way. He was just like you and me. So what made him able to love people so much that he could pray a prayer of forgiveness for his murderers? What did he have in him that allowed him to be that amazing?

Earlier in the story we were told that Stephen was full of God's grace and power and that he performed great signs and wonders among the people (Acts 6:8).

Grace and power. I think those two things are actually linked. A lot of Christians seem to want to have 'power' to do amazing things, like heal the sick and raise the dead! Now wouldn't that be something! But they forget that that kind of power is not something that is able to be demanded and just 'acquired'. It comes with *grace*.

Great grace and great power seem to be a package deal. Such grace is the quality we see as Stephen died and *still* loved his enemies! Grace is the last thing Stephen demonstrated before he died. Not great power. He did not use the power of the Holy Spirit within him to smite his enemies and prevent his death! No, he demonstrated great grace.

That reminds us that grace is actually *bigger* and more *important* than power. Grace is the reason for everything else.

Grace - undeserved love that is never ending. Great grace is the quality we should be seeking before anything else, before everything else.

As we grow in grace, we grow in the capacity to be more like Jesus. It is real. It is possible. It is accessible for us mere humans to have. Like Stephen we can show great grace even in the most horrid and impossible times.

Reading:
Read the Apostle Paul's words in 1 Corinthians 11:1.

Asking the hard questions:
Consider that rationale again: 'We can't really live like Jesus, he was God incarnate after all! We are just human!' How might this kind of line be shown to be false? How might you convince people that it is time to ditch that excuse? How could you convince someone else that such an attitude is just a cop-out for not working on problem areas in our lives?

ACTS 8

Read Acts 8 before reflecting on studies 18 and 19

18) Acts 8:2. It is okay to mourn

In the early chapters of Acts, we saw how persecution began against the Christians in Jerusalem and how it intensified until finally Stephen was killed (7:58-60). We are so used to hearing about the persecution of Christians, and the fact that Stephen was the first Christian martyr after Christ, that we can forget the enormity of this event.

It was horrible. It was devastating. It was a reality check moment. Threats and intimidation and even getting knocked around was one thing, but to have one of your people killed for their faith?

The text goes on to say that a planned persecution then began in earnest, and pretty well everyone who believed in Christ was scattered out of Jerusalem (8:1) 'except the apostles'. The text then adds, 'Godly men buried Stephen and mourned deeply for him' (8:2). One other translation puts it like this: 'Some devout men buried Stephen, and made loud lamentation over him'.

You know what that reminds us of?

It reminds us of the simple truth that it is normal to grieve. Even if you are an apostle in the church, even if you are seen as a 'devout person', it is okay to grieve. It is okay to be loud about your mourning. It is not failing as a 'person of faith' if you feel great loss and grief and pain. There is nothing deeply spiritual in being detached from your emotions. You don't have to suppress pain and sorrow because you are a church leader, or a mature member of the congregation.

Some religions, such as Buddhism, tell us to grow more detached from our emotions. Some try to say that the truly spiritual person is the one who escapes their feelings and avoids all pain and suffering in the world by becoming more and more inwardly separated from the illusion of the material realm. Sorry guys, that is just denying humanity and reality. Real people have real feelings. Real, relevant, caring people know how to mourn. In fact they know how to laugh with those who laugh and cry with those who cry. They are not trying to become detached from their emotions and avoid the realities of suffering and pain in the world. No! They accept with sadness that such things happen, but they also work through them. They are not broken by them; they become more empathetic and real because of them.

Forget the 'stiff upper lip' nonsense, and make a loud noise when you have to! It is normal, acceptable, natural, and in fact *healthy* to make 'loud lamentation' when needed.

Reading:
Romans 12:15 and John 11:33-36.

Asking the hard questions:
If we fail to weep with those who weep, what have we lost that is really fundamental to our full humanity?

If you *agree* that we should weep with those who weep (as well as laugh with those who laugh) – then how do you identify with those people who are weeping around us? What is your attitude and relationship with asylum seekers ('boat people')? Do we go along with modern indifference towards their plight? Or do we weep with them: empathise and care for them? Think about possible 'throw away lines' so common in the broader community: 'queue jumpers'; 'sneaking in the back door'; 'not really in trouble, just wanting a better life here'; 'economic migrants'; 'border security', etc?

Discuss if you have ever used such terms, or agreed with the sentiments they carry.

Who else might there be in our community who are 'weeping' who we just close our ears to? What about gay Christians struggling with the church's attitude towards them? What about the Afghani family who people look unkindly at in the street? The Muslim woman who gets slandered by ignorant Australians because she wears her traditional clothing? How do we 'weep with those who weep'? Or do we just save our weeping for our friends?

19) Acts 8:17-23. The origin of the sin of 'Simony'

Have you ever seen churches that operate like this?:

'He's a terrific giver! He is such a successful businessman who tithes regularly to the church. We should make him a board member.'

Or:

'So-and-so gave us a once-off incredibly generous gift of ten thousand dollars towards the new extension. It might be time to promote him to eldership.'

Or:

'That person has been constantly generous to all our appeals and needs in this church. Clearly that is someone with commitment and vision. Leadership material in fact.'

You know, when we read church history and find out that during the Middle Ages people with lots of money could buy themselves a church office – a position of authority, and usually a position that drew its own source of income – we often think 'Tut tut! Weren't they naughty! Fancy doing that!'

In fact, we have a name for it. We call the buying and selling of church office 'simony'. In the Middle Ages it was arguably a bit more crass than the three examples I have noted above. But the examples above are nervously close to what went on. People with money could buy themselves leadership roles in the church. We call that simony.

That word, 'simony' comes from the name of a key character in a story in Acts 8:17-23. Simon of Samaria was a magician who became a disciple at the preaching and miracles done by Philip. He was even more dazzled by the apostles' ability to lay hands on people so that they received the Holy Spirit. He asked if he could buy that power! 'Give me also this ability, so that everyone on whom I lay my hands may receive the Holy Spirit!' (8:19).

Peter was not impressed. He rebuked Simon sharply and was actually quite horrified that someone could think that money could buy them authority or power in the church!

I wonder what Peter would say today if he could see just how much money actually does get influence in churches.

Reading:

Read 1 Peter 5:1-4 (Simon-Peter's brief description of what church leaders should look like and be motivated by). Then compare it with Paul's list in 1 Timothy 3:1-7.

Asking the hard questions:

How are your church leaders appointed? Discuss the tension between appointing someone on the basis of personal character, or spiritual gifts, or worldly experience. Do worldly criteria that secular corporations use tend to apply? 'You know, he is a good businessman, so he would be good on the board'. Or, 'She has sat on the board of her company, so she would be good to have in eldership'. Or, 'He has run his own small business for years; clearly he would be appropriate for the church leadership team'.

If character is the real test of leadership (according to Paul and Peter), and not so much worldly experience – why does it seem that character is such a secondary quality for contemporary church leadership?

Part 2: The conversion of Paul to the council of Jerusalem

ACTS 9

The Conversion of the Apostle Paul

In chapter 9 we come to a crucial moment in the story of this book. It is the point where a hostile critic and persecutor of the new faith (a man named Saul) becomes a disciple.

Luke had been building up to it. He had already introduced Saul (later to be known as Paul) to us. At the end of chapter 7 and the start of chapter 8, Stephen had been killed and Saul was seen there as a member of the group that murdered him (7:58, 8:1). Not only that, but he catches the 'bug' to persecute other Christians. He was passionate and angry. 8:3 tells us that 'Saul began to destroy the church. Going from house to house, he dragged off both men and women and put them in prison.'

The story then covered other material for the rest of chapter 8, but Luke has prepared us to meet Saul again. That comes in chapter 9.

Saul is still on his witch-hunt by chapter 9. 'Meanwhile, Saul was still breathing out murderous threats against the disciples of the Lord. He went to the high priest and asked him for letters to the synagogues in Damascus, so that if he found any there who belonged to the Way, whether men or women, he might take them as prisoners to Jerusalem' (9:1-2). *That* is the setting for one of the most important events in the church's history: Saul travelling on the road to Damascus and meeting the risen Christ.

The conversion of Saul is so significant in fact, that Luke will tell the story three times in this book. Here is the first account in its historical, chronological setting. Later, Luke would record Paul sharing his testimony in various contexts to various audiences. In two such settings, Paul included the story of his conversion (22:3-16 where he speaks to an angry crowd; and 26:9-18 where he is speaking to King Herod Agrippa). It is good to compare the other two accounts to this one. You get a few extra details later that are not included here.

It really is hard to overstate the importance of this event. It changed so much. It caused so much. It led to so much! Paul would spend the rest of his life travelling from town to town and city to city telling the story of Jesus to any who would listen. He would get into all sorts of trouble and conflict, and he would see some wonderful successes. He would pen a number of letters to individuals, to churches, and to clusters of churches, and some of those letters would survive and become a large part of the New Testament. Paul in fact wrote about 20 percent of the entire New Testament.

There are 27 books and letters in the New Testament and Paul wrote up to 13 of them (a few of the 13 are highly disputed regarding authorship, so we have to say 'up to 13' to be accurate). Numerically that is about half of the books of the New Testament. But total page numbers is a different thing. The Gospels, Acts and Revelation make up the bulk of the material, and he did not pen any of those.

So this angry and passionate Jewish Pharisee, who was so hostile to the Church, became its greatest missionary. He took the new young religion, and helped embed it into the fabric of the Roman Empire. It was a grass-roots movement, working from the bottom of society upward, and its first adherents were mostly the 'nobodies' of the world. Paul would actually write to one of his churches saying, 'Not many of you were wise by human standards, not many were influential, not many were of noble birth' (1 Cor. 1:26) and such was certainly the case during the first two centuries. There were exceptions. Slaves were known at times to convert their masters, and some nobles did die for their faith during the persecutions that took place.

Despite the humble beginnings of the faith, it anchored itself, grew, and gradually caught on. It is thought that at the time of Constantine the Great becoming the first Christian Emperor (in the early 300s), about 10 percent of the population of the Empire had already joined the church. Still a minority, but a large minority.

The Apostle Paul was used by God as a critical instrument of his will. Paul tirelessly shared the gospel story, and he saw church after church begin and grow. He had a pastor's heart as well: he was constantly writing to his churches, visiting them, correcting them, encouraging them, and commending them.

The conversion of Saul to become the Apostle Paul was a profound moment in the history of the Church.

Read Acts 9 before reflecting on studies 20 and 21

20) Acts 9:10-17. Does God sometimes miss the latest news?

Acts chapter 9 is famous for the account of the conversion of Saul – who would later be known as Paul.

Here in chapter 9 we read the story of how this angry and violent man had an encounter with the risen Christ. He was, until then, killing Christians. He was on a mission to silence them, arrest them and punish them.

But Christ met him and changed him forever. The violent and angry man would later be the author of amazing teachings like, 'Do not take revenge my dear friends, but leave room for God's wrath, for it is written… "If your enemy is hungry, feed him. If he is thirsty, give him something to drink. In doing this you heap burning coals on his head". Do not be overcome by evil, but overcome evil with good' (Romans 12:19-21).

Of course, when an evil person changes to become a good person, it might not be believed straight away by people from both camps. Other evil people might think that the change is a clever ploy to 'get inside the camp of the others' and get information on them. People from the good camp might think the same!

Ananias seems to have been a bit worried about this new convert. Ironically, he found out about Saul's conversion from God himself!

'In Damascus there was a disciple named Ananias. The Lord called to him in a vision. "Ananias! … Go to the house of Judas on Straight Street and ask for a man from Tarsus named Saul, for he is praying"…' (Acts 9:10-12). Ananias was shocked. He replied to God, 'Lord…I have heard many reports about this man and all the harm he did to your holy people in Jerusalem. And he has come here with authority from the chief priests to arrest all who call upon your name' (9:13-14).

His reply is actually amusing in a way. He seems to think that the Lord has missed something. Maybe God has been busy looking after the other side of the universe for a few months. Doesn't he *know*? God! Don't you get it? If I go there he will bind me and take me in chains back to Jerusalem with the aim of having me killed! Wake up God! How did you miss the biggest news of the month!?

Well, actually it was Ananias who was the one missing the latest news. He was the one falling behind the latest gossip. He did not know that Saul had met the risen Lord and Saul's whole life was suddenly turned upside down.

I would suggest that we are all like Ananias at times. We lack faith in a big God. *We* know what has happened, *we* know what is going on, *we* know who we can trust and who is a creep, right? If we get some kind of conviction that rattles that neat and tidy understanding and maybe even threatens us a bit personally, well, 'God! Haven't you heard!? Don't you know?!'

Let us be willing to let God be God, and let's determine to trust him always.

Reading:

The gospel story of Jesus sleeping during a storm on the lake: Mark 4:35-41.

Asking the hard questions:

Have you ever felt like Jesus is asleep? Think about some time in your life when you felt like you had been abandoned by God. Left on your own. What made you feel as though God was missing your predicament? As you read this gospel story, how does it encourage you? Will you let it encourage you next time you find yourself in a horrible situation?

21) Acts 9:43. Peter stays with Simon the Tanner

The story of Paul's conversion so dominates chapter 9 that we can forget to enjoy the end of the chapter that tells us about some of the exploits of Simon Peter.

They are quite remarkable! In verses 32-43, we see two wonderful miracles done through the hands of Peter. In Lydda he raised a paralysed man (9:32-35) and in Joppa he raised a woman from the dead (9:36-42)! What an incredible pair of stories! They can't help but make us think of similar miracles Jesus did.

We can only imagine the talk and the 'buzz' that would be happening in Lydda and even more so in Joppa. I mean, think about it, raising someone *from the dead*?! Jesus is only recorded as doing that three times (Jairus' daughter; the widow of Nain's adult son; and Lazarus). Paul would do one later in the Book of Acts (Eutychus). Peter does one right here. It must have been the talk of the town!

The atmosphere in Joppa would have been electric! 'This became known all over Joppa and many people believed in the Lord' (9:42).

Peter would have been - to use a modern term - 'the toast of the town'. I reckon everyone in town would have been keen to talk to him, have him visit their home, pray for their needs, and spend time with him hearing the stories of Jesus. He would have been in big demand. In fact, he probably would have had invitation after invitation to stay at people's homes. The folk of that day and culture were very hospitable anyway, but how much more would they have been keen to have Peter stay with them! Peter probably had the pick of the town as to where he would stay and lodge. He could have stayed in the best house with the most eminent local Joppa resident.

The very next verse tells us that he 'stayed in Joppa for some time with a tanner named Simon' (9:43).

Simon the tanner is one of the many characters that appear just once in the Book of Acts. Peter stayed with Simon the tanner. In the next chapter we see that the house is by the sea (10:6).

If I think like a 21st century Australian, I think of seaside as 'near the surf'. What a view! What a wonderful way to wake up! The smell of salt and sea and the sound of birds and waves! No wonder Peter chose Simon the tanner's place to stay with a view of the sea!

But we need to try to understand it as it was *there* and *then*, rather than here and now. The smell in a tanner's home in the first century would be offensive. Tanners dealt with dead animals, skinned them, cured them, and worked with them. The reason Simon the Tanner was living 'by the sea' would have been because the rest of the town of Joppa did not want to live near him. He was not the richest man in town with the best sea view! He was the rejected man of the town, who had a dirty smelly job that also made him ceremonially unclean to good Jews.[10]

---

10   'Since tanning was a malodorous [stinking] task, it was usually undertaken outside a town and near abundant water.' *The New Bible Dictionary*, IVP. 1978, p. 92.

Peter stayed with *him*. What a wonderful testimony to the early apostles. They were not looking for the most prominent person in any location to cosy up to. They were not interested in finding the most influential man in town to become friends with. They identified with the lower class, the rejected, the unclean, the ostracized, and even the smelly!

We should too.

Reading:
Romans 12:16.

Asking the hard questions:
Did Jesus and Peter and Paul associate with the people whom the rest of society tended to reject and treat as outcasts? (Yes). Did Jesus and Paul and Peter want us to associate with the outcasts and the marginalised? (Yes). Okay, I assume there is no disagreement so far.

Next question: Do *you* associate with the outcast and with the socially ostracised? How much of *your* time is spent on *those* kind of relationships? Even if we just narrow down the question a bit: how much of your time that you spend catching up with friends or doing social activities involves associating with the lowly? Do you need to change that? Do you even want to change that?

ACTS 10

Read Acts 10 before reflecting on studies 22 and 23

22) Acts 10:28. No longer call anyone 'unholy or unclean'

Acts 10 and 11 is one of my favourite stories in Acts – the story of Cornelius' household coming to faith.

I really love the way the story unfolds. Peter is at the house of Simon the tanner by the seaside of Joppa. He is praying on the rooftop and gets hungry and falls into a bit of a trance and sees a sheet full of unclean animals that good Jews don't eat. God tells him to eat from the animals there. Peter does not doubt that it is God telling him to eat (he calls him 'Lord' in 10:14 and the voice replies, 'Do not call anything impure that God has made clean', in verse 15). But Peter politely disobeys (probably thinking it was some kind of test?). The invitation to eat happens 3 times and each time he disobeys a voice, which he acknowledges is from God! Even though he was told, 'Don't call anything unclean that God has made clean', he still disobeys. What the?

Peter was holding onto his understanding of the Scripture that he had in his day (remember, his scripture is now our Old Testament). Peter's scripture was clear about this fact: you don't eat certain animals. Read Leviticus 11 and you will see how clear it was. Yet God was saying to Peter, 'But I am *now* saying it is okay'.

This story reflects a concept that some theologians call 'progressive revelation'. God revealing more over time, clarifying earlier revelation, correcting things that were not quite fully representative of his ideals or understandings, fine-tuning teachings that might not really convey his ways.

Actually, in this particular story, God was doing this 'animals in a sheet' image, as a visual metaphor. It was really to highlight that Gentiles were now acceptable and should be seen as brothers and sisters. Non-Jews now need to be treated equally to Jews. So it is not really about food at all. Nevertheless the story is anchored in a dialogue about God finishing the food laws in the Old Testament. They had a shelf life.

The old covenant teaching and requirements had come to completion. It was actually no longer relevant now that Christ had come. (Indeed, we know from elsewhere that the cleansing of all foods did still happen – see Matt 5:17 generally, and Mark 7:19 specifically.)

So Peter holds to his understanding that the Old Testament is forever to be literally applied. He struggles with that firm view as God gives him new understanding and challenges his view of the Old Testament. Could he actually accept the possibility that it might not be an eternal Word, in the sense that it has to always be literally obeyed? Could parts of it (all of it?) have a unique application to the God-fearers *before* Christ came into the world? Now since Christ, we have a fuller understanding of things, and that even means some things that were commanded in the Old Testament are no longer relevant to the life of believers living after Christ.

When Peter came to Cornelius' home, it is instructive to hear one of the first things that is recorded coming out of his mouth. 'You are well aware that it is against our law for a Jew to associate with or visit a Gentile. But God has shown me that I should not call anyone impure or unclean' (10:28).

What a revelation! He has come to reject some of the teaching of his own faith and traditions, and even had to re-understand the law, but he *gets it now*! If God says something is no longer unclean, then it is no longer unclean. God is accepting all people, not just Jews!

When Peter made that statement, he was talking to a man who was not a Jew (though sympathetic to Judaism), was not a member of the Christian religion, did not follow Jesus (yet), was not of the same ethnicity, did not speak Peter's language as his first language, and had an occupation that would normally deeply offend a Jew (a Roman soldier: the symbol of being under the power and domination of an outside nation). Yet despite religion, ethnicity and job status, Peter said to him, 'I can't call you or anyone unholy or unclean'.

Now think about that a bit more. Cornelius was not 'saved'. According to the evangelical teaching I have grown up with, he was a sinner in need of the forgiveness of God. That would make him both unholy (imperfect, someone who sins and falls short of the high pure standard of God – someone *not* set apart for holy use dedicated for God) and unclean (a sinner who needed to be forgiven). Now I would not say that in a cruel way, more as a matter of fact. It's a doctrine. Everyone is a sinner (me included). We are all unholy and unclean until we are washed and cleansed by the blood of Christ. Right? But Peter has been shown by God that he can't call anyone – even people who have not yet committed their lives to Jesus – he can't call *anyone* unholy or unclean any more. He has to see them in a better light than that. He has to see them, I would suggest, as beloved humanity made in the image of God. Now that image might be distorted and blurred by the sin that is in our lives, but that image is not obliterated. It is still there. Sometimes we have to dig deep to see glimpses of it, but it is there, in every one of us.

Peter said he can no longer call anyone unholy or unclean. Everyone is loved by God. Not just Jews. Not just Jews who have already turned to Jesus. Not just Christians. *Everyone.* We are all flawed and imperfect. So if we go around claiming that anyone else is a sinner, depraved in their sin, fallen from God, unholy and unclean creatures, then we are actually being hypocrites because we too are imperfect and flawed.

So we don't call anyone unholy or unclean. We love all people and we treat all with respect and dignity. We show grace to all. We are not meant to be 'sin identifiers' in this world! No! We are meant to be 'grace dispensers'!

There are so many people in this world that I want to call 'unholy or unclean'. In my most honest moments it also includes me. But in my more judgemental moments it includes people like the person who shoots children in a mass shooting; or the terrorist who shot the 14 year old Pakistani school girl for advocating for women's education; or the drunk who kills an innocent bystander with his car. There are so many. I also know many Christians who enthusiastically add to that list of unholy and unclean people, others, including gays, Muslims, drug addicts, and anyone else in any 'major sin category' of theirs.

Yet, God has shown us that we can no longer call anyone unholy or unclean! We are meant to show love and grace to all. We are meant to see that part of them that is still the image of God. We are meant to remember that Christ died for the sins of the world, including *theirs*. We are meant to love all people, no matter what category they fall under.

I hope and pray that I will never again call any person 'unholy or unclean'!

Reading:
Luke 15:1-2.

Asking the hard questions:
Who do we tend to write off as 'unholy' or 'unclean'? Gays? Muslims? Drug addicts? Atheists? Drunks? The rich? Paedophiles? How does this story in Acts, and Jesus' example in Luke 15, speak to us?

Is becoming a friend to any of those people a recipe for disaster? Will it change us? If we become a friend to wealthy people who live only for money and power, will we become more like that?

If we become friends with people we personally disagree with regarding their lifestyle or beliefs, will we eventually water down our own convictions? How do we survive the friendship 'problem'?

Or are we asking the wrong questions? Maybe it is okay to become more 'grey' as we get to know more people. Maybe it is okay to mellow and not be so 'absolute' or 'certain'?

But if it is *not* that way, and we should still maintain our firm beliefs about doctrine and lifestyle, how do we actually go about *not* treating people as unholy or unclean?

23) Acts 10:34-43. Peter's other words to Cornelius

It is possible to sit in wonder at the depth of implications of our last reflection (we are not to call any person 'unholy or unclean'). We might be so overwhelmed at the magnitude of that statement that it is easy to overlook the rest of the speech Peter gave that day. So let's make sure we don't ignore it.

It starts off incredibly with yet another profound statement. Peter begins his sermon (which is without doubt summarised here by Luke): 'I now realise how true it is that God does not show favouritism' (10:34).

The first thing to note is that it does not matter if you are a Jew or a Christian, a Roman or a Greek, a man or a woman, a slave or a free person: God shows no partiality. All are seen as equal and the same in the eyes of God! That is wonderful news. It sits on a par with Paul's amazing teaching in Galatians 3:28: 'There is neither Jew nor Gentile, neither slave nor free, nor is there male and female, for you are all one in Christ Jesus.'

Peter immediately explains it a bit more: 'But God accepts from every nation, the one who fears him and does what is right' (10:35).

Now that is pretty amazing too. This verse was in the reading section of our conversation in the long devotion earlier, on Acts 4:12. Here, Peter was speaking to a Gentile, who had not actually converted to Judaism (though he was sympathetic to it). The man did not (yet) follow Jesus. He was not a member of the Christian faith (yet). But Peter said to him that people in every nation who fear God and do what is right are welcome to him.

Wow! Cornelius was already fearing God and doing what was right. Even before this speech. Even before Peter met Cornelius, he was 'acceptable to God'. Back in 10:2 we are told that Cornelius was 'devout and God-fearing; he gave generously to those in need, and prayed to God regularly.' When Cornelius' friends turned up to the house of Simon the Tanner and met Peter, they said of Cornelius that he was a 'righteous and God-fearing man, who is respected by all the Jewish people' (10:22). Cornelius was already acceptable to God *even before Peter got there*!

That is not the teaching I grew up with as a young evangelical. It sounds more like CS Lewis' enemy solider in *The Last Battle*. It sounds like the fictitious dialogue between Jesus and the father who lost his daughter in *The Shack*. It sounds like people of other faiths just might be seen by God as acceptable to him if they are sincere about their devotion to God, and if that then translates into a life that demonstrates good works – even if they don't know Jesus personally.

Such a statement in my young evangelical days would be immediately qualified. It would be watered down and changed to say, 'but you still need to embrace Jesus of course. After all, that is what the 'doing good' at least includes.'

But that is not what the text says.

Peter's speech *does* go on to talk about Jesus. Look at what Peter says about Christ after that comment:

- God sent his word of peace through the preaching of Jesus, to the sons of Israel (10:36).

- Jesus is Lord of all (10:36).

- Jesus was a real person who lived in Palestine, was baptised by John the Baptist, was anointed by God with the Holy Spirit and power, and he went about doing good and healing all who were oppressed (10:37,38).

- God was with him (10:38).

- We were witnesses to this and to his execution on a cross (10:39).

- God raised him from the dead, and various witnesses can testify to this, including us, who ate and drank with him after his resurrection (10:40,41).

- And he appointed us to preach to the people that Jesus is the one appointed by God to be the judge of the living and the dead (10:42).

- And Jesus is the one that the prophets bear witness to – through his name everyone who believes in him receives forgiveness of sins (10:43).

That last sentence in particular is the favourite for evangelicals. It helps trump over all the preceding stuff. 'See! You need to believe in Jesus for the forgiveness of sins!' None of the earlier comments mean anything at all. This is the only sentence that matters!

However, that is not a good enough way to handle the text, really, is it? Surely all that Peter is saying is significant.

So somehow, both his comments are important. It is significant that someone like Cornelius is already acceptable to God, even though he is from another nation and does not have Jesus in his heart, and yet he loves God and lives well. It is also significant that believing in Jesus brings forgiveness of sins. *Both* these sentences and ideas are important and *both* should be a part of our total understanding.

Surely.

But how does it sit together?

I wonder how we would go if we decided that we won't try to rewrite what we see, so that it fits our already determined views? If we can agree on that for just a moment, then just maybe this can be understood as follows:

God will find those who seek for him, even if they have not yet heard the name of Jesus. Jesus is indeed Lord of all, but some people have not heard of him or met him personally. Sometimes, some folk have had such a bad experience with so-called Christians that they reject the Christian message on that basis: they can't hear it for what it is, and they misunderstand it as being a part of a package deal that includes horrid people and horrible acts.

But if they love God and seek to live a good life, they are acceptable to him. Jesus' death on the cross covers the sins of the whole world after all (1 John 2:2). Jesus is Lord of all. He has made a way through the cross. And anyone who loves God and seeks to do what is right is covered because of the work of Christ on the cross. With that as the starting point, we *still* tell people about Jesus. It is impossible not to. He is incredible. He is Lord of all. He is the one who has provided the way of salvation through his death on the cross. He is the one who taught us to live the amazing ideals of the Sermon on the Mount. He is the one who reflects the fullness of God through his very life and teaching and example. We are compelled to tell you about him. He shows us how to live here and now to a higher level.

We have good news about love and grace and hope and faith. We have a message of peace and forgiveness. Our message will change your life even more here and now. We have the very Spirit of Jesus (the Holy Spirit; the mind of Christ) to offer people! His Spirit can merge with our spirit and empower us to live in radical new ways. Embracing Jesus and receiving his Spirit will lift what you do and how you live to a whole other level. We are compelled to tell you about this Jesus, it will change your life![11]

Finally, think about that last part of Peter's speech. 'All the prophets testify about him that everyone who believes in him receives forgiveness of sins through his name' (10:43).

What is it that gives forgiveness of sins? Is it the act of 'believing in him'? Or is it 'through His name'? Or both? Or either/or? One thing is certain, that *forgiveness of sins is there because of Jesus*. It is the name of Jesus that makes it all possible. His work on the cross is the deciding factor. For all who hear the message, they *can* rest

---

11   The only thing that dampens my enthusiasm here is the sad reality that many who call themselves 'Christian' – many who say they follow Christ – live nothing like what I have just described. It is a tragic testimony to the dominance of our free will and the reality of human sinfulness overriding the work of the Spirit within us. It is a sad reminder that our free will merges with our tendency to sin, and that trumps what the New Testament scriptures call on us to do. It also undermines the message we share with others. It seriously damages our witness and credibility.

assured that as they believe in Jesus they are experiencing the forgiveness of sins. What a wonderful truth!

At the same time, I do find it interesting that the text does *not* say, 'And this is the *only* way people can experience forgiveness of sins.' It simply says that, 'Whoever believes in him receives forgiveness of sins.' In the devotion on Acts 4:12 we talked about the *sure* way of salvation and asked if that means it is the absolute *only* way of salvation. The texts that speak of the link between faith in Jesus and salvation speak of the *sure* way of salvation. But in the light of the earlier comments in this same chapter of Acts, that people in any nation who fear God and live well are acceptable to him – there must be *other* things happening in the world as well.

Despite the truth that people in any nation who fear God and do what is right are acceptable to him, the apostles who taught that *were still keen to tell people of other nations about Jesus*. They knew that Jesus was the *sure* way of salvation and forgiveness. They knew that people should and would get excited about the teachings of Jesus. It would lift their lives to a whole different level and infuse them with a passion and a hope that would energise them powerfully. The disciples knew that they had something special to offer everyone; the story of Jesus, the teachings of Jesus, the truth of Jesus, the Spirit of Jesus (read 10:44-48 to see that happen here), and the wonder of deciding to follow him!

We should share in that passion and excitement as well!

Reading:
The parable of the sheep and the goats in Matthew 25:31-46.

Asking the hard questions:
The parable of the sheep and the goats is not a favourite for evangelicals. It seems to say that we are saved by our works. It also seems to imply that people who never consciously met Jesus can be saved as well (consider vs. 37-39 especially). Is this a bit confronting for you? How do you handle this parable? Could it be that it might just have a similar point to the verse in Acts that we are looking at here ('God accepts from every nation the one who fears him and does what is right' 10:35)?

ACTS 11

Read Acts 11 before reflecting on study 24

24) Acts 11:22-26. Barnabas the encourager

After the lengthy story of Cornelius that fills most of chapters 10 and 11, we then get to a short statement about how the church in Antioch started and grew. People who had fled the persecution after the murder of Stephen were scattered in all directions, and some ended up in Antioch (in modern day Syria, north of Palestine). They talked about Jesus to the locals and a church grew up there (Acts 11:19-22).

This city would become the headquarters and home base of Paul.

But before Paul ever went there, news of the growing work in Antioch reached the ears of the apostles in Jerusalem (v.22). They decided to send someone there to check it out.

The person they chose for the job was a man called Barnabas.

Barnabas pops up a few times in the Book of Acts. He is not talked about much in sermons or by the church today, but he did play a pretty important role in the early church in a few ways.

He was first mentioned in Acts 4:36. We saw earlier that, in the very early days of the life of the new church in Jerusalem, people sold land or houses to give to the poor. Barnabas was mentioned specifically there as an example of someone who did just that. In that reference to him we learn that his original name was Joseph, and that he was a Levite (the men of that tribe tended to be the priests, the professional religious men). He was also born outside of Palestine on the island of Cyprus. Most interestingly, he was a generous and encouraging man. He got the nickname 'Barnabas' because he was such a great encourager. By the time of Stephen's murder and the general persecution, and then the conversion of Saul, we see that Barnabas was clearly well established in the Jerusalem church.

Recall how when Saul (Paul) was converted, some people would have treated him *warily*. He would have been 'held at arm's length' just in case he was pretending to be a

Christian to find out who the other Christians were. He might have been hoodwinking the church to further persecute it. It does seem that the Jerusalem Christians were reluctant to meet with Saul or to trust him after his conversion. Back in chapter 9, after he met Christ, he went into the city of Damascus (also in modern Syria, north of Palestine) and preached about Jesus. Saul was finally trusted there, but he had to be secretly helped out of town when there was a plot to kill him. He went back to Jerusalem at that point and the Christians in Jerusalem were, well, let's just say, they were 'not impressed'! Acts 9:26 says, 'When he came to Jerusalem, he tried to join the disciples, but they were all afraid of him, not believing that he really was a disciple.'

Awkward! How would he break through that attitude in the church there? How could he possibly be accepted? If they did not believe he was now one of the group he had previously persecuted, what could he do? Would anyone risk their life and reach out to him?

The text goes on: 'But Barnabas took him and brought him to the apostles. He told them how Saul on his journey had seen the Lord and that the Lord had spoken to him, and how in Damascus he had preached fearlessly in the name of Jesus' (Acts 9:27).

Barnabas the encourager, encouraged Paul, and he also encouraged the rest of the church to accept Paul. Barnabas was brave and prepared to take personal risks.

The next mention of this man Barnabas is in chapter 11. He is the trusted Jerusalem representative sent to check out the work in Antioch.

I wonder why the Jerusalem church felt a need to send someone up to Antioch? Why send someone at all? Why not just let them do their thing and trust that all is well? After all, Barnabas ended up concluding just that: all was well. Why the need then?

Some say they sent him because of fears that a distorted message might have been preached there. Some suggest it was to make sure there was sound doctrine being taught. Others say it was to give an apostolic blessing to the work going on there, that somehow it was not quite 'fully a part of the church' without some kind of apostolic approval or blessing. Others say it was simply to demonstrate unity, support and encouragement. Since they sent the man known as 'Mr Encouragement', that is probably more likely the reason.

Whatever the reason or combination of reasons, the report was great. The church there was doing really well. When Barnabas got there, we are told that, 'When he arrived and saw what the grace of God had done, he was glad and encouraged them all to remain true to the Lord with all their hearts' (11:23). He was still at it, encouraging others.

You know, small-minded people can't commend a good work, unless they somehow get some credit for it. Some petty-minded Christians don't enjoy seeing others succeed in ministry, because others are in the spotlight instead of them. It is a tragic thing when leadership reflects that kind of paranoia and self-obsession. Sadly, some do find it hard to see God working in other people and other places. They want the attention on themselves.

This was not the case with Barnabas. He was able to see the grace of God at work, and he commended them and encouraged them. He joined in with someone else's work, and blessed it as well.

What a great example for us to follow.

But the story does not end there. There is a sequel. After spending some time there, he could see that there might just be room in Antioch for another full time ministry worker.

The text says, 'Then Barnabas went to Tarsus to look for Saul, and when he had found him, he brought him to Antioch', to join the church and the work there (11:25-26). Saul (the future Paul) had been accepted, firstly at Jerusalem because Barnabas extended him a hand. When no one else was interested in Saul, Barnabas was.

Saul had a brief stay in Jerusalem, but when a death threat was made against him, he left the city and moved to Tarsus (see 9:28-30). Saul then dropped out of the picture for a season – a number of years in fact – and is not mentioned in the story of Acts again, until here at the end of chapter 11. *Barnabas,* who first extended the hand of friendship to Saul, did so again. He went to Tarsus, searched for Saul, and finally found him and brought him back to Antioch.

I reckon Barnabas could not have ever imagined how important a decision that was: to get Paul on the leadership team at Antioch. It would be *that* church, and Paul in particular (along with others, including Barnabas) who would go out on famous missionary preaching tours throughout the Roman Empire. From *Antioch* all three great missionary journeys would begin. From *Antioch* the world would be changed.

Barnabas' story has not ended yet. He will be mentioned again in the Book of Acts, especially with regards to the famous 'first missionary journey' and then again at the start of the 'second missionary journey'. But we will look at those stories when we get to them.

I sometimes wonder what would have become of Paul if Barnabas had not been such a good friend to him. He might have died in obscurity in Tarsus. He might have been a part of a small work there that never did anything particularly noteworthy at all. Now of course, God is bigger than that kind of thinking and he could have called Saul from a different city. And it is worth adding that un-noteworthy work can still be vitally important work in the lives of individuals and towns too.

I personally think that God tends to use people to get things done in this world. If Barnabas had not been open to God's leading (to be gracious and forgiving and willing to take risks), well, just maybe others would have been called and used to do the things that Paul and Barnabas did!

Whatever you think regarding such things, one thing is clear. Barnabas is a wonderful example of a gracious and caring person who was prepared to give people a go, find people for ministry, encourage others in their work, and not seek the spotlight for himself. What a remarkable person! What an inspiring example of humility and encouragement!

Reading:
Hebrews 3:12, 13.

Asking the hard questions:
Are *we* encouraging people? How do we consciously think about lifting others up? How do we help others to succeed? How do we help others into ministry opportunities? Or do we think more about how much *we* want to succeed? How much *we* want ministry opportunities?

How can we increase our 'encouragement activity' to bless and build up others?

ACTS 12

Read Acts 12 before reflecting on studies 25,26,27 and 28

25) Acts 12:1-12. God does not treat us all the same

Acts 12 opens with Herod the King arresting James Zebedee, the brother of John (Zebedee's boys, the fishermen who were early disciples of Jesus), and having him executed with the sword.

It is only briefly mentioned but it is rather monumental. James was the first of the 12 apostles to be murdered. Judas had killed himself, of course, but this was the first martyrdom of an original apostle. The text then says: 'When he saw that this met with approval among the Jews, he proceeded to seize Peter also' (12:3).

James was arrested by the King and executed; Peter was then arrested by the same king and he intended to do the same to him. It did not look good for Peter!

But if you know the story, Peter was miraculously freed by an angel sent by God.

Peter thought the whole thing was a dream since he was walking past guards, and an iron gate opened of its own accord, and he simply walked out of the jail. But when he came to his full senses he realised he was free.

There are some wonderful truths that come out of this story:

1) God does miracles sometimes. I have read different theologians who don't think so, and they say that Luke is just writing in a very 'metaphorical' way and attributing to God the safe escape from jail by Peter – probably a well-planned escape carried out by the other disciples. The problem with that is that Luke is a very honest writer. When the disciples carry off a well-planned escape to help another disciple avoid being killed, he tells it as a well-planned escape. See, for example, when Paul escaped from Damascus when there was a plot there to kill him in Acts 9:23-25. In that story, the disciples lowered Paul over the wall in a basket with ropes. There was nothing metaphorical about that description. So when it is an escape orchestrated by fellow

disciples, we are not left in any ambiguity about it. When it was a miracle, we are not left in any ambiguity about that either.

Now, of course, it should be said that we can't *demand* miracles, presume miracles, or have them *'on tap'* for when we yell loud enough, or whip up a congregation to want them badly enough. It is not our call. God is sovereign and can do as he pleases, when he pleases. Sometimes he does miracles, even when the rest of us are not expecting it. (The people at the prayer meeting at the house of John Mark's mother's home did not believe Peter was at the gate when the maid said he was, for example). Fortunately God still acts even when we have no idea what his plan is.

2) This story reminds us that those who are doing much the same work, in the same place, at the same time, *are not all treated the same by God*. James and Peter were both from the original band of twelve apostles, called around the same time, both doing their work in Jerusalem, both getting on with the ministry. Then James was arrested and killed. Peter was arrested and miraculously freed! What the? How unfair for James! Why did he get it so tough and Peter got the angel and freedom?

The reality is that God has different plans and expectations and timelines for each of us. Some will be marathon runners who do the 42 kilometres. Others will be sprinters who do the 100 yards dash. James seems to have been one of the sprinters, whereas Peter was stuck on the earth for another couple of decades. (For those who don't know, Peter eventually did get executed for his faith, but not till the mid-60s during the Emperor Nero's persecution of Christians in Rome.)

You and I (and you and others in your church) are *not* all going to be treated the same by God. He will allow some of us more time on this earth. He will allow others of us more 'prominence' in ministry[12]. He will permit some of us to steward more wealth than others. He will want some of us to have a very different life and journey to others in our churches.

Really that is wonderful! God knows best after all. He has a plan and a purpose for each of us. When James was taken to be with God after such a short ministry, it was acceptable in the overall providence and sight of God.

In a nutshell, God does not treat us all the same! That is actually kind of exciting.

---

12   That really is the wrong word to use about ministry, isn't it? 'Prominence' sounds so important and worldly; so full of ambition and pride. I trust you know what I am getting at!

Reading:
James 1:2-4.

Asking the hard questions:
We might know the teaching of scripture that we should rejoice in our sufferings and troubles, *but do we*? I think I fail regularly on this one. How do we really go about being joyful in tribulations? How thankful should we be that, in comparison to our brothers and sisters in Christ overseas who are being killed for their faith, we in the West suffer little of what you could actually call persecution? How is it a two-edged sword, this lack of serious persecution in the west?

26) Acts 12:12-16. The home of Mary

In that same chapter of Acts, and in the same story of Peter's miraculous escape, we see something else that often goes by unnoticed. It is the *backdrop to the story* of Peter's wonderful release from prison, and a fascinating picture of life in the early church in Jerusalem.

When Peter was released, 'He went to the house of Mary, the mother of John, also called Mark, where many had gathered and were praying' (v. 12). It goes on to say that Peter knocked at the gate and a servant called Rhoda came to answer it. 'When she recognised Peter's voice, she was so overjoyed she ran back without opening it and exclaimed, "Peter is at the door!"' (v. 14).

Note a few things about this home that Peter went to:

1. It is described as a *woman's* home. 'The home of Mary the mother of John Mark'. Indeed, the culture of the day saw the home as the domain of the women, and public affairs outside the home (council matters, disputes, etc) as the domain of the men. So women ran the homes. Since the first churches were in homes for over two centuries, it was very common for women to be leaders of house churches. This comes out in other texts as well. Most people think that 2 John is written to a house church, not a specific woman and her biological children. It is addressed

'to the lady chosen by God and to her children' referring, we think, to the leader of the house church (the woman of the house) and the members of that group. One of the reasons we think it is probably a church and not a family is due to the last verse in the tiny letter. 'The children of your sister who is chosen by God, greet you' – probably referring to the house church John is writing from.

Then there is Titus 2:5 that reminds young women to be 'busy at home' or 'workers at home' – an easily misunderstood translation of the Greek word *oikourgous*, which means 'a keeper or guard of the house' and hence 'house-*keeper*'. (How we have domesticated that word!) And then there is also 1 Timothy 5:14 which encourages women to 'keep house' or 'manage their home' – and that is the Greek word *oikodespotein*, which simply meant 'mistress or commander of the house'.

2. The house was big and probably pretty nice compared to many homes of the time. Worth noting is that it had servant/s and a fence and gate large enough to not be able to see through or over. That means Mary would have been quite well off. Average poorer homes did not have large fences and locked gates, let alone servants attending them. This gives us a lovely picture of a believer using her home for the good of the church. She had a healthy attitude towards stewardship of the things in her care. She was, at the very least, hosting a prayer meeting in her home.

3. It may have been that all the members of the group of people praying were not all just visiting for a couple of hours before going home. Some or all of them might actually have lived there. Remember (from Acts 2:42-47 and 4:32-37) how many of the church in Jerusalem sold their homes and lands and gave the money to the apostles so that they could give it to the poor? Perhaps this larger house was seen as one of the homes that was not sold off. Resources could be better used if some folk moved in with Mary and her family, and if they sold their places instead. Maybe some or all of the prayer meeting consisted of people actually living in that house, and not just visiting for the evening. (Perhaps?)

So in the wonderful story of the miraculous release of Peter from jail, we also get a glimpse into the generous spirit of the early Christians, their communal living, and their gender equality (women could be leaders of churches – especially while churches were in homes where women naturally led and organised what went on).

None of the things I am alluding to here can be proven definitively from this story alone, but this story helps demonstrate what we read in other parts of the New Testament, and from what we know from other historical sources as well.

Reading:
Galatians 3:28; Romans 16:1-2; I Corinthians 1:11.

Asking the hard questions:
If women really are equal to men (Galatians 3:28), why do some churches still insist that women can't be leaders or preachers? If women led house churches in the earliest years of the church (Romans 16:1-2; I Corinthians 1:11), why did we allow that to change over time?

Perhaps 1 Timothy 2:12 is used as the text to trump all other texts. But 1 Timothy 2:12 is a part of the whole paragraph 2:8-15 and there are some important considerations that imply that passage is dealing with very specific problems in Ephesus at that point in time. There are good arguments to conclude that it is not a timeless 'rule' for all time[13].

Indeed Paul, in 2 Timothy 2:2 tells Timothy, 'The things you have heard me say in the presence of many witnesses, entrust to reliable *people* who will also be qualified to teach others.' That key word italicised - *people* - is very much a gender inclusive term. If Paul wanted only men to 'be trained and then teach others', then he should have used the Greek word for men (as distinct from women), which is the word *aner*. The word he used was *anthropos*, which means people (not animals). So either Paul only wants men to teach and he made a mistake in 2 Timothy 2:2, or he wants trained up men and women to teach, and we need to see 1 Timothy 2:12 as relevant to the local situation in Ephesus in that day.

Which way do you think it should go? Is 1 Timothy 2:8-15 local and limited to its immediate context in its day? Or is 2 Timothy 2:2 sloppy writing by Paul and mistaken?

---

13 See my *Women Leadership and the Church*, Melbourne: Acorn Press 2006, especially the chapter on 1 Timothy 2.

27) Acts 12:15. Faith and Prayer

In the same story where Peter was miraculously released from jail, there was a lovely moment when he arrived at the house of Mary, the mother of John Mark. Peter knocked at the outer door and a servant went to answer. She heard Peter's voice and was so excited that it was Peter, that she did not answer the door to let him in. No, she left him on the street, and ran back inside with the good news! (12:14).

The response from the people in the house church is rather telling. The people who were gathered there were praying (v. 12). They were probably praying for the safety of Simon Peter. James had recently been arrested and killed by Herod, and now Peter was in jail and facing the same fate. The church was under serious attack. So they were doing what Christians all through history have done when persecuted—they prayed.

Isn't it interesting that no one suggested that it would be appropriate to kill Herod, or wipe out the threat to their religion by armed rebellion? Think about that for a moment. No one in the life of the early church ever suggested such a pathway. Not during the first centuries at least. That erroneous line of thought evolved in the church's thinking some centuries later, and it is still strongly believed by parts of the church today. This was not the attitude of the original apostles and believers. When the early Christians were persecuted, *they gathered together, supported each other, loved their enemies and prayed*.

As they were praying, Peter turned up! What an amazing outcome! We might normally expect that miracles like this are God's response to faith. However, it does not actually appear to be the case here. When the maid shared the wonderful news that their prayers were answered, consider how these faith-filled believers reacted. 'You're out of your mind!' they told her. When she kept insisting that it was so, they then concluded, 'It must be his angel' (v. 15). When they finally opened the door and saw him, 'They were astonished' (v. 16).

The scripture says that without faith, it is impossible to please God (Heb. 11:6). It also says that if we have faith the size of a mustard seed we can move mountains if we pray, believing we will get what we ask for (Matt 17:20).

So what happened here? Clearly they did not have faith for a miracle. They must *not* have been praying, 'Lord deliver Peter miraculously from the prison and return him to us'.

I wonder just what the content of their prayer was? Maybe it was something like: 'Lord please end this persecution. Please help Peter to stand firm and not compromise. May he glorify you in his life and death. Help him to endure and please numb his pain as they kill him. Please stop this from happening Lord, if possible, if it is your will.'

I wonder.

One thing I do want to add and qualify is that I actually believe these believers *were* offering up prayers of faith. I don't think that these folk *lacked* faith. I think that we, in our time, don't define 'faith' properly.

I used to be taught that; 'faith is thanking God in advance for the specific answer to prayer that you are asking for, because you believe it will happen.' Indeed, the same teachers went on to say, 'If you don't thank God in advance for the specific outcome you expect to happen and which you specifically pray for, then you don't have faith. It won't happen. You are a double-minded doubter.'

I tried to do that for a while and it was not just hard, it felt stupid and presumptuous.

I realise now that such a definition of faith is wrong. Faith is not believing that a specific outcome will absolutely and definitely occur and you thank God in advance. No. Rather, faith is believing that God CAN do the thing you ask for, and you TRUST God with the outcome, whatever God decides about it.

Faith is seen in the story of the three boys in the furnace in Babylon. Just before they were thrown into the flames they said, 'If our God whom we serve is able to deliver us from the furnace of blazing fire and out of your hand, O king, let him deliver us. But if not, be it known to you, O king, that we will not serve your gods and we will not worship the golden statue that you have set up' (Dan 3:17,18 NASV). Faith is trusting God. Believing he *can* do the impossible, but *not* assuming you know what is best.

So faith is not convincing yourself that you believe God WILL do such and such. Rather, faith is believing God CAN do such and such. And faith is demonstrated in the act of prayer. (Why waste time praying for things that you don't actually believe can happen?)

The people praying in Mary's house that evening were people of faith. They were shocked when God answered their prayers the way he did, but they were praying faithfully, and they were wonderfully blessed in the answer that came.

We can be people of faith too. We pray. We trust God. We commit the important things specifically to him (and we commit our whole life more generally to him). While we are being people of faith, God will also surprise us sometimes!

Reading:
Mark 11:12-26.

Asking the hard questions:
Hang on, Mark 11:23-24 seems to say the very thing this devotion rebuts. So there must be some room for confident believing prayer. Surely? Is it either of them? *Either* faith is knowing in advance and believing for the specific thing asked for, *or* it is praying and trusting God whatever answer he gives. Maybe it is sometimes one and sometimes the other? Or maybe it is usually general and trusting, and occasionally there is the 'conviction of faith' that is bigger than reason? Or is it tilted the other way? What do you think?

A good friend who read this chapter wrote the following:

'I would take a further step back and say faith is knowing who it is that we serve, knowing what he has already accomplished, knowing that he is interested in our daily experiences, knowing that he is already involved, knowing that he is already active in the situation, and that he knows best about what needs to happen next, and asking for the strength to bear that which you don't like if it is for his glory and if it will make you more Christ-like, and asking for wisdom to see the situation from His perspective before going anywhere near asking for a solution.

I also think faith is a response, so when it comes down to God doing something for us, we can have confidence that if he says he is going to do something, then he will do it. In that case I think you can praise him in advance for what he has *promised*. I don't think it works when you are asking for something that is just your idea. From memory Jesus' statements in John 14:13-14 about asking anything and the Father doing it assume that we are obedient (i.e.

listening well enough to know what He wants and doing it) and abiding in him. To me that means you have to be deeply spiritually attuned for God to be answering all those prayers affirmatively. If you are that attuned I doubt you'd be asking for stuff he thinks is dumb. To limit faith to belief that "God can do such and such" in comparison to me seems like a really miniscule perspective on who He is, and isn't really worthy of the name "Faith."'

Is my friend on the ball here? Is this short reflection number 27 from Acts missing too many nuances regarding 'faith'? Is the thought in this reflection just one of many overlapping aspects regarding the topic of faith?

28) Acts 12:17. Report these things to James

We have been hovering around chapter 12 for a while now, and this will be the last reflection from that chapter.

Acts 12:17 says, 'Peter ... described how the Lord had brought him out of prison. "Tell James and the other brothers and sisters about this," he said, and then he left for another place'.

This reflection is about the apostle called *James*. Not James Zebedee, the brother of John, who was murdered at the start of chapter 12 (v.2). Not James the son of Alphaeus – one of the more obscure of the twelve apostles (of whom we don't hear anything more, after the listing of his name in Acts 1:13). It is rather about '*James*'.

There is a James in the New Testament who all other James' had to be distinguished from, this one mentioned here. There is 'James' – without qualification. He is *the* James; the most prominent one, the most important one (in a servant-hood, Christian, kind of way). He is simply, 'James'. Every other James gets a by-line, a qualification, a tag to distinguish who they are and to make sure no one mixes them up with *this* James.

So who is this James? If he was not one of the two James's mentioned in the list of the twelve apostles, then who was he?

He is *the brother of Jesus*. The child of Mary and Joseph.[14] This James is a family member of the Jesus family. He is *the* James. The James that all other James's are qualified from.

---

14   Catholics will dispute this and say he is not the brother of Jesus, but rather the cousin of Jesus. Or, if he is the brother, then he is the older half-brother of Jesus by Joseph and a first wife. He is not a child of Mary who stayed a virgin all her life.

Here in this tiny verse in Acts 12:17 we see that he has become a key leader in the early church in Jerusalem. That only continues and deepens as time goes on. James becomes the 'first bishop of Jerusalem'. He would pen the little letter by his name at the end of the New Testament.[15] He would be known all through history as, 'James the Just', and, 'James the man of prayer' (one of his nicknames was 'camel knees' because he hardened them so much from all his praying).

It is interesting for our studies on Acts, that by Acts 12 James has more or less replaced Peter as the key leader of the church in Jerusalem. You see it hinted at here. Peter reminds the house church to tell James the news of his escape as he heads into hiding for a while. If there is any doubt about James being the key leader of the church in Jerusalem, you only need to read Acts 15, the chapter about the council of Jerusalem. James is not just the MC who runs the council, he also decides the outcome at the end. He is well and truly the main leader of the Jerusalem church.

So how come Peter dropped down a bit in leadership status? What might have led to the change from Peter to James?

We have to speculate a bit, but it is very interesting that this all happens almost immediately after Peter has been to the house of the Gentile soldier, Cornelius (chapters 10 and 11). Visiting a Gentile in his home and treating him as an equal was a huge thing for Peter to do. He had to be convinced by a vision from God, and even then he found it hard. But he did it. He would struggle more in the future with the same issue. It was not solved for all time in his heart or in his practice (Galatians 2 tells us a story about Peter where he was struggling with treating Gentiles equally, and that story told by Paul in Galatians happened after Acts 12). Despite his shaky response, Peter was still a long way ahead of most other Jewish Christians in Jerusalem when it came to this radical equality for Gentiles.

It is worth noting that it cost him quite a lot to follow God into that Gentile arena. It seems to have probably cost him the leadership of the Jerusalem church in fact. He befriended Gentiles, ate with them, and didn't expect them to keep all the laws of Moses. This was too much for a lot of other Jerusalem Christians (such as James) to handle.

---

15   Though it has to be admitted that there is considerable debate over the authorship of the Letter of James.

Our lesson from this reflection is simple isn't it? When you stand with those who others shun, you will probably get shunned too. Expect it. It can even happen in the house of God.

But it is worth it!

Reading:
I Peter 2:20-24.

Asking the hard questions:
What is Peter's point in 1 Peter 2:20-24? How can we be empowered to live that way?

ACTS 13

The start of Paul's missionary journeys

We have come to a key moment in the Book of Acts. It is the start of the three great missionary journeys of the Apostle Paul. The first one begins at the start of chapter 13.

This juncture in the book turns our attention away from the first apostles, and the work done mostly in Jerusalem. Now we will be focusing on the Apostle Paul – a late comer to the role of Apostle (and one who felt very unworthy of that description. He called himself 'the least of the apostles' in 1 Corinthians 15:9). Now we will be reading about Paul's travels and the conversion of Gentiles in the Roman Empire.

Each of the three missionary journeys is more ambitious than the one before it, and each of them sees Paul and his different travelling companions go further and further afield.

The first missionary journey is described in Acts 13 and 14.

It is followed in chapter 15 by an important 'council meeting' of the church leaders, to work out what they are to do with Gentile converts coming to faith.

The second missionary journey is described in Acts 15:36-18:22.

The third one is described in Acts 18:23 until Paul's arrest in Jerusalem in Acts 21.

After that point the last main section of the book begins: Paul's prison time! It fills the last 7 chapters.

Read Acts 13 before reflecting on studies 29 and 30

29) Acts 13:13. Handling people who disappoint us

Chapter 13 sees the start of the 'second half of the book'. It is not quite half way chapter-wise, but there is definitely a change of emphasis now. The rest of the book really focuses on Paul and the great missionary journeys he undertook.

The focus of the book moves away from Jerusalem and Peter and centres on Antioch (north of Palestine) and Paul. Paul has settled down in Antioch, and is one of the elders ('prophets and teachers') of the church there (13:1).

The text informs us that while the leadership team were praying together, the Holy Spirit said to them: 'Set apart for me Barnabas and Saul for the work to which I have called them.' (v. 2). I would love to know *how* the Holy Spirit spoke to them. It is said so 'matter-of-factly' by Luke. You know, like it just happens all the time... ho hum... the Holy Spirit spoke again... (Remember Forrest Gump's famous lament? 'I had to see the President, *again*'). But really, how did the Holy Spirit speak? Through tongues and interpretation like Acts 2? Or by a prophetic word like Agabus would bring (Acts 21:10,11)? Or by an impression one of the elders might have got while they were all praying and talking together (like what seems to be happening in the Council of Jerusalem in Acts 15, especially v. 28)? We just don't get told the details.

However, they heard and discerned the message, they were soon on their way and it becomes clear that the team was bigger than just the two of them. In verse 5 it says, 'John was with them as their helper'. That reference is actually to John Mark, usually called Mark. Luke was not being all that clear here when he called him just 'John'. But the first readers knew exactly who he was referring to. We do too from the rest of the story as it unfolds. It is the same Mark as the son of Mary, the owner of the house that Peter went to after he was freed from prison (Acts 12:12 – there we see both names for John/Mark).

When the team reached Salamis, they had a rather confrontational encounter with a magician who had the ear of the proconsul of the area. The power contest that seems to have happened between Saul and the magician results in a very rare 'negative' miracle in the New Testament. By negative, I mean a miracle that hurt someone. Paul declared to the magician 'You are going to be blind for a time, not even able to see the light of the sun' (13:11). It was a strange miracle. Hard to explain really. Does God strike bad people blind when it is called out for by faithful missionaries? Commentators go to great lengths to tell us it was 'only for a time and not permanent'. Some teachers and writers will remind us that it was similar to Paul's blindness back in chapter 9. Paul was hindering the way of Christ and he got temporarily blinded by God for that too. This negative miracle here in Salamis certainly led to the proconsul believing in Christ!

Whatever we do with that 'strike him blind miracle', the next paragraph tells us that soon after this incident, John Mark left them and returned to Jerusalem (v. 13).

It is said so 'blandly' and briefly, that we can miss it entirely. If it wasn't for a comment in chapter 15, we would not think twice about it. No big deal, John Mark headed home after this incident. Cool. He must have had his reasons. Perhaps he only intended to go this far and then return, perhaps he got news that his mother was ill, perhaps he was doing a couple of things at the same time and the main other task was finished so now he could return. Perhaps he was sent back by Paul and Barnabas.

But in chapter 15, when Paul and Barnabas decide to go on their second great missionary journey, Barnabas suggests that they take, 'John, also called Mark, with them' (15:37). At that point Paul insisted on not taking John Mark, because he had 'deserted them' on the last trip and 'not continued with them in the work' (15:38)! It led to a massive argument and fall out between Paul and Barnabas (15:39).

John Mark going home during the first missionary journey was not so innocent after all! John Mark 'deserted them' according to Paul. He was clearly not sent back by the team. He had not pre-arranged to go so far and then return. His mother was not ill. Mark *deserted* them. That is a pretty harsh thing to say of someone.

Barnabas was not as concerned about the supposed 'desertion' as Paul was. Barnabas did not judge it that badly. We see in chapter 15 that when Paul adamantly refused to have Mark on his team, Barnabas took him on instead. Barnabas and John Mark went off on their own missionary journey to Cyprus (15:39). Paul took Silas with him on his missionary journey instead (15:40).

Isn't it reassuring that even the great apostles had their fights and fall-outs! Isn't it worthy of a sigh of relief? These great apostles were human too! They had their disagreements and their fights. One of them (John Mark) disappointed another (Paul) to such an extent that Paul wanted nothing more to do with him.

At least for now.

The sequel is also encouraging. If you read the later letters of the New Testament, you see that Paul always speaks well of Barnabas after this incident. He speaks of him honestly, but respectfully. You sense that Paul still really does appreciate Barnabas. What's more, Paul later speaks well of John Mark also!

Reconciliation clearly took place. Paul's final letter was 2 Timothy. It was written just before Paul was killed by Nero. Paul wrote that last letter from jail while he was awaiting execution. He wrote it to Timothy and asked him to try to get to him before he was killed. He really wanted to see one other person as well: a person who is also dear to him. Guess who that was? None other than John Mark! 'Get Mark and bring him with you, for he is helpful to me in my ministry' (2 Tim 4:11).

One of the last people Paul wanted to see before he met his Maker was Mark! Something had happened in the intervening years. Clearly reconciliation had taken place.

So this story is encouraging in two ways. Firstly, even great Christian leaders are human and have fights and fall-outs. But secondly, (and here is the challenge for us) we are inspired to be forgiving and to work for reconciliation too.

If we are in damaged relationships with other Christians in our church, or in our life journey, then just maybe there is room for forgiveness and reconciliation. It might not mean you end up back in the same church together or do the same ministry together, but it will mean that the hurts and pain are left behind, and you let that heavy baggage drop from your back. You can be friends again even if the friendship is different to how it was originally. The relationship will be different, but that is okay too. It might take some years to repair (as it seems to have done with Paul and Mark) but it is always possible.

Is anything too big for God to handle, especially in the department of reconciliation?

It is a challenge to apply this to one's own life. It is much easier leaving it as a lovely story from our church beginnings, but if you *do* let it infect you and change you, then it can actually be quite liberating.

Reading:
Romans 8:28.

Asking the hard questions:
Romans 8:28 might just be the most over-used verse in the Bible. It has been waved in our faces way too often during troublesome times, and it does not seem to bring much comfort! How can the living Word

of God seem so ... so ... empty of power? So frustrating at times? Am I doing something wrong if it falls flat on my ears? How can I get past this hurdle? How can I let the actual meaning of this text impact me for my good? Does reading the whole paragraph and surrounding context help us see how we should apply that text?

30) Acts 13:43. Continue in the grace of God

After Mark left them during the first missionary journey, Paul and Barnabas reached Pisidian Antioch (This is a different Antioch to the home base city of these guys).

Here Luke records a long speech given by Paul. It is a summary, but it is a long summary. It goes from 13:16 to 13:41. It is one of the longest speeches in the Book of Acts. If you have a look at the whole speech, you will see that it is spoken to Jews (mostly) in a synagogue.

The summary Luke provides starts with recounting the great things God has done with the ancient Hebrew people and raising up David, and then raising up Jesus from David's offspring. Jesus is highlighted, and the death and resurrection are noted and expanded upon, and the reality of forgiveness of sins is described. 'Through Jesus the forgiveness of sins is proclaimed to you. Through him everyone who believes is set free from every sin, a justification you were not able to obtain under the law of Moses!' (13:38,39).

After the talk is over, the Jews in the synagogue are buzzing. The people wanted more on the following Sabbath (v. 42). As the meeting broke up for the day, 'Many of the Jews and devout converts to Judaism followed Paul and Barnabas, who talked with them and urged them to continue in the grace of God' (v. 43).

What a great thing to emphasise: *continue in the grace of God.*

I mean, think about the alternative. *Not* continuing in the grace of God.

What would *not* continuing in the grace of God look like? Well, specifically to these Jews living in a Gentile city, *not* continuing in the grace of God would mean staying locked into trying to observe all the Laws of Moses to win God's favour and approval. For those hearers, to continue in the grace of God would mean to continue to trust that God has already forgiven them through Christ, and there is nothing they can do now to earn God's approval. God's approval is already freely poured out on them! They did not deserve it. They did not earn it. But they received the generous gift of the love and mercy of God without having to win it by various feats and deeds. Continuing in that grace would mean not falling back into the trap of thinking they have to earn points with God, or slipping back into the belief that the works of the law are somehow tied to salvation.

Paul would write along these lines to the Galatian Christians some time later. 'Are you so foolish? After beginning by means of the Spirit are you now trying to finish by means of the flesh?' (Gal 3:3). And, 'But now that you know God - or rather are known by God - how is it that you are turning back to those weak and miserable forces? Do you wish to be enslaved by them all over again? You are observing special days and months and seasons and years! I fear for you, that somehow I have wasted my efforts on you' (Gal 4:9-11). And, 'It is for freedom that Christ has set us free. Stand firm, then, and do not let yourselves be burdened again by a yoke of slavery' (Gal 5:1).

'Continuing in the grace of God' means not relying on your own efforts to be acceptable to God.

We received the Spirit of God upon our conversion. Let that Holy Spirit guide and renew and lead you. You don't need to keep a list of 'do's and don'ts' to win God's favour. Yes, you will choose to live for him in thanks for the grace and mercy he has poured out on us. But no, you don't live for him in an effort to win a place in his kingdom. It is freely given by his grace!

'Continuing in the grace of God' means living as a free child of God, one who voluntarily chooses to live a life holy for God. We live a life that is joyfully outworked, as Christ would want us to live – *because* God has loved us, *because* God has sent Jesus for us, *because* God has saved us while we were yet sinners, *because* God has shown us such grace and mercy and forgiveness.

We are no longer paranoid rule-keepers trying to appease the wrath of an angry God. We are grateful children, overwhelmed at how much God loves us!

Reading:
Ephesians 2:8-10.

Asking the hard questions:
Is continuing in the grace of God easy? It sounds simple enough. Grace… faith… not works… But then, at the same time, we *are* meant to live a life of good works after experiencing the grace of God. We do that in gratitude for the grace. Living a life of good works then, is not to *earn* our place in heaven. It is not to win God's favour. It is, rather, a response of love. So, easy hey! Isn't it?

If it is so simple, then why is it that so many of us fall back into legalism and rules and lists of 'do's and don'ts'? Why do we become so judgemental of others who don't live successfully according to our lists? If it really is all about *grace*, what is going wrong with the way we 'live our life of good works' in response to it? How do we actually walk a lifestyle of grace without becoming obsessed by works, but still living a life of good works?

ACTS 14

Read Acts 14 before reflecting on study 31

31) Acts 14: 8-20. Cross-cultural blunders

We are now deep into the famous 'first missionary journey' of the apostles Paul and Barnabas. There are a lot of good stories recorded in these two chapters (13 and 14), but one in particular makes me both smile, freak out a bit, and feel that in some ways, it speaks to us today and encourages us to hang in there as we live in a multicultural society.

In Chapter 14, verse 8, the apostles get to Lystra. A wonderful miracle takes place. A cripple from birth is healed! Now you would think that such a miracle is a good and wonderful thing, right? It would help open the door to the hearts of the people there - right? Well, sometimes miracles did just that. However, not this time.

There was an old story associated with the general region of Lystra that Paul and Barnabas were probably not aware of. The story was about how two gods, Zeus and Hermes, had visited the area, and how they were rejected by nearly everyone in the town. The gods came in the appearance of weary travellers needing food and shelter, but people did not help them. House after house turned them away. The gods had come to the earth and had been rejected by many. Finally, an elderly poor couple called Philemon and Bacuis took them in and fed them. The gods struck the rest of the town with a flood and killed everyone, except the old couple, who were rewarded for their kindness.

Well when Paul and Barnabas came to town, and they were used by God to do an amazing miracle – can you imagine what the people thought?! In the town of Lystra, a cripple *from birth* was healed in a moment. The townsfolk thought (not unreasonably I would add) that the gods were revisiting the city. This time the people witnessing such a wonder would *not* be judged as ungrateful! This time they would honour the gods! They would offer sacrifice to them! They called Barnabas 'Zeus', and Paul 'Hermes', and they tried to sacrifice to them.

Good Jewish - now Christian - disciples of Jesus could not accept worship. They stopped the proceedings and utterly confused the townspeople! 'They had difficulty keeping the crowd from sacrificing to them' (v. 18). Not long after, some Jews from Antioch arrived and poisoned the people against Paul. The disappointed and confused townsfolk were swayed, and they actually stoned Paul and left him for dead! (v. 19).

Bummer hey?

So how does this rather sad story encourage me? Well, I am a bit of a master at cross-cultural *blunders*. I have offended a number of people on a number of occasions and I have said the wrong thing, done the wrong thing, and embarrassed myself too many times to remember. I have thought I was wishing Indian Fijians a warm welcome, and found that I mispronounced the words and was cursing them with one of the worst insults you can say to an Indian! I have crossed my legs in the presence of Korean men older than myself. I have sat on the floor and revealed the soles of my shoes to Thais. When I thought I was offering to be 'bold' in front of a group of Filipino teenagers, I was saying a word that in their language meant that I wanted to be 'naked' in front of them. I have misheard people with accents and made a fool of myself trying to say the same words back. For example, I once called a pet dog of Sri Lankan hosts 'Jesus' for a week before I found out his name was actually 'Caesar'[16].

I have made mistakes, and at times I have been utterly unaware of the cultural practices and sensitivities of so many people.

Here in Acts 14, Paul and Barnabas blew it too! Only their mistakes and lack of local understanding had bigger implications. They so confused the folk of the town they were visiting that the people there turned against them altogether!

If the great Apostle Paul could make cross cultural blunders – and yet keep going – well, *so can I*! If Paul could make such a monumental mistake like this one, then my smaller mistakes are simply good stories to tell, and look back on, and even laugh about.

I will aim to learn from my mistakes, not repeat them, and move on. I will not be

---

16   In my defence, when I asked one of the workers in the house what the name of the dog was, and he said what I thought was 'Jesus', I did seek to clarify that with him. 'Did you say the dog's name was 'Jesus'?' I asked slowly and deliberately. 'Yes sir, Jesus,' he replied. I asked a second time. 'Jesus?' 'Yes sir. Jesus.' I thought, 'This is a very religious family!' Of course he was actually saying 'Yes sir, Caesar'!

turned off befriending those from other cultures, religions, and ethnicities. I will just accept the fact that I will make (new) mistakes, and I will get over it and keep going!

Reading:
I Corinthians 9:19-22.

Asking the hard questions:
Paul seems to have tried hard to bend to accommodate others – 1 Corinthians 9 seems to be a carefully thought out philosophy of mission. Is it workable? How do we bend without breaking? How do we really apply that teaching of being 'all things to all people'? Isn't it just a recipe for compromise?

ACTS 15

Read Acts 15 before reflecting on studies 32 and 33

32) Acts 15:1-29. When the church has to solve a contentious problem

A particular problem kicked off the first great council meeting of the church. That gathering is recorded in Acts 15. The problem they were grappling with was all about the place of Gentile believers in the church. Were Gentiles fully equal to Jews? Were they able to be seen as brothers and sisters in Christ, even if they did not embrace the Jewish law? If the men did not get circumcised, were they truly following Christ? If they did not keep all the laws of Moses, could they be called brothers and sisters?

The problem was hinted at with the conversion of Cornelius' household in chapter 10. But that was an isolated incident. However, with Paul and Barnabas going out on the first great missionary journey (chapters 13 and 14) it really brought the problem to a head. Now, because of their work, there were lots and lots of Gentile churches. That reality was clearly a problem for some of the first Christ-followers (some of the Jewish ones). Since their particular expression of faith in Christ was so deeply embedded in their cultural and religious past, then surely everyone who became a Christ-follower must become just like... well... just like *them*! Right? They had to become kind of 'Jewish Christians' because that is what these Jewish Christians knew and were experiencing for themselves.

Paul disagreed. He saw the bigger picture. This debate would haunt his ministry and follow him around like a bad smell for his entire life. The Jew/Gentile problem is 'everywhere' in the letters of Paul throughout the New Testament (Well, not really 'everywhere' but in lots of places!)

Paul was really quite a remarkable person. Just right for the job he got. He was a good strict Jew by upbringing, but he had spent some of the formative years of his life in Tarsus – and that is a fair way from Palestine. He had been privileged to have had a cross-cultural upbringing. It made him a bit more understanding of Gentiles than many of the Jews in Palestine. Multiply that by ten when you think of the Jewish Christians in Jerusalem, especially.

Paul knew that Gentiles could become Christians and they could express their new-found faith *differently* to Jews who became Christians. They did not need to get circumcised or keep all the rules of Moses. They could love God and love their neighbour *in their own cultural context.*

Convincing the Jerusalem Christians, however, and even many of the apostles, seemed like a big task!

Remember that Paul was now living in Antioch, north of Palestine. So too Barnabas. While they were there, 'Some men came down from Judea and began teaching the believers, "Unless you are circumcised according to the custom taught by Moses, you cannot be saved"' (15:1). It is quite possible that this is the story that Paul alludes to in his letter to the Galatian churches, and that the letter to the Galatians was written soon after this visit, but before the council of Jerusalem[17].

In the letter to the Galatians, Paul mentions a visit to Antioch by 'men from James' (Gal 2:12). Those men expected good Jewish Christians to *not* have table fellowship with uncircumcised Gentiles, even if they were Christian brothers and sisters. The presence of these 'Judaisers' caused Peter and even Barnabas to momentarily compromise on treating all believers as equal in Christ (Gal 2:12-13)[18].

As you can imagine, a great dissension and debate occurred with the visitors from Jerusalem. It was soon decided that a trip to the capital city was needed to sort out the issue.

The meeting that decided this debate was made up of 'the apostles and elders' (Acts 15:6). Interestingly it was not made up of *only* the apostles, nor was it made up of *every* Christian in Jerusalem. The meeting listened to a lot of people (15:7) and then finally Peter shared the Cornelius story again (15:7-11). Barnabas and Paul also shared

---

17 This is not the only theory about how Galatians and Acts fit together, but we will work with this for now.

18 There are two main theories about the writing of Galatians: this one here (that it was written just before the council of Jerusalem) and a different theory that says it was written a bit later by Paul – during his third missionary journey – in which case he would be writing to northern Galatian cities, rather than the southern Galatian ones assumed here. I tend to go with the early writing of the letter since there is no reference whatsoever to the Council of Jerusalem's findings on the Gentile question – and that would have been a very important point to remind his readers of. The debate about the time of Paul penning Galatians is more complex than just that, of course, and there are good arguments for both positions.

stories from their travels and work, stories we would love to know more about but which are not elaborated on here by Luke (15:12).

Finally James stood up and his speech is given the most space (15:13-21). Paul's position is accepted with a few very minor impositions being asked of the Gentile believers. The four requests were mostly to do with food laws, so that table fellowship would be possible for Jewish Christians going into Gentile homes (15:20).

The Jerusalem Council was quite a victory for Paul. More importantly, it was a massive victory for *a broader more culturally sensitive response to conversions of different people groups.*

By verse 22 the meeting of apostles and elders seems to have 'opened up' for other Christians, because now, 'The apostles and the elders *with the whole church* decided to choose some of their own men and send them to Antioch with Paul and Barnabas'. They would be delegates who would present the decision with a united front.

Big disagreements and controversies will come and go in the life of the church. But we can work through them, just as the first Jewish Christians did here. In working through them we can either seek to be bigger than our own bias, or we can stay entrenched in our already worked out worldview. We can be bigger than our own upbringing and cultural conditioning, or not. We can be bigger than our own 'all worked out' theology at times too, or not. If we allow the wisdom and stories of the Christian community to guide us, as they do here in this story, we too can rise above such cultural constraints.

We know from other scriptures that the guidance of the Holy Spirit and the guidance of Scripture must also inform and guide us. We see reference to the Scripture even here in Chapter 15 as James summed up the final decision (15:16-18). We also see a reference to the Holy Spirit working with them in reaching their decision (15:28).

Right here in this chapter, clearly the sharing of stories, the wise reflection and genuine grappling of the mature members of the Christian community, Scripture, and the Holy Spirit, all contributed to them finding the right decision.

When we do that too, like the church back then, we can also 'be glad' (15:31).

Reading:
Romans 12:18.

Asking the hard questions:
It is a wonderful idea to aspire to 'be at peace with all people'. But how do we really go about doing that? What about that pain in the neck at work? Or the pain in the neck at church? (I know, I know, that is not supposed to happen!). What about that annoying, critical, cynical person on the church board? Or in the office at work? The bully at school? How do I really live that out? The start of the same verse says 'as far as possible as it depends upon you' then it says 'be at peace with all'. What does that actually mean? Is it up to me? What should I do from my side? What if the other person does not want to be at peace with me? Does it let me off the hook? Or do I keep on showing grace and love even if it is not reciprocated?

33) Acts 15:36-40. A friendship is severed

We have already touched on this passage when we looked at Acts 13:13. So I won't go over it in detail here. I thought instead I would have some fun and offer a 'radical paraphrase' of the argument between Paul and Barnabas. I am using a very broad poetic licence as I invent an imagined conversation between the two great apostles of the early church.

Here we go. The detailed transcript of the argument between the two men. (Someone had their iPhone on them, and recorded the whole thing I guess!)

Paul:	I don't want Mark coming along. He deserted us on the last trip, at Pamphylia.
Barnabas:	Deserted us? That's a bit harsh isn't it? He left after careful reflection. He had family concerns and was still grappling with the whole Jew/Gentile thing.
Paul:	He wasn't reliable. I don't want to risk it this time. We need a team that will work well and not be distracted.

Barnabas:	I think you should give him another go Paul. It has been over three years since that all happened. He has matured a lot during that time.
Paul:	But not to a point where I can be confident about him. No. He can't come.
Barnabas:	He can't come? So who made you the dictator of the group? What Paul wants, Paul gets? Is that how it works now?
Paul:	I have prayed about it Barnabas. I don't think he should be coming along.
Barnabas:	I have prayed too. And I think he should be coming.
Paul:	He is your kin Barnabas. You are not seeing this objectively.
Barnabas:	He's your kin too, in the Lord. And you have decided to write him off and never let him mature or change.
Paul:	I just want a reliable team. He hasn't won my confidence yet.
Barnabas:	Perhaps he's won the Lord's confidence. Can't we see this as a chance to mature him and all the others on the team? I think he will make the distance this time.
Paul:	I don't. Sorry. But I just don't. I don't want to take any chances.
Barnabas:	If I hadn't taken a chance with you, you might have never ended up in ministry either!
Paul:	Wow! Where did that come from Barnabas? You know that God always intended to have me end up where I am. It wasn't you who got me here. You were the instrument God used to help, but whether it was you or someone else, I was always going to be here.
Barnabas:	Look, use all the theology you like. At the end of the day I saw the potential in you and helped you to be accepted by the rest of the church. I see that same potential in Mark.

Paul:	You know Barnabas, when I hear you talk like that it makes me think that you are a bit jealous of me. I mean, you were in Christ before me, and you were prominent in Jerusalem and then Antioch, but then I have become a more noticed leader than you. It is undeserved and I am the least of the apostles, but it is the way things have turned out. Are you just chaffing at the bit?
Barnabas:	Give me a break Paul! I'm not jealous of you. I'm glad that God is using you the way he is. But the simple truth is that we gave you a chance when a lot of the brethren wanted to ignore you and keep you buried away in Tarsus. A lot of people were finding it hard to get past your involvement in the persecution of so many of the first disciples. But I found you and helped get you into your ministry.
Paul:	Don't think my past life doesn't haunt me still! But you are missing the point – let's refocus on the issue at hand here. The mission work is at stake and I won't put it in jeopardy.
Barnabas:	You're the one missing the point. There is a man and his ministry at stake too. God is more concerned with people than programs Paul. He is concerned with Mark just as much as with our unknown future brothers and sisters. I will not write Mark off just because you don't like him.
Paul:	I never said I don't like him – don't start accusing me of things that are not true. I don't want him on the team because I don't think he is up to it. It is not fair on him!
Barnabas:	Not fair on him? What? Maybe it is not fair on him to box him in to some pre-formed opinion of him, and never let him change. That is what is 'not fair'.
Paul:	No, it is not fair on him if he fails and deserts us again. He will lose any self-respect he still has, and it might undermine his future ministry if he becomes too despondent.

Barnabas:	He will only become unsure and despondent if we say he is so useless that he can't come now! Can't you see what you are doing here?
Paul:	Yes! I can see! I can see I am trying to protect the work of the mission trip.
Barnabas:	All you seem to be protecting is your own pride!

So it went on, and on, and on. Back and forth – for ages. It got very heated.

If the above captures even some of the things that they argued about that day, then the frustrating thing is that they both had good arguments! They had such a sharp disagreement, however, that they ended up parting company. That was both sad and, in a strange sort of way, good at the same time. It was sad because it was a tragic example of disunity over the work of God. But it was good because God turned it around and got two mission journeys out of it. As we know from hindsight, all three men ended up reconciled, and even Paul ended up respecting Mark for his 'usefulness in ministry' (2 Tim 4:11).

Personally I think Barnabas was more right than Paul. If a few years had passed and Mark had matured during that time, there should be every reason to give him another shot at the work. Indeed, time proved Barnabas right. Mark would become a trusted friend and a good worker. Paul himself would admit that in his final letter to Timothy. Not only that, Mark also left us the gospel of Mark. Many historians believe that Mark was the first of the four gospels written (and that it then served as a key source for both Matthew and Luke).

Mark proved his mettle, and he left the world with one of the most important documents ever written!

Reading:
Philippians 4:1-3.

Asking the hard questions:
In Philippians 4:1-3, Paul really wants these two quality women in the church of Philippi to reconcile. Interestingly, he himself did not have a perfect track record in staying reconciled with others. Even in Philippians, we see that he has problems with some of his own team (Phil 2:20, 21 and see also 2 Tim 4:10). Is Paul a hypocrite to ask this of these women? Or is there a difference between being imperfect, working on our own problems, and still encouraging others to work on theirs too? What is the difference between *hypocrisy* and *growing together,* helping each other do better?

Part Three:
The second and third missionary journeys of Paul

ACTS 16

Read Acts 16 before reflecting on studies 34-39

34) Acts 16:1-3. Paul has Timothy circumcised. What is going on?

Paul and his new travelling companion, Silas, are now on the 2nd famous missionary journey. It will take us from Acts 15:41 to 18:22. This 2nd missionary journey is probably more famous than the first because of some of the much loved stories in it (the next 10 studies will cover a number of them).

For now, at the very start of this long and amazing journey, we come across a new character in the story. When Paul and Silas get to Lystra, we meet *Timothy*. This is where Paul first meets the young man, and this man will become like a son to him.

Years later, when Paul is in prison awaiting execution, he writes to this same Timothy, his close friend and travelling companion of many years. In the letter he asks if Timothy might be able to get to the jail in time to see him, to say goodbye before his death (2 Tim 4:9). Here is where these two men first met, and here is where their friendship and ministry together began.

'Paul came to Derbe and then to Lystra, where a disciple named Timothy lived, whose mother was Jewish and a believer, but whose father was a Greek. The believers of Lystra and Iconium spoke well of him. Paul wanted to take him along on the journey …' (16:1-3).

Timothy was a Christian before Paul met him. So Paul was not his spiritual 'mother' who helped him in his initial 'rebirth'. But Paul would become his spiritual 'father' as they forged a deep bond over the coming years.

Did you see that his mother was Jewish (but also a Christian) but his father was a Greek (we don't know if his biological father was a Christian or not. Possibly not). Because his father was not a Jew and this young man had grown up in a Gentile city, Timothy was not circumcised. He probably did not speak Hebrew either, and he probably did not have a strict attitude towards the Law of Moses.

Paul had gone to great lengths to win the debate at the council of Jerusalem. He had argued with Barnabas and Peter that Gentile believers did not have to be circumcised or follow all the laws of Moses. In fact, all they were actually asked to do was keep four specific things outlined in the letter that was drafted after the council of Jerusalem. Three of them were to do with food laws and the final one was to not live a sexually immoral life (15:29). That was it.

Then, virtually straight after that victory, we read here that Paul, 'wanted to take him on the journey, so he circumcised him.'

Why on earth did he do that?

He made Timothy get circumcised? After all that big fuss that he made in Antioch (15:1), and after all he said (or will say later) in the letter to the Galatians? Even after James had agreed it was not necessary? Paul *then* goes and circumcises Timothy? He is actually on a journey that includes, 'Delivering the decrees, which had been decided upon by the apostles and elders who were in Jerusalem, for them to observe' (16:4). While telling Gentiles who get saved that they don't need to be circumcised, he goes and circumcises Timothy.

Why?

The rest of verse 3 says, 'he circumcised him because of the Jews who lived in the area, for they all knew that his father was a Greek.' That is it. That's the explanation.

I would have liked a bit more detail here.

We can speculate and unpack that short explanation a bit, and I think we can reach some pretty solid conclusions from other things Paul says in his letters as well.

Paul's typical method of evangelising a new town or city was to first find the synagogue (if there was one), and then preach to the Jews there. Usually – but not always – the Jews would reject him. Then Paul would end up on the streets or in halls or buildings or market places, speaking to Gentiles as well. He seems to have had that pattern, to the Jews first and then to the Gentiles. You see this happen time and again as he goes from town to town (e.g. 17:1; 17:10; 17:17; 18:1-4; etc). If there was no synagogue he changed tack (e.g. 16:11-13) but he clearly wanted his Jewish kinsmen and women to know about Jesus!

If Timothy was going with him, Paul wanted Timothy to be accepted by the Jewish congregations that he met. He needed to have Timothy circumcised to facilitate that. Even though Paul knew it was not necessary, he did it anyway. Even though he knew it was old covenant and was meaningless in the big scheme of 'our relationship with God', he still did it because it would open doors to Timothy to minister in amongst Jewish congregations. Remember that the Jewish synagogues that they would be going to had not learnt about the new covenant yet. Timothy was half Jewish: circumcision would be expected of him.

This is actually a very good example of being free in Christ, but choosing, for the sake of witnessing, to not use some of your freedom in Christ. It was a personal sacrifice Timothy made to help advance the Gospel.

There do seem to be mixed signals in the letters of Paul about all this. For example, Paul would say later that, 'Not even Titus, who was with me, was compelled to be circumcised' (Galatians 2:3). So why Timothy but not Titus? Well, Titus was all Greek. Timothy was half Jewish. Paul encouraged Timothy to do what Jewish congregations would expect him to have done: to have the knife! Titus would never have been expected to have done that.

Paul would also write lots of really negative things about circumcision. 'Mark my words! I, Paul, tell you that if you let yourself be circumcised, Christ will be of no value to you. And I declare to every man who lets himself be circumcised, that he is obligated to obey the whole Law' (Galatians 5:2, 3). That sounds a bit hard and fast! So was Timothy now obligated to keep all the Law? Had he given up Jesus? Was the cross meaningless to Timothy because Paul went and had him circumcised?

No. If you read all of Galatians you see the context. Jewish Christians who wanted Gentile Christians to follow all the Law were insisting that they get circumcised as a sign of their commitment to the Law of Moses. Paul is very upset when writing the letter to the Galatians. He sees the Gentile Christians there abandoning the way of Christ and the Spirit. He feels that they are abandoning the path of grace, and they are replacing it with rules and laws and rituals.

What was happening with Timothy was different to that. It was a concession. It was not needed as far as reconciliation with God was concerned, but it was needed for the sake of the Jews they would be meeting. Timothy was half Jew. He needed to be circumcised to be accepted by Jews who had not yet found faith in Jesus Christ. It was a concession. Not a requirement.

Indeed, Paul would later write a very famous paragraph in the letter of 1 Corinthians that sums up this very kind of behaviour. Consider 1 Corinthians 9:19-22:

> Though I am free and belong to no one, I have made myself a slave to everyone, to win as many as possible. To the Jews I became like a Jew, to win the Jews. To those under the law, I became like one under the law (though I myself am not under the law), so as to win those under the law. To those not having the law, I became like one not having the law (though I am not free from God's law but am under Christ's law), so as to win those not having the law. To the weak I became weak, to win the weak; I have become all things to all people, so that by all possible means I may win some. I do all this for the sake of the gospel.

That is why Timothy was circumcised!

It is a good policy for us to embrace too. We will find that there are times when we bend a bit this way, or that way, to be able to connect to those around us. Perhaps we will watch a particular movie or series that we don't really like, and actually find offensive in parts. We do it so that we can talk about it with people who want to talk about it and are passionate about it. We hope that in so doing we are building relationship with them so that we can share Christ with them too.

Perhaps we will go to some venue that we would prefer never to set foot in. We do it to be the friend of 'sinners', just as Jesus was. Perhaps we will visit some location that is associated with unacceptable practices. If our motive is to win people for Christ, then we are doing just what the Apostle Paul did. The trick is to be able to bend without compromising. Bend without breaking. Be 'a Jew' sometimes, without actually being under the law. Be a 'Gentile' sometimes, without actually forgetting that we are under the 'law of God and Christ'.[19]

---

19 Wisdom should be used in applying this. It is best to follow the "go out two by two" pattern in scripture. This is especially so if you have a particular weakness in a specific area. In that case think twice about where you go, and definitely take a stronger friend with you.

It might be a tricky tight-rope to walk sometimes, but the key is *to walk it*, and hopefully you don't fall off one side or the other!

Reading:
1 Corinthians 10:31-11:1.

Asking the hard questions:
How is this passage similar to the passage in chapter 9 of 1 Corinthians, quoted above (9:19-22)? Note how this 10:31-11:1 passage leads straight into the discussion about head coverings (1 Corinthians 11:2-17). How does it help us understand that difficult passage? If we see the head covering passage as coming out of these introductory comments, discuss how that impacts the teachings in chapter 11.

Consider: Paul could be asking the church in Corinth to bend to what is culturally expected (and culturally neutral as far as God is concerned) and not press their freedom in Christ to do whatever they liked.

35) Acts 16:10. Luke becomes a character in the story

Have you noticed that I like to tell stories about some of the characters in the Book of Acts? So far we have met Theophilus, Simon Peter, John, James Zebedee, Barnabas, Gamaliel (the Jewish elder in the Sanhedrin), Ananias and Sapphira, Stephen, Simon the Magician of Samaria, Saul (Paul), a second Ananias (9:10), Simon the Tanner of Joppa, Cornelius, James the brother of Jesus, John Mark, John Mark's mother Mary, their servant girl Rhoda, Timothy, and others—and there are more to come! Each one of them has lessons for us to learn from. Their stories teach us principles to apply to our own life. What to do in our context, and sometimes what not to do.

Well, now it is time to meet Luke, the author of the Book of Acts (and the author of the gospel by the same name). Luke finally comes into the story of Acts in chapter 16. It has taken over half the book. So far, all he has told us has come from him interviewing others, recording stories from the people he met, and using reliable sources. Now he will be able to share with us parts of the story as an eye witness.

He does not enter the story by name. Luke does not use the name 'Luke' to describe himself. He more humbly just changes the *person* of the writing: from 3rd person to 1st person plural. From 'Paul went here and Paul went there and did this and that', to '*We* went there and *we* went here and *we* did this and that'. The very first 'we' section starts at 16:10.

Prior to that verse, the context tells us that after Timothy had joined the group of travellers, they went to various cities strengthening the churches they visited. They were delivering the decree from the Jerusalem Council, so we assume that they were visiting some of the churches they had started on the first missionary journey. The text then says that, 'Paul and his companions travelled throughout the region of Phrygia and Galatia, having been kept by the Holy Spirit from preaching the Word in the province of Asia.[20] When they came to the border of Mysia, they tried to enter Bithynia, but the Spirit of Jesus would not allow them to' (16:6-7).

Like earlier in the book (13:2-4), Luke again does not explain *how* the Spirit directed them and forbade them. He just says the Spirit said 'no'. We might end up speculating (rather pointlessly I would add) about whether or not these early apostles and missionaries were charismatic, Pentecostal, or 'generally guided by the Spirit' evangelicals, or something else altogether. We just don't know.

However it was happening, they were more or less 'stuck' in Troas (16:8). Finally, Paul received *a vision*. Perhaps that is one of the ways, or the only way, or an unusual out-of-the-blue, once-off exceptional way, that Paul got direction. (Luke, why aren't you answering the questions we 21st century Western Christians want you to answer? How dare you just present material for your own church generation!) Whatever you decide about that, the great news is that they got past their blockage. The Spirit guided them.

The vision came to Paul at night, and it was of 'a man of Macedonia standing and begging him, "Come over to Macedonia and help us." After Paul had seen the vision, **we** got ready at once to leave for Macedonia, concluding that God had called **us** to preach the gospel to them' (16:9, 10).

That is all written quite strangely isn't it? Paul had a vision of a man from Macedonia come to him and ask for help, and *we* concluded God was calling *us* to that location.

---

20 That would be what we call 'Asia Minor' not modern day Asia of China, India, Pakistan etc.

Luke had not been mentioned until after the vision was noted. But suddenly he is a part of the team and involved in the decision making. When did he join the team?

There is a bit of speculation and reasonable guess-work from the data we have on Luke.

Luke was clearly a Gentile. His name gives that away. But not just that. He is listed with Gentile co-workers of Paul in the letter to the Colossians.[21] He was a doctor (Colossians 4:14). That is interesting in itself, and has led to other speculation. Perhaps he had been a slave and was now freed, because trusted slaves were often trained to be the household doctors in those days. Medicine was not a 'glamorous' job in the Roman world.

More certainly, Luke was not an original apostle or converted by Jesus personally. He was not a 'first generation Christian,'[22] but seems to have been converted either by Paul or around the time when Paul was passing through. We do know that he became a devoted friend and travelling companion of Paul, and that he is with Paul right at the end of Paul's life (2 Tim 4:11). When others deserted Paul to save their own skin, Luke stayed on and remained at Paul's service while Paul was in jail.

Let's re-focus back on Acts 16. When did Luke turn up to this company of missionaries? Some suggest that he might well have been the man from Macedonia who appeared in the vision. He might have been the Macedonian who asked Paul to come and minister there. If so, then just maybe the story went something like this:

Luke turned up and met the travellers on the road. They shared the wonderful news of Jesus with him, and converted him. Luke got so excited about it that he wanted them all to go back to his home town (Philippi in Macedonia – the place they end up going to next), to convert his friends and family there. Then that night, while Paul was drifting off to sleep, the events of the day were used by God to give him a confirmation dream to go to Macedonia with Luke. So when he shared the vision (the dream) with the rest of the group, all of them concluded that it was the Spirit confirming their direction.

    Maybe?

---

21   See Colossians 4:14, but read all of 4:7-14 noting that Jewish co-workers are listed up to verse 11 and then Paul clearly notes that the following people he mentions are 'not circumcised'.

22   Luke 1:1-4 admits as much when he talks of speaking to those who were eyewitnesses and servants of the Word, and those eyewitnesses having handed down the stories to *us*.

Whatever we might decide about the details of Luke's life, or this story before us, we can certainly admire the man who becomes a new friend and companion of Paul's. He would not be with him for *all* the rest of the Book of Acts, but he would be with him for *much* of it. The 'we' sections start and finish and start again, and then continue on until the end. Luke would be with Paul through his numerous trials before governors and the King, and he was with Paul on the boat trip to Rome. He endured the ship wreck with Paul, and he witnessed the miracles on the island of Malta. He stayed with Paul during his two years of open imprisonment in Rome, recorded at the very end of the Book of Acts.

Luke was a faithful, hard-working friend. He was never the leader or top guy. He did not even think to name himself in the Book of Acts. That very humility and commitment and dedication is our lesson from this study. We should be of that spirit too. Humble, committed, dedicated, fearless, and someone who sees it through to the end!

Reading:
Luke 1:1-4.

Asking the hard questions:
As you read Luke's slightly longer introduction to his first book (the Gospel of Luke), what does it tell us about Luke himself? Discuss the following things about Luke that surface in that introduction: (1) he was not a personal eye witness of Jesus Christ[23]; (2) he was a methodical researcher; (3) he wanted to get his facts and stories right; (4) he is very self-confident about his own ability to do what he sets out to do; and (5) he was 5 feet 10 inches tall, and slightly balding? (Just kidding about number 5).

Does this boost your confidence in the writings of Luke? Can we have a sense of certainty that he is telling us what really happened? Is his material reliable? On the other hand, any one can say they are a serious and careful researcher. Maybe he just said it but wasn't one really? Is that possible?

What is your attitude towards the historical reliability of the gospels and Acts?

---

23 That actually dispels one ancient conflicting tradition about Luke: that he was one of the famous 70 disciples that Jesus sent out (Luke 10:1).

36) Acts 16:16-18. A demon-possessed fortune-telling slave girl

With Luke now in the party, the group of missionaries travelled to Philippi. A woman called Lydia was converted by Paul, and she and her household were all baptised (16:14-15). That in itself is a wonderful story, especially the phrase 'the Lord opened her heart to respond to Paul's message' (v. 14). But what happens next is an even more well-known story.

'Once when we were going to the place of prayer, we were met by a female slave who had a spirit by which she predicted the future. She earned a great deal of money for her owners by fortune telling' (v. 16). The slave girl was following after Paul and she was calling out behind them saying, 'These men are servants of the Most High God, who are telling you the way to be saved' (v. 17). She did this 'for many days' (v. 18).

Now before we look at how Paul got 'greatly annoyed' by this, and what he did about it, it would be good to think about what that slave girl was doing and saying.

This poor girl was truly oppressed. She was first and foremost, a slave. Not a good status to have. She was also a *woman* in slavery – not a good combination at any time in history. Woman + slave = a recipe for exploitation and abuse. On top of this, the girl was also demonized! Talk about a triple whammy! The demon within her gave her a capacity to do 'demon-inspired prophecy' and the slave owners made good money out of her fortune-telling.

Interestingly, it seems that what she said about Paul and the others was all true. They *were* servants of the Most High God and they *were* proclaiming the way of salvation. So she was not saying anything that was erroneous, as far as we know. The facts of the matter were true enough.

Then why did Paul get greatly annoyed?

Perhaps the slave girl was saying it in a mocking tone. You know, 'Hear ye hear ye… here is Paul! He is here to represent *the Most High Gggggooooood*! He is here to tell us about the way to get *saaaaved*!' in a cynical and mocking way.

Or maybe Paul got greatly annoyed because the owners were capitalising from this. She had correctly predicted the work and plans of these missionary strangers who came to town, so others should come back and have *their* fortunes read (for a price)!

Or just maybe Paul was grieved at her plight. He saw her being exploited and would have understood how she would also have been a victim of abuse by her owners. Perhaps he was angry at the very structure in the community that permitted all this.

Or perhaps Paul just did not see it as all that important. Could Paul have had some parts of his upbringing still rearing their ugly heads at times? The part that just accepted that slavery was 'the way things were', and there was nothing to be done about it? Might he have been blinded, unable to see past an annoying person practising divination? Was he still personally growing in some areas of his life? Could we be seeing here Paul wearing some 'cultural blinkers' that limited his grasp of injustice and desperate human need?

Then again, perhaps it was not like that at all. Maybe she was just saying what she was saying, without lots of sarcasm or cynicism. Perhaps Paul simply did not want advertisements from a demon-possessed fortune teller any more than Jesus wanted demon-possessed people to identify his mission (e.g. Luke 4:34-35).

The other question asked though, is why did Paul wait a number of days before casting the demon out? 'She continued doing this for many days' (v. 18). I wonder how many? Three or four? Seven or eight? Ten or twelve? Twenty or thirty? Just how many days passed before Paul cast out the demon? Why did he not just do it on day one?

When Paul got 'greatly annoyed', he 'said to the spirit, "In the name of Jesus Christ I command you to come out of her!" At that moment the spirit left her' (v. 18).

Perhaps we get a clue to the answer (of why Paul delayed the exorcism) when we consider how the masters of the slave girl reacted so badly to this event. They caused great pain for Paul and his missionary work in Philippi. It all led to a riot, a beating, jail, and being asked to leave the city. Paul knew (I suspect) that freeing the slave girl from the spirit of divination would not be received well by the slave owners who made money out of her plight. Paul would have known it would cause a stir and it would get the owners very angry. Recall when Jesus saved a demon-possessed man by casting the demons into a herd of pigs (Matthew 8:28-34). It led to the pigs running into the sea and drowning. That, too, got the owners upset, and the local townsfolk asked Jesus to move away. Disrupting economic profits is almost guaranteed to create hostility from those making the profits!

But if that is so, then did Paul hold off helping someone because of the goal of avoiding conflict with vested interests? Do we really want to think that of Paul?

Well, no one is perfect, including Paul. Paul did work in complex arenas, where conflicting goals and problems were always being juggled. Maybe he did have an inkling of how bad it might get if he released the slave girl from demon possession. Maybe he knew what kind of reception that he would get from the owners. So he hesitated. Others were being saved and impacted by the work in Philippi in the meantime – during the 'many days' before he cast the demon out. If Paul helped one girl here, all that might stop (and in fact did stop, as far as Paul doing work there). Was the slave girl 'sacrificed' for the greater need of spreading the message through the town and establishing the church first?[24]

Whatever way we try to explain the delay in assisting the slave girl, the wonderful thing is that Paul *did* finally get to the source of her problem, and he *did* free her from the demon of divination. Yes, it unleashed a huge backlash that cost him personally. But perhaps he chose the right time, when enough work had been done to establish the new church in Philippi, and he could leave this work to continue on without him.

Reading:
Colossians 3:22-25.

Asking the hard questions:
The New Testament does not ever unambiguously condemn slavery as an evil institution. Isn't that a bit disappointing? Isn't it a problem for us? How do we explain that possibly embarrassing acceptance of such an evil social structure? Before reading the next indented paragraph, discuss your thoughts on that. Once that has been teased out, only then have a read of the following, and discuss if you think it is an adequate explanation:

---

24 Paul does call on people to restrict the things they do for the sake of spreading the Gospel more successfully. He wanted people to voluntarily not use all their freedom in Christ at times, for the sake of helping the Gospel advance and not causing hurdles in the community for people to be reached. Perhaps he is applying something of that principle here. Though here, of course, it is not something the slave girl was asked to do voluntarily. So it is quite different. Paul just did not help her 'for many days'.

Paul, in various letters, exhorts people to work within the common social structures they find themselves in. This does *not*, however, mean that Paul is focused on *maintaining* social structures and hierarchical distinctions. It does not mean that God has *ordained* those particular social structures. Paul and all the early Christians were living in a society that was imperfect and full of divisions. He wanted to give advice on how to live as a Christian in those social realities, in an imperfect world. He told slaves and masters how to live, and husbands and wives, and parents and children. But he did not see the social distinctions and structures as God-ordained. They were the way things were… and Christians have to live today, and each day, in the midst of an unjust world. So here is advice on how to do it at a higher level. Masters, treat your slaves well, remembering that you too have a master in heaven. Slaves, work hard for your masters as if to Christ, and not just when they are watching you. Husbands, love your wives like Jesus loved the church and gave himself for her. And so on. Paul's advice lifts the individual Christian to a higher level of experience in the midst of unjust and imperfect human structures that he could not change in his day. Paul accepts that real world social divisions exist, but he does not want Christians, who belong to a new created order, to put any *significance* in those worldly structures. We will live in the midst of them, yes, but we will live to a higher call. We will not use existing social inequalities and structures to dictate how we live in relationship to one another. Paul did not have the opportunities to do what Wilberforce would later do. Nevertheless, he did what he could do: he instructed Christians how to rise above the imperfect structures and demonstrate Christ-likeness in the situations they found themselves in. For Paul to acknowledge the realities of social distinctions around him is *not* him endorsing them or promoting them. It is Paul *working within them and calling Christ-followers to live to a higher ethic*.[25]

---

25   From: Jim Reiher, 'Galatians 3:28: liberating for women, or of limited application?' *Expository Times* 123.6 (March 2012), pp. 272-277.

37) Acts 16:16-18. Paul's laid-back attitude to demons

There is something else that should be thought about regarding the way Paul handled this situation with the demon-possessed slave girl.

Let me ask you what *you* think. Does it seem like Paul is a bit, well, 'relaxed' about a demon-possessed girl? I mean, the demon does not seem to faze him. He seemed all very 'laid-back' about it.

If a demon-possessed person started following me around and calling out correctly the things I was doing, I think I might be a bit freaked out by it all. I would not be nearly so easy-going about it! However Paul was not perturbed. Think about what he did *not* do. He was not driven to a 24/7 prayer meeting to learn the spirit's name before he cast it out. He was not calling up his prayer warrior team to pray and fast for a few days before he cast it out. He did not even address the girl or the demon for many days!

He just *ignores* it all. He ignores it until it bugs him too much (and maybe until he has established the new church enough) and then he very simply, matter-of-factly, casts it out. He made an authoritative statement and demanded it leave her in the name of Jesus. And it did. No hullaballoo, and no fancy meetings to have her on a stage to cast it out. No hours of conversation with the demon (and the girl obviously) in a quiet room first. No making a big deal out of it. No recording it on his iPhone to put it up on YouTube later, so as to use it for self-promotion and ministry support. (Okay.... No iPhone or YouTube back then, but you know what I mean.) He just … does it.

The lesson for us here is that we do not have to be worried about, or particularly bothered about, the spiritual realm. If we cross paths with it, we can choose to ignore it or we can choose to deal with it, but we certainly don't have to be frightened or perturbed by it.

There are good sound reasons for this. First, the Holy Spirit within us is more powerful than any other spiritual force. 'The one who is in you is greater than the one who is in the world' wrote the Apostle John some years later (1 John 4:4). Further, as we know and experience the love of God and as we grow in love for others, nothing can make us frightened. 'There is no fear in love. But perfect love drives out fear' (1 John 4:18).

We do not have to fear the spiritual realm. We can actually ignore it for most of the time. If we have to confront it, we do so with authority, and we can do so decisively.

Reading:
Mark 1:21-28.

Asking the hard questions:
Clearly Jesus does not seem to have much problem with dealing with demons. Mark 1 is just one of many stories where Jesus is confronted by the dark spiritual realm, and where he deals with it somewhat simply. If Paul and Jesus both seem to have very little problem dealing with evil spirits, without ignoring them, how has the church today turned away from their example?

How have churches that never talk about the spiritual realm ignored this kind of story?

How have churches that *do* believe in the spiritual realm and demon oppression, how have they possibly run in a different direction as well? Could some of that group be taking the whole doctrine of demons a bit too dramatically, making it all unnecessarily complex and scarier than it actually is? What part have *fictions* played in creating a different theology on this issue? (Consider movies like *The Exorcist*, or novels like *This Present Darkness* by Frank Peretti). Shouldn't we rather be influenced by the examples of Jesus and Paul?

38) Acts 16:25. Rejoicing in troubles

A huge uproar happened after Paul liberated the demon-possessed slave girl from her spiritual oppression. She was still a slave, and still a woman, but she was suddenly of no real economic value to her owners who made money from her fortune telling! They were furious and they whipped up good-old-reliable anti-Jewish racism against Paul, resulting in him and Silas being dragged to the local magistrate for punishment. Part of the slave owner's accusation to the magistrate was, 'These men *are Jews* and are throwing our city into an uproar…'

Paul and Silas were then beaten. The chief magistrates of the city oversaw the beating. They had the two men 'stripped and beaten with rods… they were severely flogged …' (16:22-23).

It did not end there. The two men were thrown into prison, put into the inner prison and fastened by the feet in stocks (vs. 23-24). They would have been in agony.

Think about it. They were beaten with 'many blows' with rods. Their backs would be cut, bruised and bloody, and their clothes would be sticking to their wounds. They were then dragged to the inner prison (the darkest, dirtiest part) and fastened by their feet into stocks. They could not, therefore, even try to position their bodies into more comfortable positions as they waited for the pain and swelling of their injuries to settle.

What would we be doing at a time like that? Maybe praying? Maybe calling out to God? Our prayers might be something like, 'Oh God, what is going on? Please get me out of here!' Or, 'God, please save us from further pain and get those guys back for what they have done to us this day!' Maybe we would just be complaining or crying. Or we might feel confused and even abandoned by God. Perhaps we would even be too upset to pray.

Well, Paul and Silas *were* praying (16:25). We don't know the content of the prayers, but I have a feeling it was more like, 'Help us to be a strong witness and not cave in under pressure.' Or, 'Give us strength to do what is right and to never betray Christ, no matter what comes. Forgive our torturers and jailers, as they do not realize what they are doing.' Or, 'Help us endure suffering and pain for the sake of the gospel and to share in the troubles of Jesus himself. Thanks for that privilege.'[26]

Whatever they were praying, they were also 'singing hymns to God' (16:25).

Singing! At a time like this? Singing hymns? *Praise* songs? When they have just been beaten and left to rot in jail? I might have been singing a lament ('nobody knows the troubles I have seen....') but certainly not a praise song? Really?

Their singing captured the interest of the other prisoners (v. 25), but not the old jailer, who was sleeping through it (v. 27)[27]. It seems that while Paul and Silas were singing, an earthquake occurred that caused all the chains to fall from the prisoners' bodies, and all the prison gates to come off their hinges and swing open (v. 26). Did the singing actually *cause* the earthquake? Did God respond to such faithfulness and

---

26   I am basing my speculations on the prayers and actions of the other apostles when they threatened and beaten, back in Acts 4:23-31, and 5:41-42.

27   I say 'old' jailer, because the task of overseeing jails was often done by older soldiers who were no longer as fit and agile, as needed for battle, and also because we meet this jailer's family a bit later in the chapter.

trust, expressed in singing, and provide an earthquake to free the prisoners? Or did God just provide the earthquake because God wanted the next sequence of events to happen? Or was it just a bizarre coincidence and Paul and Silas used the earthquake as an opportunity to preach the Gospel to the guard?

The jailer ended up getting converted after Paul and Silas stopped him from killing himself. (He thought that the prisoners had escaped and he would be held accountable). It is a wonderful story. The jailer took them home and bathed their wounds. That is interesting isn't it! The wounds still needed attention, and yet they were singing praise songs during this time.

What could be happening to these men that they are so relaxed about getting beaten? How could they be so calm? How could they sing praise songs? Isn't that literally *rejoicing* during this time of great trouble, persecution and physical pain? Are we *really* meant to live that way?

Perhaps they had talked about their next move and were feeling okay about the immediate future. Maybe they had worked out the strategy they would employ the next day. Perhaps they even derived some comfort from the plan, thinking about how the Roman officials, who had ordered them to be beaten, would be feeling when they found out that it was illegal for them to be beaten without a trial first (since they were Roman citizens). Perhaps they were reasonably confident that all would be well.

Maybe that was part of it. But it could not have been all of it. They were beaten, bruised, cut and sore. They were chained by their feet in a dingy, dark and stinking jail. There must have been something else *sustaining* them at this time.

I would suggest that Paul and Silas had such a close and abiding relationship with Jesus Christ that they did not mind what happened to them in the here and now. I think that they were genuinely comfortable at the thought of taking the bad with the good - and not being perturbed by either. When things hit rock bottom for them, it was a good excuse to wait and see what God would do! Perhaps they were so full of faith that they really did not care much about the things of the world and the power politics being played by men like the Roman officials in this town.

Paul would pen a letter back to this very church in Philippi some years later. He would write: 'I have learned to be content whatever the circumstances. I know what it is to be in need and I know what it is to have plenty. I have learned the secret of being content in any and every situation, whether well fed or hungry, whether living in plenty or in want. I can do all this through Him who gives me strength' (Phil 4:11-13).

Now that is a great definition of 'Christian living'! How challenging for us to wonder how we would react if things got really hard for us, or when painful and uncertain challenges arise in our lives. In a safe Western democracy like Australia it is not likely to be physical persecution for our faith, but it might be a different kind of pain and a different insecurity. It might be a long-term illness, or the tragic loss of a loved one. Whatever our pain and whatever our uncertain circumstances, would we react like Paul and Silas did that day? Would we rejoice and sing hymns of praise to God?

It can't be done mechanically, or parrot-like. It can't be done just because 'these guys did it, so I will too'. No. To be meaningful and really sustaining, there has to be a genuine relationship with Jesus at the very core of our being. Only then can we join with Paul in saying, 'I can do all this through *Him who gives me strength*'.

Reading:
Philippians 4:4.

Asking the hard questions:
Paul was the one singing, and Paul is the one saying, 'Rejoice in the Lord always'. That seems consistent enough. But how did he do it? How can *we* do it? *Whatever* comes our way? What is the 'trick' or 'secret' to success here?

39) Acts 16:35-39. Paul used the legal system

Before we leave Acts 16 and the trip to Philippi, there is one more thing I would like to highlight. After the slave girl had the spirit of divination cast out of her, and after Paul and Silas were beaten and imprisoned, and after the earthquake and the conversion of the jailer and his family, and after the jailer washes the wounds of the apostles, *they went back to the jail and waited there.*

Note that they did not use the earthquake to escape.

Why not? Peter had used doors swinging open by a miracle of God to escape back in Acts 12. Why would Paul and Silas not use this opportunity to escape as well?

A few things should be noted.

For starters, their new brother in Christ, the Roman jailer, would probably have been killed for losing prisoners. That is what happened to the guards who lost Peter back in Acts 12. Herod ordered them to be led away to execution according to 12:19. I can't imagine that Paul or Silas would have wanted that for their new friend and brother.[28]

It is important to also consider what might have happened if Paul and Silas had just disappeared. The authorities who had been so cruel to them had proven themselves to be happy to listen to racist slurs and act on them. If Paul and Silas just disappeared, those same authorities might just treat the small young Christian church and its members with contempt as well. The small church and its new members would be possible targets for more persecution.

I think Paul and Silas made a deliberate decision to go back to the jail cell that night, and await the new day. Perhaps the jailer and his family prayed for the safe deliverance of Paul and Silas as they did so. Perhaps Paul and Silas themselves were praying for wisdom and God's hand to be with them. Perhaps too Paul had a plan. He had a 'trump card' that he could play, one that Simon-Peter could not have used back in Acts 12. Paul had something Peter did not have: *Roman citizenship*.

Paul had been born in Tarsus. He had been a Roman since birth, courtesy of where he was born (cf. Acts 22:28). Roman citizens had rights and privileges as well as responsibilities. One of the rights of a Roman citizen was that he could not be beaten or shackled in a prison without a fair hearing. In fact, if someone did that to a citizen, the person who did it could be severely punished. Even face the death penalty.

Paul might well have agreed to go back to jail because of that fact as well. Indeed, we see him play that very card as the story unfolds. He possibly did not even let the jailer in on his plan when he went back to the prison during the night. However, he was ready to go with it. He would expose the proceedings of the day before as illegal and punishable – because they had beaten and shackled a Roman citizen without a fair hearing.

---

[28] I actually wonder if Peter would have consciously wanted that for the prison guards who were guarding him as well. Recall how he thought it was all a vision or dream, until he was out of the jail and was clear of the area – see 12:9-11. Then again, Peter did not go back to the prison and offer himself up again!

If you read 16:35-40 you see the sequel play out. The chief magistrates sent the police to the jail with a message, 'Release those men'. The jailer was pleased to hear that nothing more was going to come of it, and excitedly told Paul and Silas that they could go (v. 36). It is at that point, however, that Paul digs his heels in. 'They beat us publicly without a trial, even though we are Roman citizens, and threw us into prison. And now do they want to get rid of us quietly? No! Let them come themselves and escort us out!' (v. 37).

The police told these words to the chief magistrates, and everyone started to panic. How could they cover their butts? How could they get out of this predicament (v. 38)? They ended up going personally to the jail, tails between their legs, and they brought Paul and Silas out and then begged them to leave the city (v. 39).

I remember the first time I read this story. I thought that Paul was being a bit arrogant. He seemed to be quite unforgiving. He kind of played these men and got them quite distressed before he complied with their requests. He seemed to be enjoying making them squirm. He seemed to be happy to humiliate them. I wondered if that was a very Christ-like way to behave. Jesus did not humiliate his jailers or torturers. He asked God to forgive the men who had nailed him to a cross. Was Paul being a bit 'immature' and carnal here?

Well – possibly. However, as we reflect more on this story, I think Paul might be doing this for strategic reasons, not just to 'stick the knife in and twist it,' regarding these Roman officials. I think Paul is attempting to protect the small church that he will be leaving behind. He does not want them to be the target of persecution. He wants the Roman officials in charge of law and order to think twice before hurting the members of the new church congregation. He is probably making this stand as a strategy to protect his friends from similar treatment.

Is there a lesson we can learn from this story?

I think it is clear that Paul felt comfortable using the legal system to protect himself and his friends. He would take advantage of his Roman citizenship, and he would use it for the cause of the Gospel as well, if need be. If it helped serve the goal of furthering the Gospel, then he would use it. Otherwise, it was not all that important. Paul really was a citizen of *heaven,* not of Rome. He says just that in Philippians 3:20. But he was, in the here and now, also a citizen of Rome. If that fact was useful for the work of God, then he would use it accordingly.

We can too.

Reading:
Romans 12:14-13:7.

Asking the hard questions:
Romans 13:1-7 is often read for advice on how to live in the world as a citizen in your own country. Essentially it is all about being a good citizen and not breaking the law of the land. But is that all there is to it? We saw in an earlier study that sometimes we have to disobey governing authorities. (It can be a healthy practice to read Revelation 13 whenever you read Romans 13, in fact.)

We should also not neglect the material that comes immediately before Romans 13. It is interesting that the material that leads into the Romans 13 teaching is all about loving your enemies, not cursing those who curse you, and not repaying evil for evil. Even from governments it seems.[29]

If that is the case, then is there really any room in our faith for trying to kill evil dictators in the world? American Christianity was nearly unanimous about killing Saddam Hussein and Osama Bin Laden. Were the churches in that country wrong to support such actions? Was Bonhoeffer right in joining in an assassination attempt to kill Hitler? Or was that one of the biggest mistakes of his Christian walk? Should we be praying for our enemies instead of bombing them? Or is that just not practical? Or is it not actually the meaning of the text? Maybe the call to be pacifist is for individuals, not governments? What do you think?

---

29   The chapter break is very artificial and here it certainly seems to interrupt the flow of thought. Remember that chapter breaks were not put into the Bible until the 1200's. Sometimes they are in rather strange places that interrupt the flow of thought on the same topic.

ACTS 17

Read Acts 17 before reflecting on studies 40 and 41

40) Acts 17:10-12. What makes us 'noble minded'

In chapter 17 Paul and his group leave Philippi and reach Thessalonica. Their time there is briefly described in 17:1-9. It was a tumultuous short visit! But out of it a new work was planted that took root and grew.

The new church in Thessalonica would have the wonderful privilege of having Paul write two of his future letters to them (1 and 2 Thessalonians).

After the travellers left there, the missionaries came to Berea. Even though this visit is only mentioned in three verses, I would like to home in on it for this reflection.

Berea was not the most famous of the cities Paul visited. There are no letters addressed to them. There are no detailed stories or anecdotes about miracles or persecution that happened there. Just three verses.

But one thing is said about the Jews in that city that stands out and is worthy of reflection. They are called 'noble minded'. What a nice way to be described and remembered!

Why do you think did they get called 'noble minded'?

The Jews of Berea were actually compared to the Jews in Thessalonica (some of whom believed Paul, but most of whom rejected the message, and stirred up a crowd to attack the Christians in the city – see verses 5 and 6). The Jews in the synagogue in Berea, 'were more noble minded than those in Thessalonica' (17:11). The reason is given straight after that. 'Because they received the message with great eagerness, and examined the Scriptures every day to see if what Paul said was true. As a result, many of them believed.'

It seems that Luke would call you noble minded *if you are prepared to listen to someone exploring and explaining the Scripture to you*. It is even okay to 'check the Scriptures closely' to 'make sure the things said were okay'. All of those attributes combined make Luke conclude that these people were indeed 'noble minded'.

It is a great example to aspire to. Do we listen and evaluate? Do we allow someone to offer their interpretation of Scripture and then study it closely ('every day') to see if the things said are sound or not? Are we prepared to accept what is said if they are offering a convincing and well-anchored use of the Word? Or are we so locked in to our own traditions and doctrines that nothing or no one could ever change us?

If we are happy to participate in exploring issues, and grappling with the text with an honest and open spirit, then we are like the Bereans: noble minded!

I wonder how someone would summarise my faith community if they visited us. I wonder what phrase they would apply to us. We could do a lot worse than being called 'noble minded'! We could be pretty happy if we were summed up as a group of people who check the Scripture closely to see if the things we are told are true or not.

Reading:
2 Timothy 2:15.

Asking the hard questions:
Paul encourages Timothy to be diligent in the way he 'accurately handles' the Word of God. How can we be more diligent in that task? Isn't Bible reading all about just 'opening it up, reading a passage, and applying it to your life'? What is there to be so diligent about anyway? Why do we have to 'study' it? Some folk who spend a lot of time 'studying the Word' seem to end up killing the Word, and turning it from investigation into more of an autopsy. So shouldn't we avoid that danger?

41) Acts 17:18-34. How to live in a multicultural/ multi-faith community

After Paul left Berea, he headed off to Athens. In chapter 17 we see one of the best stories in the New Testament of how to relate to people of other cultures and other faiths.

This is a terrific example of encountering people who are different to you. What a great story of cross-cultural communication and tolerance. It is much more successful than the story we read earlier when Paul was nearly stoned to death in a different city.

Let's note a few things from this story of Paul in Athens. It is extraordinarily relevant for us today as we live in a multicultural community.

1) There are lots of religions in the world, and they are not the same as each other

Firstly, we can see that not all religions are the same. In verse 16 Paul sees the city full of idols and 'he was greatly distressed'. His spirit was *grieved*. You see, Paul was a Jew who had become a Christian. Both Jews and Christians find idols problematic. The belief is that God is so awesome and so huge (infinite in fact), and that God is spirit, not made of any matter, and that God does not want anyone to try to create an image of him. So to make any idol is considered wrong. It can't capture God. It must *limit* God. It offends him for us to imagine that we can possibly represent him with a human-created image.

2) The immediate response to other religions: discuss and debate

When Paul's spirit was provoked and saddened because of the idols, note what he did *not* do. He did not get a sledgehammer and start knocking down the idols. He did not lobby the town council to get them removed. He did not organise the like-minded people in town to form a faction and seek to get representation on the local town council to have them removed that way. He did not by stealth, under the cover of night, plant bombs and blow them up. No. He did nothing hostile.

Note what Paul actually did instead. He *talked*. Verse 17 says, 'So he *reasoned* in the synagogue with both Jews and God-fearing Greeks, as well as in the market place day by day with those who happened to be there.' Paul talked about religion to people. He talked to the Jews, trying to expand their minds. Their Messiah had come and he wanted everyone – non-Jews as well as Jews – to follow him. He also talked to Gentiles, presumably about the idols and true religion – verse 18 tells us it included Jesus and the resurrection.

The locations are important. The Jews would hang out around the synagogue. It was the common meeting place and social centre for Jews. The market place was likewise a really busy and central place to talk to others as well. Paul strategically chose the busy places for the two people groups he would be targeting.

Paul created considerable interest by talking to whoever crossed his path. He received an invitation to speak to a larger crowd of men in Athens. He was invited to speak at the Areopagus. Verse 19 shows us that they were curious about his 'new teaching'.

What he says and what he does not say at the Areopagus is most revealing.

3) Commend others for their spirituality

The very first thing[30] that we read Paul saying to this crowd is a compliment—and it is a compliment about their religious behaviour. 'People of Athens! I see that in every way you are very religious.'

Now that is fascinating. Paul did not like the idols. We know that from verse 16 (and he gets around to saying it to this crowd very gently in v. 29). He was grieved and he knew that idols offended God. He saw the Athenians as 'lost' and following dead ends. He wanted to share Jesus with them, *but he compliments their religious sincerity*. Even though they practised other religions, and even though he was utterly confident that he had found the truth about life in Christ, he was gracious and positive towards people of other religions.

Note that! We don't have to agree with another person's religion to be kind and affirming to them. We are not saying, 'I agree with all you say and do,' simply by being friendly to others. But we can and *should* be friends. We can compliment religious

---

[30] Of course the speech, like all recorded speeches in Acts, is a summary. No one believes that Paul only spoke for just over 1 minute (all you need if you read the speech as it is here out loud). We believe that Paul said much more, but that Luke has faithfully recorded the essence of what he said. So 'the first words' that are recorded here may or may not have been the actual first words Paul said. They are very introductory in nature and so they would certainly have been early in the speech.

sincerity, and we can honestly admire religious zeal and passion, without it meaning that we have converted to their world-view.

4) Understand their world-view

The next thing Paul says is equally stunning. He admits to having studied their religion and idols. 'As I walked around and carefully observed the objects of your worship…' Paul took the time to observe, examine and to understand the religion of the Athenians. He did this, presumably, so that he could talk intelligently about their religion to the people of the city.

It is not wrong to study and understand other people's religions. It is not un-Christian to examine and grapple with the world-views of others. It is not 'sin' to look at the idols of other religions, and try to get inside the thinking of those who pray to them. It is okay to visit places of worship of other religions to seek to understand what they believe and do.

Note too, that there is a difference between studying and observing, and *participating* in and *worshipping* with. We don't see Paul do the latter. He would study, observe, check things out and discuss. He did not sacrifice to the idols, or leave offerings on idol altars. That would have been too great a compromise for this Jewish Christian to do.

Studying and understanding and examining and thinking about, is a good thing! It shows those of other faiths that you have taken some time to try to understand them. It is usually appreciated.

5) Start where people are at, and use that to lead to a discussion about Jesus

In verse 23 we see that Paul found a link; a link from their faith to his. He found a spring-board to bounce from their world view to his. He found it because he had examined the objects of their worship. He found it because he had taken the time to understand a bit about their idols.

'As I walked around carefully observing the objects of your worship, I found an altar with this inscription: "To an unknown god". So you are ignorant of the very thing that you worship – and this is what I am going to proclaim to you.'

He then went on to a discussion that eventually ends up at Jesus.

What a clever connection! He found an altar to an 'unknown god'. The Athenians had all the main gods and goddesses in idol form. Yet someone must have said something like, 'But what if we have left one out? What if we are offending a god out there by not worshipping him or her, too? Maybe they will smite us!' Or something like that! For whatever reason, there was an altar to an unknown god. Paul jumped on the opportunity to tell them about the one true invisible, infinite, spirit God who made all things; the one true God who proved his truthfulness by raising Jesus from the dead.

6) Don't quote the Bible to people who don't give it any authority

The next thing to note is a point that sometimes does not get mentioned. *Nowhere* in this summary of Paul's talk to the Athenians, do we see him quoting the Bible.

Paul's Bible was, of course, what we now call the Old Testament (The New Testament had not been written yet). Paul's Bible at that point in time was the collection of Jewish sacred writings that were considered especially inspired by God. Paul used his Bible a lot whenever he was with an audience that accepted it as Scripture.

But in Athens, in the Areopagus, he did not use it.

What he did use, interestingly, were a couple of quotes from Greek poets.

> *'In him we live and move and have our being'*, (from Aratus a Greek poet who lived from about 310 BC to 240 BC. He was probably from Cilicia. This quote is from his poem 'Phaenomena').

and

> *'For we are indeed his offspring'*, (from Epimenides, a philosopher and poet from Crete who lived earlier than Aratus, approximately around the 6th or 7th century BC. He may even be a mythical creation who had ancient poems attributed to him. Probably he was a real man who had mythical stories added to his memory. For example: he supposedly slept for 57 years in a row, and it was said that he lived to be over 300 years old. This line quoted by Paul is from his poem 'Cretica').

So, Paul was not quoting Scripture, but was quoting non-Christian sources, when talking to non-Christian people.

Interesting.

We should learn from that. Some people are so keen to quote Scripture at non-Christians that they forget this important point. If the person hearing the Scripture does not give it any credibility, then what is the point? It is like a Muslim trying to convince a Christian of the Muslim faith by quoting the Koran. Or a Buddhist trying to win an argument with an atheist by quoting Buddha, and then expecting that to be the end of the discussion.

It is sometimes not all that helpful to use Scripture, particularly if the listener has no respect for it, or knowledge of it. Use illustrations from their world, just as Paul did when he quoted their poets. Use material that they can respond to with, 'Yes, that makes sense!'

Now, when the speech was over, some people did become disciples of Jesus. Even though it does not say it, I reckon Paul would *then* have taught them about the sacred writings, the Scripture. However, he does not seem to do so until it is going to *mean something to them*.

The end of the story

Well, the talk is over, and people reacted in three different ways:

1. some people mocked Paul
2. others were prepared to listen to him some more ('the jury was still out')
3. and some became disciples of Jesus that day

We can expect the same three reactions with all that we do. As we try to be cross-culturally sensitive, as we seek to commend things that we can commend, as we work to understand other faiths and religions, as we try to find keys to bounce from one world view to another, and as we seek to be wise in all that we say - we too will find that some people will hate us, some will love us and some will listen again.

Reading:
Jude 9, 14.

Asking the hard questions:
Jude's little letter is warning his readers against false teachers in the church (vs. 3, 4). In verses 9 and 14 he cites stories from ancient Jewish writings that are not in the Old Testament. Verse 9 comes from the Assumption of Moses and verse 14 comes from The Book of First Enoch. Does that seem a little weird to you? Why quote non-Scripture to church folk? Surely it would be better if he quoted the Bible to them? Why cite those two particular books? Couldn't Jude have illustrated his point with other examples?

Or maybe, on the other hand, those two books he cites should be in our Old Testament?

Whatever you decide about that, how does what Jude is doing here serve as a further illustration to our discussion above of Paul in Athens? How is it similar to what Paul did?

ACTS 18

Read Acts 18 before reflecting on studies 42, 43 and 44

42) Acts 18:1-3. Meet Priscilla and Aquila

After Athens, Paul ended up in Corinth. Now this is an important city in the life and ministry of Paul. Two of our longest New Testament letters are written to the church in Corinth (1 and 2 Corinthians).

When Paul reached Corinth, he made friends with a married couple named Priscilla and Aquila (Aquila is the husband just in case you are wondering). They were Jews who had been living in Italy, until the Emperor Claudius decided to ban all Jews from Rome (18:2). Paul ended up staying with them while he was in Corinth (v. 3). In verse 11 it says that he was in Corinth for 18 months, and then in verse 18 we see that he stayed there for some time longer, before he left. He was in this city for a considerable length of time: more than he spent in most of the other locations he visited. Perhaps about two years.

Priscilla and Aquila are mentioned about six times in the New Testament. This is our first meeting of them. They become lifelong friends of Paul, and he crosses paths with them on a number of occasions.

When Paul finally did leave Corinth, this couple joined his wandering missionary team and left the city with him. 'Paul left the believers and sailed for Syria, accompanied by Priscilla and Aquila' (18:18). They all ended up in Ephesus briefly, where Paul left them (v. 19). Paul would come back to Ephesus on his third missionary journey, and he ended up staying there for even longer than he had stayed in Corinth. But we will get to that story in due time.

For now, we note that Priscilla and Aquila were in Ephesus, helping to found and then contribute to the life of the church there. If we read ahead, we come across this married couple again in verse 26. In that brief story that occurred in Ephesus (when Paul was not there) Priscilla and Aquila are seen accurately sharing the Scripture and doctrine with a man called Apollos. It is an encouraging story on so many levels.

Apollos was a fantastic speaker who dazzled his listeners. He is described as an 'eloquent man' (v. 24), who 'had been instructed in the way of the Lord', was 'fervent in spirit', and 'spoke and taught accurately the things concerning Jesus' (v. 25). So he was a good guy! But he did have a slight problem in that he was not fully up to speed with the Baptism of the Holy Spirit, it seems. The text says that he was acquainted only 'with the Baptism of John' (v. 25). The following story that is about to be given in 19:1-7 makes it pretty clear that this meant that he did not have an understanding of the *empowering work of the Holy Spirit*. Apollos taught people to repent and be baptised and to believe in Jesus (see 19:4 – the Baptism of John) but he did not know about receiving the empowering presence of the Holy Spirit (again: see 19:1-7).

The thing is—when a married couple, tent-makers by trade, nobody special, pulled this eloquent speaker aside and humbly and methodically taught him 'the way of God more accurately'—he accepted their teaching and instruction. Now that is impressive! It is impressive in so far as Apollos is concerned. Despite being a bit of a draw-card and a well-loved speaker, he was not too proud to learn more and to be corrected in areas where he was lacking. It is impressive, too, for what it says of Priscilla and Aquila. They were gifted teachers of the Word and able to teach others well.

It should go without saying that we see here both a wife and a husband teaching a man. The text does *not* say that the wife listened to her husband as he accurately taught the truth to Apollos. It does *not* say that the wife had some ideas and bounced them around and looked to her husband for approval to see if they were doctrinally correct or not. The text does *not* say the husband did the teaching while the wife made the tea. No. The wife and the husband *both* taught Apollos. Men and women are both able to teach doctrine and Scripture.

This married couple get mentioned three more times in the New Testament. They don't come back into the story in Acts, but we see them mentioned in 1 Corinthians 16:19, Romans 16:3, and 2 Tim 4:19.

1 Corinthians was probably written when Paul was back in Ephesus in Acts 19 (about verse 10, when he had been living in Ephesus for over two years by then). Writing from Ephesus, Paul gives greetings to the people in the church of Corinth. He also sends greetings from people the church would have known, who were with him at the time in Ephesus. Remember that Priscilla and Aquila were originally from Corinth (when Paul first met them). Since they were founding members of the Corinthian

church before they moved on to Ephesus, we would naturally expect to see Paul say 'hi' from Priscilla and Aquila. He does exactly that. 'The churches in the province of Asia send you greetings. Aquila and Prisca [the shortened version of the name Priscilla] greet you warmly in the Lord, and so does the church that is in their house' (1 Corinthians 16:19).

We see that they were still at it; teaching and helping others in the church. There was even a church in their house. They are faithfully ministering as a couple, building up the local church.

Romans was written (we think) when Paul was in Corinth on the third missionary journey (probably about Acts 20:3, to be exact. We will talk more about the writing of Romans in a future devotion when we get to Acts chapter 20). When Paul writes to the Roman church he sends greetings from those who would be known to them, too (just like he did with the Corinthian letter.)

Recall how Priscilla and Aquila were originally from the Roman church, before Claudius kicked out the Jews, and before they were in Corinth. Well, Claudius changed his mind on that decision and made a new decree allowing Jews to return to Rome and live there and do business there once again. It had been a bad decision economically and he flipped on it. Priscilla and Aquila seem to have travelled back to Rome after that change of policy. They were living there again by the time Paul wrote to the Roman church. And so *this* time when he mentions them by name, he is not saying, 'Hi from these guys', but rather he is saying 'hi' *to* them; 'Greet Prisca and Aquila my co-workers in Christ Jesus' (Romans 16:3).

Paul's comments about them do not end just there, however. Paul adds another sentence about this couple that make us admire them all the more. He adds, '… They risked their lives for me. Not only I, but all the churches of the Gentiles are grateful to them' (Romans 16:4).

Wow! Something happened in Ephesus! We will see more about Paul's travels in Ephesus soon, but let me just say one thing briefly. While Paul was there for over three years in total, a lot seems to have happened. Indeed, when we consider how Luke just gives us about a chapter on Paul in Ephesus, there must have been so many stories not told to us! Here we get the hint of something big. There was the riot that Luke describes in Acts 19, but Priscilla and Aquila are not mentioned by name in that incident. (Other church members who get caught up in it are named.) Perhaps it has something to do with that riot. Perhaps Priscilla and Aquila were working behind the scenes trying to encourage a solution to the tension while it was happening. We really don't know and can only speculate. But what we *do* know is something pretty impressive: whatever the incident, this couple risked their own lives to help Paul. Clearly, he would be forever indebted to them.

The last mention of Priscilla and Aquila is in 2 Tim 4:19. This is Paul's final letter, that was penned probably just a month or two before his execution. He was writing from prison, in Rome. It was a bad time for Christians in Rome. The church members were being rounded up by Nero and killed – blamed for starting the terrible great fire of Rome. Paul was awaiting his execution. He was writing to Timothy who was overseeing the work of the churches in Ephesus. It seems that Priscilla and Aquila were back in Ephesus again. Perhaps they fled the persecution and managed to get out before they were grabbed. That is a perfectly legitimate response to have (after all Jesus said, 'When they persecute you in one town flee to the next' Matthew 10:23). If you can get away without compromising your faith, then it is quite acceptable to do so.

So Paul's final words about this much admired couple are from his prison cell in Rome. He is about to die and, like many who have been aware of their impending death, he thinks about the people whom he has grown to love and care about. He wants to see Timothy (2 Timothy 4:9), he wants to see Mark (4:11), he is glad that Luke is with him (4:11), and of the small number of people he thinks of to greet, in this his last letter, top of the list is none other than Prisca and Aquila. 'Greet Prisca and Aquila and the household of Onesiphorus.' Clearly this couple were his dear friends from the first day they met him until his last day on this earth.

What a terrific example. We should identify their strengths – faithfulness, courage, commitment, service, handling the Word accurately, correctors of error, perseverance, loyalty - and seek to imitate them!

Reading:
Proverbs 18:22. 1 Corinthians 7:32-34.

Asking the hard questions:
Don't these verses say opposite things? Is it better to be married? Or better to stay single?

Women in the Book of Acts.

As we have been travelling through the stories in Acts, we have encountered a lot of women in different contexts. In summary, recall:

Mary the mother of Jesus – Acts 1:14.

Women mentioned at the outpouring of the Holy Spirit at Pentecost – Acts 2:17-21. 'Your sons and daughters will prophesy... upon my menservants and maidservants I will pour out my Spirit...'.

Sapphira and her husband Ananias – Acts 5:1-11.

The persecution against the first Christians was against men and women both. Acts 8:3

Tabitha – Acts 9:36-43.

Mary the mother of John-Mark – Acts 12:12-16.

Rhoda the servant in Mary's house – Acts 12.

Lydia, the seller of purple goods in Philippi - Acts 16:13ff.

The slave girl in Philippi – Acts 16.

Priscilla and her husband Aquila – Acts 18:1-3, 18-19, 23-26.

And there are also **Philip's 4 daughters** who had the gift of prophecy - Acts 21:8-9.

As we think about the above stories, we see such diversity of gifts and such breath of activity! Mary the mother of Jesus, listed with the other leaders of the early church, reminds us of God's grace extended to women and men equally; Pentecost (and Philip's daughters) remind us of the equality of *gifting* in, and service to, the church; Sapphira's death reminds us of equality of responsibility before God; Tabitha reminds us of the ministry of serving the poor; Mary, Rhoda, and Tabitha remind us of *different* giftings for *different* women; Jewish businesswoman Lydia and the Gentile slave girl remind us of equality across social strata and ethnicity; and Priscilla (and Aquila) remind us of equality and partnership in marriage, as well as the fact that women can teach in the church.

43) Acts 18:3. Paul was a 'tradie'

In the story where Paul met Priscilla and Aquila, we also see that Paul was a tentmaker by trade. So were Priscilla and Aquila. '… and because he was a tent-maker, as they were, he stayed and worked with them' (18:3).

This comment about his trade is a small aside, but it has led to a *lot* of discussion about 'models for mission'.

Should missionaries have a trade or skill that they can use to support themselves with, like Paul does here? Or should they depend on the giving of friends and family back in their home base, more like Jesus in Luke 8:1-3?

It is interesting that Paul was a tent-maker. We are told that in those days all Jewish boys were taught a trade, usually their father's trade, to make sure they always had a way to support themselves and their loved ones. Jesus, we know, was the son of a carpenter and he would have learnt that trade from Joseph as he grew up. Paul was a tent-maker.

It certainly proved to come in handy at times for Paul, like here in Corinth. He could live and work with Priscilla and Aquila and not be a burden on them. He worked with them and 'every Sabbath he reasoned in the synagogue, trying to persuade Jews and Greeks' (v. 4).

It does go on to say that when Silas and Timothy caught up with him there, 'Paul devoted himself exclusively to preaching, testifying to the Jews that Jesus was the Messiah' (v. 5). Paul might have received some support at that point through the hands of Timothy and Silas, and so he was freed up to devote himself completely to the work of sharing the Gospel.

It seems to me that the two models for doing mission work are in fact biblical. Each should be used or not used depending on the situation. It is good to be supported because it can free you up for more mission work, more sharing the good news, more teaching and debating and persuading. But it is also good to have a trade and be able to work and earn some money to support yourself. That way you are not a burden on others, and critics of the Gospel can't accuse you of being in it for the free money you get from your gullible listeners. It is good to have a skill so that you can survive financially if there is no one there to support you.

We do not need to see the two models as competing. They are not either/or: either the Paul model of tent-making, or the Jesus model of being supported. No, such an either/or explanation is a bit simplistic. It seems for example that Paul moved from one to the other as the occasion lent itself, or as the need was there. He actually took care in not collecting any money from the Corinthian church itself while he was there. He either worked on his trade, or had support from *other* churches outside of Corinth. Consider what he says about that in 2 Corinthians 11:7-9.

The lesson from this simple truth is that there can be more than one way to skin a cat. Some things don't just have the one preferred model for all occasions. Sometimes, we can move between models and ways of doing things. We just need to search our motives, and act accordingly.

Reading:
2 Thessalonians 3:6-10.

Asking the hard questions:
Okay, Paul does it one way, and Jesus does it another way. One is a tent-maker and the other depends on support. We have said that both models are scriptural and it is not an 'either/or' but a 'both/and'. But here in 2 Thessalonians, it sure does seem like Paul is promoting his way as the preferred way. Is Paul overstepping the mark here? Or is it legitimate to say what he is saying?

How might the circumstances of the people he is writing to in Thessalonica affect how we interpret this? Could it be that some circumstances call for his emphasis, and other circumstances might call for the supported model? If so, what kind of circumstances could support either model?

44) Acts 18:17. Persecution that backfired

Paul was in Corinth for a couple of years it seems. In Acts 18:11 he had already been there for 18 months, and after that he continued on a bit longer. Some of the details in Luke's brief account are blurry and we would love a better explanation. But we can get the gist of the story most of the time.

For example, in 18:7 we see that Paul had moved out of Priscilla and Aquila's home and was now living next door to the Jewish synagogue. In verse 8 we are told that Crispus was the leader of the synagogue, and Crispus and all his household believed and were baptised! Wonderful news!

What we are not told is that Crispus probably lost his job as the leader of the Synagogue for converting, for believing in Jesus as the promised Messiah. We get a hint of this in v. 17 where the leader of the synagogue is now someone else, a man named Sosthenes. Luke did not blatantly say, 'And Crispus got forced out of his role as leader of the Jews because of his conversion', but it seems very likely that something like that was the case.

Anyway, when Sosthenes was the leader of the Synagogue, Gallio was proconsul of Achaia (v. 12). During that time, 'The Jews of Corinth made a united attack on Paul and brought him to the place of judgment' (v. 12), complaining to the Roman Gallio about him. From what follows we can piece together the likely scenario.

Sosthenes it seems, decided that the Roman proconsul would be a good person to use to hurt Paul. Sosthenes probably promised Paul's blood to his fellow Jews who hated Paul! He possibly incited them to take action and they hatched a plan to drag Paul to the proconsul and have Paul whipped, or worse!

But the whole thing backfired horribly for Sosthenes. The Jews complained to the Proconsul that 'this man is persuading people to worship God in ways contrary to the law' (v. 13). Before Paul could even say a word, the proconsul was clearly bored and uninterested in Jewish/Christian theological debates. He replied dismissively, 'If you Jews were making a complaint about some misdemeanour or serious crime, it would be reasonable for me to listen to you, [but not this]....I will not be a judge of such things' (vs. 14-15). So 'he drove them off' (v. 16).

How disappointing for the angry Jews who wanted blood! They were probably promised it and now they were bitterly disappointed. In a fit of frustration and anger at not getting the outcome promised, the text says, 'the crowd there turned on Sosthenes the synagogue leader and beat him in front of the proconsul; and Gallio showed no concern whatsoever' (v. 17).

The Jews that Sosthenes had led turned on him! He had probably incited them and whipped them up into an angry crowd wanting action, but when they did not get it, they took it out on their failed leader.

The story ends there, as far as Luke's account goes. Sosthenes had been beaten and left lying in the street, as far as we know. Verse 18 changes tack and tells us that 'Paul stayed on in Corinth for some time. Then he left the brothers and sisters and sailed for Syria…'.

But the story does not end there. I want to know what happened to Sosthenes.

Well, Paul would later write two letters to the church back in that city. When Paul wrote to his churches, he tended to send greetings from the people who were with him, who were friends of the church in the city he was writing to. (We saw that with the way he noted Prisca and Aquila in various letters, for example.) Paul does just that in the first letter to the Corinthians as well.

Paul is writing back to the church in Corinth, probably from Ephesus (see Acts 19:10). He had been with the Corinthian church for a couple of years. This letter we call 1 Corinthians was penned about 4 or 5 years after he had left them.[31] As usual, Paul passes on greetings from people who are with him, whom the Corinthian church would know.

Note how that famous letter of 1 Corinthians begins: 'Paul, called to be an apostle of Jesus Christ by the will of God, and our brother *Sosthenes*, to the church of God in Corinth…' (1 Corinthians 1:1-2).

One of the people who was with Paul was none other than…. can you believe this… *Sosthenes*! Paul calls him 'our brother'!

What happened between the failed lynching of Paul (by Sosthenes and others) and Sosthenes becoming a travelling companion and 'brother' to Paul!?

We can only speculate.

You know what I *want* to believe happened? Here is how the rest of the story might have taken place, after Sosthenes was beaten by his own people:

---

31 There were other letters in-between that are lost to history. It was not as if this letter we call 'First Corinthians' was actually his first letter to them. Note 1 Corinthians 5:9 for example, where he refers to an earlier letter.

The proconsul ignored the beating and the Jews left the scene. Sosthenes was lying on the ground beaten and bruised , close to unconsciousness. He might have died if no one had helped him that day. His own men had beaten and abandoned him. So who helped him?

Paul and the church did. Crispus and Paul and a few others carried Sosthenes back to their home and tended to his wounds. They spent time looking after him until he recovered. As Sosthenes regained enough strength to prop himself up on the couch, he surveyed the room of people whom he had brought before the tribunal the day before. Paul, sitting on a couch opposite, was able to share with Sosthenes his own story. He identified with Sosthenes' passion to protect Judaism and destroy this heretical Christian teaching! But then he described the pivotal moment in his own life, when just as he was in the throes of hunting down those followers of the Way, he met the risen Messiah on the road to Damascus. As Paul spoke, and Crispus tended his wounds, somehow Sosthenes' heart and mind softened. He was converted. This probably meant he could no longer be the synagogue leader any more. But it did not matter now. He had found new life in the Messiah! So Sosthenes rose from the couch, joined Paul and became his travelling companion..

That is what I think might just have happened. If something like that is the explanation, then it teaches us the same lesson that we see in the parable of the Good Samaritan. Love in action, even to those you would not normally help. That is the key to winning hearts and minds. You can argue until you are blue in the face and it just won't change some people. *Acts* of unconditional love however, even in the face of hostility, combined with the truth *spoken* in love, can soften the hardest heart.

Now that is an example to imitate!

Reading:
1 Peter 3:9.

Asking the hard questions:
We all seem to love the stories of Christians who forgive their enemies after great suffering and pain – especially if they are stories that happened a long time ago, or in countries a long way from us. But how do we go personally about loving *our* enemies? The people who hurt *us*?

ACTS 19

The 3rd missionary journey that does not end well

At the end of chapter 18 Paul was finally back in Antioch, his home town. He had completed the 2nd missionary journey. He had left Corinth (v. 18) and passed briefly through Ephesus (vs. 19-21) and then travelled home. That 2nd missionary journey ended where it had begun; in verse 22 he landed 'at Caesarea, he went up to Jerusalem and greeted the church and then went down to *Antioch*'.

It seems that Paul was not there too long this time before he headed off again. Luke tells us, 'After spending some time in Antioch, Paul set out from there and travelled from place to place throughout the region of Galatia and Phrygia, strengthening all the disciples' (v. 23).

So begins the 3rd Missionary Journey of Paul. No mention of a prayer meeting and words from the Holy Spirit like what happened at the start of the first one (13:1-3). No big fight between apostles like happened at the start of the 2nd one (15:36-40). Just after 'some time' they headed off again.

This would be their most ambitious missionary journey yet—and this one ends badly for Paul. After travelling around for some years, just before he was about to get back home to Antioch, he was passing through Jerusalem. While in Jerusalem he found himself in trouble (again) and ended up arrested and in Roman imprisonment. He would stay in prison for about 5 years this time!

The 3rd missionary journey then, starts in Acts 18:23 and it comes to a premature end in 21:33 when Paul is arrested by the Romans in Jerusalem.

Paul's prison time was split between different prisons and locations. He was held in a prison in Jerusalem for a relatively short period of time and was then transferred to a prison on the coast at Caesarea (in 23:33). He was held there for over two years (24:27). He was then transferred to Rome (27:1). The Book of Acts ends with Paul still in open imprisonment in Rome, for over two more years (28:30).

If we divide the Book of Acts up into 'big chunks' then, we might do this:

The church begins in Jerusalem and starts to spread out slowly (Chapters 1-12)

Paul's 1st missionary journey and the council of Jerusalem (13-15)

Paul's 2nd missionary journey (15:36-18:22)

Paul's 3rd missionary journey (18:23-21:23)

Paul's imprisonments (21:34-28:31)

Read Acts 19 before reflecting on studies 45 and 46

45) Acts 19:19. Is book-burning ever a good idea?

Paul was now on his biggest and most dangerous missionary journey so far. It did not take too long before he ended up in Ephesus. He immersed himself in the work there, and he would stay for over three years. Paul arrived in Ephesus in 19:1 and the whole chapter (of 41 verses) is devoted to some of the highlights of those three years. In 20:1 he departs Ephesus and heads for Macedonia.

The things Luke highlights in Ephesus make for exciting reading.

19:1-7 tells the story of followers of John the Baptist being converted to the way of Jesus. It is an interesting story that reminds us that there was actually a 'John the Baptist cult' (or at least 'following') that had reached into Jewish and mixed communities a long way from Palestine. It is interesting that the Gospel of John is thought to have been written for the churches around Ephesus as well, and in that gospel we get the most information about John the Baptist. We also get that line from the mouth of the Baptist that Jesus 'must become greater and I must become less' (John 3:30). Some argue that John Zebedee, the author of the gospel, was writing for an audience that included the followers of John the Baptist.

19:8-16 tells us about extraordinary miracles and exorcisms (vs. 11-12) and then copy-cat attempts to exorcise demons that backfired on the Jewish exorcists trying to do it.

19:17-20 tells us about how people caught up in witchcraft and magic changed their ways, gave up their previous activity and embraced Jesus Christ instead.

19:21-41 (half the chapter) is then given over to a frightening riot that nearly had some of the church members torn to shreds by an angry crowd. We will talk more on that in the next study.

There must have been so much more that happened in those three years in Ephesus. We get some broad brushstrokes, but there is obviously much we are not being told! Three years of a missionary's activities in a major volatile city? You could surely write a whole book on it! Luke gives us 41 verses. From what we do have, we know Paul had some exciting adventures. One unusual verse that I would like to highlight is to do with some people who practised magic, and how they gave up their art and became Christians.

Note what verse 19 says in full, 'A number who had practised sorcery brought their scrolls together and burnt them publicly. When they calculated the value of the scrolls, the total came to fifty thousand drachmas.' (A 'drachma' was a silver coin worth about a day's wage).

It is always exciting to see people radically saved and passionate about their new-found faith. Also, when you have 'traded in' an old world-view for a new world-view, it is common to make 'a clear break' from your past views and practices that are now seen as inconsistent with the new world-view.

In this case, for some of these folk who gave up their magical arts, they decided to burn their 'books' (their scrolls). They made it a public burning, and the value of the books was considerable: 50,000 pieces of silver.

Having said all that, I have to admit that I still cringe a bit when I read that short note about the book-burning. I think I cringe for two reasons:

(1) As a historian, I know that the times in history where there have been massive book-burning events have not been good times. They have been times of cultic propaganda and evil dictatorships. Whether it is Hitler burning the works of Jews

and anti-Nazis, or Romans burning the Library of Alexandria, or the Middle Ages Catholic Church with its Inquisition and list of banned books—not much good can ever come from book-burning.

(2) When I was a young Christian in my early 20s I had quite a collection of primary source books on other world religions. I had books on Buddhism by Buddhists; books on Islam by Muslims; etc. It was quite a collection of second-hand books that I had built up over a year or two. But as a young and somewhat idealistic young Christian, I got this sudden feeling that I should not have those books any more. So I burnt them. Like these guys did to their books in Acts 19. In fact, as a very young Christian, I think I was even inspired to do it because of this story. However, some years later I really regretted that I had done that. I became a theological college lecturer and one of the subjects I taught was an introduction to the world's religions. I began collecting the same kinds of books all over again!

When I think back to my sudden desire to 'burn the books of other world-views' I get a feeling of regret and a sense that I was experiencing naive youthful zeal.

Perhaps if you have been saturated in a world-view or practice that you now think is seriously wrong or even evil, then you might feel a need to destroy the stuff that you collected and used in that lifestyle. Maybe these folk in Acts 19 did the right thing for them, since they would have no further use for books detailing practices they were forsaking. In my case, however, I had not come out of any of the other world religions. I was just interested in understanding them. I don't think my situation was actually like these people's situation at all. I could have donated the collection to my nearest theological college, for goodness sake!

Some have suggested to me that perhaps I was too immature in my faith to be able to handle those books back then, and maybe they would have 'led me away' from Christ if I had kept them. Years later, as a lecturer at a college, I can now supposedly handle such material and won't be misled or taken down paths I should not tread. So maybe I did the right thing for myself back then. Maybe.

Whatever we decide about Acts 19:19 and whatever I decide about my own youthful zeal all those years ago, I guess I will always continue to have just a bit of discomfort as I read this story.

The one thing that is *unambiguously good* and that can be the general principle we draw from the story is this: It is wonderful to see people experience a radical conversion to Jesus and have a firm determination to turn away from their sins. The joy, the zeal, the passion and the change of focus is inspiring. How we express that… well, that might be open for more discussion!

Reading:
Philippians 4:8.

Asking the hard questions:
Paul's words here in Philippians seem to encourage us to apply a kind of 'personal censorship' to ourselves. What is the difference, though, between personal decisions about what we do and don't put into our heads, and burning books that might be deemed bad?

46) Acts 19:37. Living side by side with other faiths

We are up to the story of the riot in Ephesus. What a frightening few hours this must have been for the Christians dragged into it.

It starts at 19:23. 'About that time, there arose a great disturbance about the Way.' The movement of Christ followers had a few nicknames, and one of them was 'The Way'.[32] It is interesting that this never really 'caught on' like the other nickname Christians'.[33]

Here in Ephesus, followers of the Way got caught up in 'a great disturbance'. That is an understatement when you read the story that follows.

The trouble was triggered by craftsmen who made religious items for the worship of the Greek gods. These craftsmen were angry at the Christians because they believed the Christian teaching was shrinking their market. 'A silversmith named Demetrius, who made silver shrines of Artemis, [the main goddess of Ephesus, also called Dianna] brought in a lot of business for the craftsmen there. He called them together along with the workers of related trades…' and he whipped them up into a frenzy, blaming the Christians for falling business profits! (19:24-25).

---

32   'The Way' is used as a title for the followers of Christ in a number of verses in Acts: 9:2; 19:9; 19:23; 22:4; 24:14; and 24:22.
33   'Christian' is only used twice in the Book of Acts: 11:26 and then later in 26:28.

What a crafty and clever speech he delivered. He was motivated primarily by money, as seen in his opening words: 'You know my friends, that we receive a good income from this business…'

Driven by a need to maintain his prosperity, he then wove a religious argument into his speech, to whip up religious devotion and sentiment in his hearers:

> Paul has convinced and led astray large numbers of people here in Ephesus and in practically the whole province of Asia. He says that gods made by human hands are no gods at all. There is danger not only that our trade will lose its good name, but also that the Temple of the great goddess Artemis will be discredited; and the goddess herself who is worshipped throughout the province of Asia and the world, will be robbed of her divine majesty (vs. 26-27).

Demetrius was clever. He had tapped into a formula that many throughout history would tap into. It is the old trick of cloaking your selfish motives in religious devotion. It is the trick of pretending to be concerned for the welfare of your religion, when other more hedonistic motives are actually at work. If it was not for the material gain you were getting or the prestige you were acquiring among your peers, then you would not be bothered about the religious arguments at all.

Like so many other times in history, it worked here too. The crowd got upset! 'When they heard this they were furious and began shouting, "Great is Artemis of the Ephesians!"' (19:28).

The city was soon filled with confusion (v. 29) and the angry, incensed mob was looking for Christians to beat up or kill. They dragged Gaius and Aristarchus (two of Paul's travelling companions) into a theatre, and were screaming at them (vs. 29-32). Paul had not been grabbed, and when he speculated about going into the theatre to speak to the crowd, his friends who lived in the city begged him not to (vs. 30-31). They must have seen things like this before and they probably knew that usually it did not end well.

Meanwhile in the theatre, it was looking bad for Gaius and Aristarchus. A third man, Alexander, was also there and he attempted to speak to the angry crowd (v. 33). As he began speaking it was clear to the crowd that he was a Jew; so the crowd started screaming all the louder to drown him out (v. 34). They were clearly racist to the core.

The crowd continued shouting, 'Great is Artemis of the Ephesians!' And they kept it up for two hours! (v. 34).

Finally they quietened down. What made them stop screaming? Perhaps they were tired. But what we are told is that 'the city clerk' spoke to them (v. 35). The town clerk. He is not named, but clearly he was neither Jew nor Christian, because the townsfolk stopped and listened.

The cheeky side of me likes to picture in my mind a small weedy frail guy with big glasses, pushing his glasses down just a little bit to look over the top of them, scanning the angry crowd that want to kill these men, clearing his throat and beginning in a squeaky voice, 'Fellow Ephesians...' (v. 35). He was probably not small or frail and he definitely would not have had a thick pair of glasses, but whatever he looked like and whatever his stature, he *did* quieten the crowd.

> Fellow Ephesians, does not all the world know that the city of Ephesus is the guardian of the temple of the great Artemis, and of her image which fell from heaven? Therefore, since these facts are undeniable, you ought to calm down and not do anything rash. You have brought these men here, though they have neither robbed temples nor blasphemed our goddess. If, then, Demetrius and his fellow craftsmen have a grievance against anybody, the courts are open and there are proconsuls available. They can press charges. If there is anything further you want to bring up, it must be settled in a lawful assembly. As it is, we are in danger of being charged with rioting because of what happened today. In that case we would not be able to account for this commotion since there is no reason for it (vs. 35-40).

What a great speech! It is Luke's summary, of course, but what a great emphasis. The result was that the assembly was dismissed and the whole thing settled down (v. 41).

I love what that little guy said! I love the two big points he makes about the Christians in Ephesus. The things he says that saves their lives. The things he notes about them that are a wonderful example to us of how to live as Christians in a community where we are a minority and where there are other faiths and other religions. This small speech by the town clerk of Ephesus reminds us of two really important things we should be doing in our lives as we live together in a multicultural community.

The two things that the Christians of Ephesus did NOT do were:

1. Rob their temples.
2. Blaspheme their goddess.

The Christians who lived in Ephesus did not rob the temples of other religions nor blaspheme the gods and goddesses of other religions.

Now that is an example the Church would have done well remembering over the centuries. Pity they did not notice this part of their Bible.

In recent years, in the council area where I live, some angry Christians petitioned Council and higher state bodies in an effort to stop some Afghani members of the community from building a mosque. The Christians did not want a mosque in the same street as their church. So they were fighting them tooth and nail in the court to try to block it. Council initially passed it, but they took the fight higher. It was in all the local news, and it was most unpleasant.

To me those angry Christians trying to block a mosque seems to be an action consistent with 'robbing their temple'. It is not literally going into an existing mosque and stealing all the furniture or stripping it of valuables. But it is akin to the idea. It is being hostile and damaging to other faiths. It is hindering them. It is hurting them. The early Christians in Ephesus definitely did *not* do that.

It seems to me that Christians should be willing to live and let live. 'Do unto others as you would want them to do to you' (Matthew 7:12). If we would not want a church application to be blocked by Council, then we should not try to block other religions from having their places of worship either.

The same group of Christians I am referring to in my local area were also notorious for their 'blaspheming of other religions'. Some of their spokespersons have, to their shame I would add, held seminars on 'the evils of Islam', and how bad a person Mohammed was.

The Christians in Ephesus were saved from an angry mob when the town clerk reminded them that these men had neither 'robbed our temple nor blasphemed our goddess'. We Christians today would be wise to take a leaf out of their book. It is not 'Christian' to rob temples (or want them demolished, or try to block them being built) and it is not Christian to 'blaspheme the gods of other religions' or mock their prophets.

What *should* we be doing, instead of getting distracted by such negative activity? We should be getting on with the positive work of shining the light, of sharing the wonderful news of Jesus. We should be living witnesses to the transformation that can happen when you embrace Jesus in your life. We should be people who love everyone and never do any harm in the world. We should even love our perceived 'enemies' and do good to them.

Instead of trying to block a mosque next door to our church, for example, we should meet the leaders of the proposed mosque, get to know them, befriend them, offer to help them, and host a picnic for them the first day the work begins next door! We should not waste our time cursing what we deem to be 'the darkness', but rather we should get on with 'shining the light'. We need to be *grace dispensers*, not negative mean-spirited angry people who only see evil everywhere we look. Let us be living examples of Christ to those around us!

Reading:
Matthew 5:14-16.

Asking the hard questions:
If Jesus wants us to 'shine the light', why are so many Christians so miserable and more known for 'cursing the darkness'?

ACTS 20

Read Acts 20 before reflecting on studies 47, 48, 49 and 50

47) Acts 20:2-3. Paul writes the Book of Romans

Paul wrote a lot of the New Testament. There is debate about the authorship of some of the letters that are attributed to Paul, but there is virtually no debate about the main group. Here are the ones we think he wrote (in the order I personally think he penned them in[34]):

> **Galatians** – about 49 A.D. – around the start of Acts 15 (though there are some good arguments to place it later too).
>
> **1 Thessalonians** – from Corinth, about 50 or 51 A.D. – Acts 18:11.
>
> **2 Thessalonians** – from Corinth, about 50 or 51 A.D. – a month or two after the first one to them.
>
> **1 Corinthians** – from Ephesus, about 56 A.D. – Acts 19:10.
>
> **2 Corinthians** – from Troas about 57 A.D. – Acts 20:1 (assuming Paul went from Ephesus to Corinth via Troas). See 2 Corinthians 2:12-13 and 1 Corinthians 16:5-6.
>
> **Romans** – from Greece about 58 A.D. (and probably from Corinth in Greece) – Acts 20:2-3.
>
> **Ephesians** – from the first Roman imprisonment at the end of Acts – about 61 A.D. from Rome – Acts 28:30.
>
> **Colossians** – at the same time as Ephesians.
>
> **Philemon** – at the same time as Ephesians and Colossians.

[34] Other scholars will argue for a different date or dates for one or more of the letters. If it interests you, any Introduction to the New Testament will outline various views.

1 Timothy – after the end of the Book of Acts, while Paul was travelling and ministering again, and before his second Roman imprisonment (that second imprisonment began about 64 or 65 A.D.).

Titus – after the end of the Book of Acts as well, in similar circumstances to 1 Timothy.

Philippians – after Paul was re-arrested and again in a Roman prison – about 65 A.D.[35]

2 Timothy – Paul's last letter from the second Roman imprisonment, probably a couple of months after Philippians.

Of all the above letters, the ones with the most debate around them regarding authorship are 1 Timothy, 2 Timothy and Titus. The rest are pretty solidly seen as Paul's real letters. The ones most soundly agreed on are the earliest ones, up to and including Romans.

That brings me to the letter of **Romans**.

Why pause in these reflections on the stories of Acts to digress and talk about Romans?

Because it was written during Paul's travels in Acts and also because it is the most important thing he ever wrote. If we had to save just one book or letter from the pen of Paul, it would be almost unanimously agreed that we should save the Book of Romans. That is not to say that there is not great material and value in all his writings, but the Book of Romans is so solidly a presentation of his understanding of 'the Gospel' that it is without a doubt the single most important contribution he left the church.

This book has had an amazing impact on church history. For example, a passage from this book was used by God to convert **Augustine** – the early church father who would become the greatest thinker in the church for the first 1,000 years! The Book of Romans was also used to convert **Martin Luther** – a monk in the later Middle Ages who struggled with the sins of the church and with his own imperfect life. He

---

[35] I have not found any scholars who agree with me on this; most put the letter of Philippians earlier, about the same time as Ephesians, Colossians and Philemon. Some put it even earlier still during the imprisonment of Paul in Caesarea (around Acts 24:27). Some say earlier still in a speculated imprisonment in Ephesus (around Acts 19:10). For my arguments as to why it should be seen as a second Roman imprisonment letter, see Jim Reiher, 'Could Philippians have been written from the *Second* Roman Imprisonment?' *Evangelical Quarterly*. Vol. LXXXIV. No. 3 July 2012. pp.213-233.

was reading Romans when the Spirit of God opened his heart to understand the lost message of grace and forgiveness, salvation by faith not works, all based on the grace and mercy of God. This Book of Romans was also used to radically convert **John Wesley** – one of England's most influential preachers and teachers ever.

Romans was probably written about the time of Acts 20:2-3. Paul had left Ephesus and 'he came to Greece [we assume Corinth]. And there he spent three months...' During that three months we think he penned the most important document he ever wrote.

The letter of Romans is a long letter to a church Paul had never visited. He knew some people in the church of Rome (people moved around then, just as they do now). Priscilla and Aquila had moved back to Rome by then, for example, and he says hello to them by name in the final chapter (16:3). But he had not been there personally at the time of writing (1:11-13). The church had a significant minority of Jewish Christian members, coexisting with the Gentile majority. References to tensions between Jewish Christians and non-Jewish Christians permeate the pages of Romans. That tension is most clearly seen in chapters 1, 4, 11 and 14.

What motivated this lengthy and detailed letter? Different scholars and readers of the letter offer different theories:

- Some see it as a 'self-introduction'. Paul was planning to visit the place and he wanted to make sure the church would accept him, and allow him to minister amongst them while there.

- Others say it was his chance to pen his understanding of the message of the Gospel of grace, and he wanted to share that with the church that was in the capital city of the entire Roman Empire.

- Others think he wanted to put an apostolic stamp of approval on a church that had sprung up without any actual apostle's input or guidance.

- Still others say he wrote because he had heard of the tensions between the Jews and Gentiles in the church, and he wanted to provide input to that situation.

I tend to go for the first and last of those explanations: it was a self-introduction; it was giving the Roman church a chance to 'get to know' Paul and his message. It was also an appeal for different Christians (Jews and Gentiles specifically) to get on well together even if they were not exactly the same; even if some were more legalistic than others, even if some seemed more 'slack' and easy-going than others.

Whatever his reasoning, he gave the church then and forever, a brilliant and inspiring document. It reminds us of such important things as: the undeserved love, grace and forgiveness of God; the wonderful work of Jesus Christ; and the incredible promise of the Holy Spirit to live in the lives of believers. It inspires us to do good in the world, to accept suffering and troubles and let that shape us into better people, to love our enemies, to serve others, and to be tolerant of difference. Let me quote just a few of the gems that I personally love:

> 'All have sinned and fall short of the glory of God, and all are justified freely by his grace through the redemption that came by Jesus Christ' (Romans 3:23, 24).

> 'Therefore since we have been justified through faith, we have peace with God through our Lord Jesus Christ, through whom we have obtained access by faith into this grace in which we now stand. And we boast in the hope of the glory of God. Not only so, but we also glory in our sufferings, because we know that suffering produces perseverance; perseverance, character; and character, hope. And hope does not put us to shame, because God's love has been poured out into our hearts through the Holy Spirit, who has been given to us. You see, at the right time, when we were still powerless, Christ died for the ungodly. Very rarely will anyone die for a righteous person, though for a good person someone might possibly dare to die. But God demonstrated his own love for us in this: while we were still sinners, Christ died for us' (5:1-8).

> 'There is therefore now no condemnation for those who are in Christ Jesus' (8:1).

> 'If God is for us, who can be against us? He who did not spare his own son, but gave him up for us all - how will he not also, along with him, graciously give us all things? Who will bring any charge against those whom God has chosen? It is God who justifies. Who then is the one who condemns? ...

Who shall separate us from the love of Christ? Shall troubles, or distress, or persecution, or famine, or nakedness, or peril or sword? ... For I am convinced that neither death nor life, neither angels nor demons, neither the present nor the future, nor any powers, neither height nor depth, nor anything else in all creation, will be able to separate us from the love of God that is in Christ Jesus our Lord' (8:31-39).

'Do not repay anyone evil for evil. Be careful to do what is right in the eyes of everyone. If it is possible, as far as it depends on you, be at peace with everyone. Do not take revenge, my dear friends, but leave room for God's wrath, for it is written: "It is mine to avenge, I will repay," says the Lord. On the contrary: "If your enemy is hungry, feed him; if he is thirsty, give him something to drink. In doing this, you will heap burning coals upon his head." Do not be overcome by evil, but overcome evil with good' (12:17-21).

'Accept the one whose faith is weak, without quarrelling over disputable matters. ... Who are you to judge someone else's servant? To their own master servants stand or fall. And they will stand, for the Lord is able to make them stand... Therefore let us stop passing judgment on one another. Instead, make up your mind not to put any stumbling block or obstacle in the way of a brother or sister. ... For the kingdom of God is not a matter of eating and drinking, but of righteousness and peace and joy in the Holy Spirit. ... Therefore let us make every effort to do what leads to peace and to mutual edification' (14:1-19).

I encourage you and plead with you to *read the Book of Romans* and *savour its incredible content*. It can change your life!

Reading:
2 Peter 3:14-16.

Asking the hard questions:
Peter mentions Paul's writings in his second small letter. He makes the fascinating observation that some people find some things he writes hard to understand! He also calls Paul's writing 'scripture' when he says that unstable people distort Paul's writings, just as they do 'other scripture'. How does that affect how we should see the writings of the New Testament?

It seems that as far as the early apostles were concerned, fellow apostles or the immediate disciples of fellow apostles, could write 'scripture'. Would it have been seen as equal to the Old Testament material? Less important? Or more important?

48) Acts 20:17, 28-31. Church leaders can be the problem!

I am jumping past a pretty amazing story in Acts 20:6-14. (In that story, Paul passed through Troas and gave a sermon on the third floor of a building. The sermon went way too long, and a young man fell asleep during it. He was in the window-sill and he fell to his death. He was then restored to life! Well worth the read.)

I want to look at the *next* story in this chapter, instead; Paul's only recorded sermon, in this long book, addressed to *Christians* (20:18-36).

Normally we see Paul speaking to Jews, or to Gentile crowds. Here in this one spot in Acts, Paul speaks to a group of church elders. We are privileged to listen in to the talk; it is fascinating. Paul does not think he will ever see these people again (v. 25). It is, in his mind, his last chance to give them input and to guide them. So what we have is effectively Paul's 'last words' to these church leaders. That being the case, the words he says are clearly of huge importance to Paul. They are worthy of our close attention.

Paul had by-passed Ephesus knowing that if he visited there he would get stuck there for longer than he had time to give (v. 16). So he went to Miletus and called the elders of the Ephesian church to meet him there (v. 17). They gathered, and he gave them this speech. It is full of significance for us still today.

Of the numerous things Paul talked about, verses 28-31 stand out:

> Keep watch over yourselves and all the flock of which the Holy Spirit has made you overseers. Be shepherds of the church of God which he bought with his own blood. I know that after I leave, savage wolves will come in among you, and not spare the flock. Even from your own number some will arise and distort the truth in order to draw away disciples after them. So be on your guard!

One of the recurring themes and concerns of Paul was the tragic reality of 'wolves in sheep's clothing' (a phrase coined by Jesus in Matthew 7:15). 'Savage wolves' would come in among them and seek to hurt the church members. Not just that, some of the very people in the room, some of the current leaders and elders, would also 'turn' into such savage wolves. The reality and the danger of false teachers and false leaders in the church has been going on for 2,000 years.

The problem is very real: members of the Christian community getting lost in their own importance, and leading fellow members of the community astray. We are talking about people who started well, but who wandered off the track. Even though they had wandered off the straight and narrow, *they were still in the church*. These are people who were leaders, prophets, teachers, pastors – but who had become dangerous examples in either their teaching, their lifestyle or both.

This problem surfaces time and again throughout the letters of Paul. A few examples:

To the Ephesians:

(From the letter to the same church that this group of people were from – the people Paul is actually addressing in Acts 20):

> '[If you allow yourself to mature in Christ] ... then we will no longer be infants, tossed back and forth by the waves, and blown here and there by every wind of teaching and by the cunning and craftiness of people in their deceitful scheming. Instead, speaking the truth in love, we will grow to become in every respect the mature body of him who is the head, that is, Christ' (Ephesians 4:14-15).

To Timothy:

Consider also some of his words he would write some years later to Timothy - who was by then overseeing the churches in the same city of Ephesus:

> Stay there in Ephesus, so that you may command certain people not to teach false doctrines any longer, or to devote themselves to myths and endless genealogies. Such things promote controversial speculations, rather than advancing God's work – which is by faith. Some… want to be teachers of the Law, but they do not know what they are talking about or what they so confidently affirm (1 Timothy1:3-7).

> The Spirit clearly says that in later times some will abandon the faith, and follow deceiving spirits and things taught by demons. Such teachings come through hypocritical liars, whose consciences have been seared as if with a hot iron. They forbid people to marry, and order them to abstain from certain foods.' (1 Timothy 4:1-3).

> If anyone teaches otherwise and does not agree with the sound instruction of our Lord Jesus Christ, and to godly teaching, they are conceited and understand nothing. They have an unhealthy interest in controversies and quarrels about words that result in envy, strife, malicious talk, evil suspicions, and constant friction between people of corrupt mind, who have been robbed of the truth, and who think that godliness is a means to financial gain! (1 Timothy 6:3-5).

Then from the second letter to Timothy: 'evil-doers and impostors will go from bad to worse, deceiving and being deceived. … (2 Timothy 3:13).

> For the time will come when people will not put up with sound doctrine. Instead, to suit their own desires, they will gather around them a great number of teachers to say what their itching ears want to hear. They will turn away their ears from the truth and will turn aside to myths. (2 Timothy 4:3-4).

Clearly it was a problem for the Ephesian church, but not just for them. It is all through Paul's letters. It is an ever-present danger in every church. Consider his words:

To the Corinthians:

> If someone comes to you and preaches a Jesus other than the Jesus we preached, ... or a different gospel from the one you accepted, you put up with it easily enough. ... such people are false apostles, deceitful workers, masquerading as apostles of Christ. And no wonder: for Satan himself masquerades as an angel of light. It is not surprising, then, if his servants also masquerade as servants of righteousness. (2 Corinthians 11:4-15).

To the Galatians:

> I am astonished that you are so quickly deserting the one who called you to live in the grace of Christ and are turning to a different gospel ... some people are throwing you into confusion and are trying to pervert the gospel of Christ (Galatians 1:6-7).

To the Philippians:

> Join together in following my example, brothers and sisters, and just as you have us as a model, keep your eyes on those who live as we do. For as I have often told you before and now tell you again even with tears, many live as enemies of the cross of Christ. Their destiny is destruction, their god is their stomach, and their glory is in their shame. Their mind is set on earthly things (3:17-19).

To the Colossians:

> I tell you this so that no one may deceive you with fine-sounding arguments. ... See to it that no one takes you captive through hollow and deceptive philosophy, which depends on human tradition and the elementary spiritual forces of this world, rather than on Christ. ... Do not let anyone who delights

in false humility and the worship of angels disqualify you. Such a person also goes into great detail about what they have seen; they are puffed up with idle notions by their unspiritual mind. They have lost connection with the head [Christ]. (2:4, 8, 18, 19).

To the Thessalonians:

We ask you brothers and sisters not to become easily unsettled or alarmed by the teaching allegedly from us – whether by a prophecy or by word of mouth or by letter – asserting that the day of the Lord has already come. Don't let anyone deceive you in any way ... So then brothers and sisters, stand firm and hold fast to the teachings we passed on to you, whether by word of mouth or by letter. (2 Thessalonians. 2:1-3, 15).

In the name of the Lord Jesus Christ, we command you brothers and sisters, to keep away from every believer who is idle and disruptive and does not live according to the teaching you received from us. For you yourselves know how you ought to follow our example. (2 Thessalonians 3:6-7)

And to Titus who oversaw the churches on Crete:

For there are many rebellious people, full of meaningless talk and deception, especially those of the circumcision group. They must be silenced because they are disrupting whole households by teaching things that they ought not to teach – and that for the sake of dishonest gain ... They claim to know God but by their actions they deny him. They are detestable, disobedient and unfit for doing anything good. (Titus 1:10-16)

Warn a divisive person once and then warn them a second time. After that have nothing to do with them. You may be sure that such people are warped and sinful; they are self-condemned. (3:10-11)

Paul does not want Christians to go off the track and become 'false teachers' or 'wolves in sheep's clothing'. He wants us to be careful, to watch out for ourselves. He wants us to be aware that any one of us can wander off the right path, and deceive ourselves, and deceive others with us. If we stay alert, humble, open to the guidance of the Holy Spirit, open to the Word of God, and open to the wise advice of our church community, we should be able to survive that temptation and danger. But be on your guard. It really could happen to any one of us.

Reading:

It is not just Paul who is concerned about false teachers emerging out of the church. Consider John Zebedee's words in 1 John 2:18-20.

Asking the hard questions:

If John says that many *antichrists* have already come and they are *false teachers in the church*, how does that impact what we have been told about the antichrist? Does it change your thinking about it? Haven't we been told that the antichrist is a political figure who will take over the world and make everyone follow himself? What is that based on? Are you aware that in the entire book of Revelation, the word 'antichrist' never appears? (There is a beast in chapter 13. And that beast has an off-sider, a false prophet (19: 20). But neither is actually called 'The Anti-Christ'.)

How does this text in 1 John fit in or reshape your thinking on all that?

More importantly, this text also tells us a key to avoiding being deceived by false teachers. What is that key? (v. 20).

What is the anointing that we have that can help us stay discerning and on the right track?

49) Acts 20:33-34. Money is not our focus

One of the other things Paul emphasised to the Ephesian church elders in this speech to Christians in Acts 20, is the following:

'I have not coveted anyone's silver or gold or clothing. You yourselves know that these hands of mine have supplied my own needs and the needs of my companions. In everything I did, I showed you that by this kind of hard work, we must help the weak...' (Acts 20:33-35a).

We noted in an earlier study that Paul was a tent-maker by trade, and that when he was in Ephesus he worked for his own keep with other tent-makers (Priscilla and Aquila). We talked about Paul's way of life being a model, but not always *the* model to follow. Indeed, that is still true. He would not take money from the people he was with, but he did at times take money from established churches as gifts towards his work in other cities. That was an important distinction for Paul. He did not take money from new churches that he was visiting and living with. He would work with his hands or accept gifts from other more established churches away from where he was currently living.

Paul took this aspect of his ministry quite seriously. He did this because he wanted to be an example to those around him. He would find at times that some Christians were lazy and wanted to sponge off the church coffers. He saw a number of people who liked to live off the goodness of the church community's heart. They exploited the church when they actually could have been looking after themselves. Paul really did *not* like what he saw. This theme resurfaces in many of his letters as well as in this speech here.

When Paul wrote to the church of Thessalonica, he said to them:

You yourselves know how you ought to follow our example. We were not idle when we were with you, nor did we eat anyone's food without paying for it. On the contrary, we worked night and day, labouring and toiling so that we would not be a burden to any of you. We did this, not because we do not have the right to such help, but in order to offer ourselves as a model for you to imitate. (2 Thessalonians. 3:7-9)

Paul was keen to set a good example to the churches he spent time with. He worked to provide for his own needs (if other churches were not supporting him) and he expected that example to be followed. He calls it 'a model' like we did, but he *does* anticipate that the Christians he has taught will actually take it seriously and follow it.

When Paul wrote to the Corinthian church they had had some trouble with people who they thought were 'Christian missionaries – good preachers'. Actually they were con-artists: people who came through the church and fleeced the flock! They did not *feed* the flock. They *fleeced* it.

Paul became really upset by the gullibility of the Corinthian Christians not to be able to see through this deceit. He wrote to them comparing the money-focused ministry of false teachers, to *his* ministry:

> Was it a sin for me to lower myself in order to elevate you by preaching the Gospel of God to you free of charge? I robbed other churches by receiving support from them in order to serve you. And when I was with you and needed something, I was not a burden to anyone; for the believers who came from Macedonia supplied what I needed. I have kept myself from being a burden to you in any way, and will continue to do so. (2 Corinthians 11:7-9)

He adds a bit later in the same letter:

> How were you inferior to the other churches, except that I was never a burden to you? Forgive me for this wrong! Now I am ready to visit you for the third time and I will not be a burden to you, because what I want is not your possessions, but you. After all, children should not have to save up for their parents, but parents for their children. So I will very gladly spend for you everything I have and expend myself as well. (2 Corinthians 12:13-15)

Paul refused to be seen as someone who 'peddled the word of God' (2 Corinthians 2:17). He saw his ministry as way too important to be brushed aside by the astute outsider. He knew that some people would look in and see the preachers or leaders making lots of money from gullible members of the church. Talk about a turn-off from wanting to get involved in something like that! No, Paul refused to take money from any church he was with, so that no one could accuse him of such a selfish worldly motive as material gain. He went to great lengths to keep that guiding principle in place. No one could ever accuse him of 'making money out of his new religion'.

Hear his heart when he wrote this passage in 2 Corinthians:

> For we are to God the pleasing aroma of Christ among those who are being saved and among those who are perishing. To the one we are an aroma that brings death; to the other an aroma that brings life. And who is equal to such a task? Unlike so many, we do not peddle the word of God for profit. On the contrary, in Christ we speak before God with sincerity, as those sent from God. (2:15-17)

Christ-followers are not meant to be money-followers. They can't serve two masters, God and money (Jesus said that in Matthew 6:24). They are meant to be free from the cares of the world. Jesus and Paul both had so much to say on this topic that it would fill a book to explore it all. The simple truth seen here in Acts 20 is that Paul expected church leaders to be driven by motives other than worldly gain.

Leaders in the church should not be interested in savings and investments, share portfolios and appreciating property. They should not be distracted from their calling. When we minister we remember the words of Jesus, 'Freely you received; freely give!' (Matthew 10:8). The tragic materialism of the Western Church today is a sad reflection on how much we have forgotten the words of Jesus and Paul.

Let us resolve *never* to be seen as a 'peddler of God's Word'.

Reading:
Matthew 10:5-10.

Asking the hard questions:
Paul really did try hard to never let anyone accuse him of 'being in ministry to make money'. Why are we so laid back about that same criticism today? It *is* a criticism that non-Christians level against us, *a lot*. Shouldn't we be just as concerned as Paul was? Even more concerned? Shouldn't we try to *avoid* that criticism just like Paul avoided it? Why are we so easy-going about it? Could it be that some of the big name ministries out there doing the circuit are really more about making money than representing Jesus faithfully? Should we avoid supporting them?

Okay, taking this a bit further, even when some of us don't show much interest in money, why do we still play the game of paying big gifts to visiting ministries? Or accepting bigger gifts than we intuitively sense (Holy Spirit convicting perhaps?) we should receive when we do ministry elsewhere? Is it really all that easy to just slip into that kind of compromise?

50) Acts 20:35. A quote from Jesus

Before leaving Paul's speech to the Ephesian elders at Miletus, there is one more gem worth noting in verse 35. It comes straight after the comment about Paul not being a burden on anyone. Starting at verse 34 again, listen to the extra statement he makes:

> I have not coveted anyone's silver or gold or clothing. You yourselves know that these hands of mine have supplied my own needs and the needs of my companions. In everything I did, I showed you that by this kind of hard work, we must help the weak, remembering the words the Lord Jesus himself said: 'It is more blessed to give than to receive.' (Acts 20:33-35).

What a wonderful treasure to find in the Book of Acts—a saying of Jesus that is not in any of the four gospels.

The short quotation from Jesus is an important reminder about caring for others. The actual teaching should not be lost in the discussion that is about to follow. We *should* care for the poor and for anyone less well off than ourselves. It is a solid and repeated teaching of Jesus. He had a lot to say about caring for the poor, sharing your possessions, using money wisely to help others— all that and more.

One of the 'more' things he said was, 'It is more blessed to give than to receive'. Our culture has turned that around to some extent and makes us believe it is better to get things rather than give things. Our highly materialistic society wants us to believe it is great to *get stuff*. The reality is that a more lasting satisfaction and joy comes from helping others; *giving* to those in need, *sharing* with those less well off.

It really is more blessed to give than to receive.

The fact that this teaching would not be known to us were it not in the Book of Acts reminds us that Jesus must have said so many other things, given so many other parables, so many other teachings and instructions that we just don't have. We have four wonderful gospels, but as the writer of the fourth gospel said at the end of his book, 'Jesus did many other things as well. If every one of them were written down, I suppose that even the whole world would not have room for the books that would be written' (John 21:25).

What a fitting way to close the fourth gospel. I love John's hyperbole here. I smile as I read his deliberate exaggeration to drive home a point. Jesus did *so much more*. He said so much more. His life had so much more to it! Here are some of the stories, here are some of the teachings, here are some of the great adventures and miracles, conversations and controversies - but not all of them!

We can be grateful for what we have, but we don't have it all. In fact, it seems we have only a small proportion. How full those years must have been. How exciting a life to have been a part of!

I wonder what else Jesus said that we just don't have recorded? Perhaps his most dominant themes *are* all represented. Even in regards to this saying of Jesus, it is not a surprise teaching. If Luke had not included it, we would still know that Jesus taught us about the importance of giving and caring for those in need. If this lovely short saying was missing, we would not really be lacking in plenty of material from Jesus on caring for the poor.

Let me offer you a thought about *another* passage of Scripture that will take us on an apparent tangent. It is only an apparent tangent though, because it will circle back around to this idea about extra teachings of Jesus.

There is an interesting passage in one of Paul's letters where he initially quotes Jesus. Then he specifically does not quote Jesus, because he has nothing to draw on from Jesus for the situation he is confronted with.

In 1 Corinthians 7, Paul reflects on the difficult and messy questions of divorce and remarriage, and celibacy. Talk about hot potatoes! Paul is offering some solid advice on how to navigate around difficult and complex situations. Note what he says in 1 Corinthians 7:10-40 (The whole passage should be read for the full context and discussion, but let me highlight 10-13, 25 and 40):

> To the married I give this command, (**not I, but the Lord**): A wife should not separate from her husband. But if she does, she must remain unmarried or else be reconciled to her husband. And a husband must not divorce his wife. To the rest **I say this (I, not the Lord)**: If any brother has a wife who is not a believer and she is willing to live with him, he must not divorce her. And if

a woman has a husband who is not a believer, and he is willing to live with her, she must not divorce him ... Now about virgins: **I have no command from the Lord, but I give a judgment** as one who by the Lord's mercy is trustworthy. ... **I think** ... **In my judgment**, she is happier if she stays as she is - and **I think** that I too have the Spirit of God'

What an insightful glance into Paul's writing! Paul knows certain teachings of Jesus. Jesus taught people to not divorce (e.g. Matthew 19:3-9). He is aware of that and he says so: 'I give you this instruction, ... actually not me, but this is from the Lord.' A bit later he wants to talk about the difficult situation where a Christian and a non-Christian are married and it just isn't working. It may be that the non-Christian can't stand being married to someone with the Christian faith. In this case Paul says it is okay to divorce. Note how he introduced it though: 'Not the Lord, but I say'. Paul did not have a saying of Jesus to lean on in that situation. He knew that Jesus had commandments that pushed no divorce. However, Paul did not see that as being relevant or applying to a mixed faith marriage that was failing. Jesus' apparently 'black and white' statement was not so 'all encompassing' as some have tried to make out, it seems. At least that was Paul's feeling about it. So Paul created his own rule of thumb for the situation he was addressing. Paul allowed divorce in those circumstances.

A bit later in the same chapter he gives advice to the unmarried ('virgins'). He admits again he had no command from the Lord, but he was giving his opinion as 'one who by the mercy of God is trustworthy'. He concludes that long section recommending celibacy, with the final comment, 'So that is my opinion, but I reckon that I also have the Spirit of God'.

When Paul could quote a saying of Jesus, he did. When he did not have a saying of Christ to help inform him on how to respond to a situation, he gave his opinion. Both those kinds of writing are in the Scripture - direct commandments from Christ (that have contextual limitations it seems) and opinions from a wise mature Christian, guided by the Holy Spirit. Both kinds of 'material' are in the Bible.

You and I have to decide what that means for our interpretation and application of any of the material we come across in the Bible. In this short discussion we are really confronted with a number of complex implications and considerations. Consider:

- If Jesus' apparently 'black and white' teachings are not actually applicable to *all* situations after all, then how does that affect the way I apply Christ's sayings to any situation?

- If Paul admits in 1 Corinthians that sometimes he gives his own personal opinion and trusts it is guided by the Spirit, then are we obligated to follow that teaching as much as we are obligated to follow the teachings of Jesus?

- If Paul does this in 1 Corinthians (gives his personal informed opinion) and he admits he is doing it here, perhaps he is doing it elsewhere and just does not spell out that this is what he is doing. Can we decide to reject some of the things Paul says because we feel he is offering his informed opinion that may or may not really be God's perfect teaching?

- Is there something else going on bigger than all this? Has God, in his providence and sovereignty, overseen things so that even when Paul is sharing his opinions, those opinions are exactly what God wanted written and collected for his Holy Scripture?

- Is the previous point just a simplistic way to avoid the more challenging questions of how we discern the material in the Bible? Is it a rationale to get ourselves off the hook regarding seriously thinking about the content and teachings in the Bible?

The issue of how we see, handle, interpret and apply Scripture is huge. We will be grappling with that all our lives.

Before we end this devotion, let me change tack one more time.

It is good to remember every now and again that we have a lot of 'snap shots of Jesus' in the gospels. They are like a nice thick photo album overflowing with memories of Christ.

We can know a bit or even a lot about someone from a photo album. However, it is one thing to browse a photo album and it is quite another to *know* the person in the pictures. Paul had a very real relationship with the risen Jesus Christ. Paul was not just a clever man who knew a lot of things Jesus said. He was someone who had met the risen Christ (way back in Chapter 9) and in a real, spiritual way had continued to walk with him. He did not just study the sayings of Jesus and quote them when needed. He did not just have an intellectual grasp of the Christ. No, that would not have been enough to sustain him during the toughest times of persecution and trial. He not only knew *about* Jesus, he actually *knew* him personally. The difference between knowing *about* him and knowing him is in the way the relationship is sustained. Prayer, silence, meditation, reflection, daily conversation, sensing his presence in all the things he participated in, sensing his presence in the lives of others— all that and more.

That is a wonderful example for us to imitate. We should not just know *about* Jesus but we should actually *know him* too. That will sustain us as we walk through our life journey as well.

Reading:

2 Corinthians 8:1-15 (and you might read all the way through to 9:15).

Asking the hard questions:

As you read through 2 Corinthians 8, note the reasons why it is great to give to others in need. List as many different reasons as you can find. If you are keen, finish off the rest of chapter 8 and all of chapter 9 as well. Those two chapters are dedicated to the theme of 'giving'. If you make it to the end of the two chapters you might notice that *tithing* is never mentioned. In fact, it is almost impossible to find any positive reference to tithing in the New Testament.[36]

Why, then, do many churches teach tithing as if it is a New Testament principle? It was an Old Testament law to provide for the Levites. It is not taught as a Christian practice in the New Testament.[37] Clearly if we follow the principles of 2 Corinthians 8 and 9 and the teaching of Jesus, 'That it is more blessed to give than to receive' – we would give *more* than 10%! Wouldn't we? *Do* we? If not, why not?

---

36 Tithing is mentioned by Jesus in his criticism of the religious formalism of the Pharisees and scribes in Matthew 23:23 and Luke 11:42, and it is mentioned by Jesus in the parable of the proud and self-righteous Pharisee in Luke 18:11. But that's the only mention of it in the gospels.

37 For more on this see my "The Eye of the Needle: Discipleship and Wealth". UNOH publications. 2005. Especially chapter 11: "Do Christians have to tithe?"

ACTS 21

Read Acts 21 before reflecting on study 51

51) Acts 21:4, 10-12. *Not* listening to the Holy Spirit

The speech to the Ephesian elders ended and Paul left Miletus. In Chapter 21, we were told how Paul and his companions travelled through various places until they got to a place called Tyre.

'We sought out the disciples there and we stayed with them seven days. Through the Spirit they urged Paul not to go on to Jerusalem' (21:4).

If the Holy Spirit of God gives a message and it is genuinely believed to be from the Spirit of God, then you would think that would be worth listening to, wouldn't you?

Paul, however, ignored it. Or to put it more bluntly, he chose to disobey it. The short summary of the message was that Paul was told 'not to set foot in Jerusalem'. He was *not* recommended to reconsider his plan. He was *not* simply given a vision of what *would* happen when he got to Jerusalem (as if that was God's will so be ready for it). No, it is very difficult to ignore the fact that *he chose to disobey it*. He decided to go to Jerusalem despite this message.[38]

As the story unfolds, Paul did in fact go to Jerusalem. The prophetic word proved to be true, he was caught up in a riot, nearly killed by the crowd, saved by Roman soldiers, and then imprisoned. He would stay in prison for about five years! It really did seem to be a word from God to 'not go to Jerusalem'.

Some interpreters will soften this. Perhaps the statement *'they kept telling Paul through the Spirit, not to set foot in Jerusalem'* actually meant that the believers had a Spirit-led vision of trouble awaiting Paul in Jerusalem and nothing more. Since they saw what would happen to Paul if he went there, those believers then decided to tell Paul not to go.

---

38 Interestingly, Paul was not unfamiliar with the Holy Spirit blocking his travelling plans in the past. Recall Acts 16:6-10.

That is possible. It is making the text say something else, though. What the text actually says is that the believers in Tyre told Paul 'through the Spirit' not to go to that city. That sounds like a prophecy or a word of knowledge. The word from the Spirit was simple: 'Don't go!'

The prophetic word Paul received about not going to Jerusalem was reinforced a second time some days later. After leaving Tyre, the group made their way to Ptolemais (v. 6) and then Caesarea (v. 8). When they got to Caesarea, they stayed at the home of Philip the Evangelist, one of the original deacons back in Acts chapter 6. Philip now lived out of Jerusalem on the coast, and he had four daughters who were prophetesses (vs. 8-9). Note what happens next:

> After we had been there a number of days, a prophet named Agabus came down from Judea. Coming over to us, he took Paul's belt, tied his own hands and feet with it and said, 'The Holy Spirit says, "In this way the Jewish leaders in Jerusalem will bind the owner of this belt and hand him over to the Gentiles."' When we had heard this, we and the people there pleaded with Paul not to go up to Jerusalem. (21:10-12)

If this incident in Caesarea was the only reference to Paul being warned, and we did not have the comment about the Spirit's instruction that happened back in Tyre, we might say that Paul was *not* commanded to avoid Jerusalem. Rather he was just being shown what to expect if and when he went. Yes, he would be arrested and handed over to the Romans, so be ready for it. If we only had this Caesarean incident, we might not conclude that Paul was doing anything wrong. He was not disobeying God in going up to Jerusalem. He was simply being forewarned and prepared for some serious persecution.

The fact that this second incident shows us a vision/warning rather than a command, actually reinforces the point that the first occurrence in Tyre was *not* such a picture that Paul could simply 'be ready for'. Luke describes them differently. In Tyre he was warned, 'Don't go'. Now he is being shown what will happen if and when he goes.

Paul seems adamant that he is going. He replied to the prophecy and the appeals not to go, with this: "'Why are you weeping and breaking my heart? I am ready not only to be bound, but even to die in Jerusalem for the name of the Lord Jesus." When he would not be dissuaded, we gave up and said, "The Lord's will be done'" (21:13, 14).

Some might suggest that it was actually the Lord's will for Paul to go to Jerusalem because of that final statement there by the disciples in verse 14. I can just imagine the moment: after trying to talk Paul out of going, the disciples eventually give up, shrug their shoulders and sigh. 'The will of the Lord be done.' Does that mean it really *was* the will of the Lord, just because they decided to stop arguing and fall back on that line? Maybe the will of the Lord was for Paul to stay out of jail for five years and do a lot more ministry establishing more churches, visiting the ones already up and running, and struggling with various problems. Maybe the will of the Lord was expressed back in Tyre when Paul was told through the Spirit not to set foot in Jerusalem.

If that is so, then the disciples were either convinced by Paul that they were wrong, and they finally came around to Paul's view, or maybe they saw 'the will of the Lord' a bit differently to how we might think about it. Perhaps they saw the *actual* will of the Lord (to keep Paul out of jail and continuing in his ministry) as being ignored, but they also saw that if people do not follow the will of the Lord, then a *secondary* 'will of the Lord' still kicks in.

You see, even in our moments of disobedience and failing, the Lord will still do what *he* wants to do. He will use other people to do what we should have done. We will end up somewhere else *and he will still use us there if we are willing to be used.* God can see all things. He could see that Paul was not going to follow the direction through the Spirit to stay out of Jerusalem. It would mess up the plans God had for him, but God knew that. So God had other plans, and implements them despite Paul's stubbornness.

I think it is hard to conclude anything other than that Paul failed to obey God on this occasion. Just like you and I do at times too. We know what we are meant to do, but we just don't do it. Perhaps, like Paul, our motives are actually pretty good—or at least, mixed. Paul seems to mix love for his fellow Jews with pride that he can handle tough situations, and he would show his friends that!

Paul certainly loved his fellow Jews, and it grieved him greatly when they stubbornly refused to embrace their own Messiah. In the Book of Romans he laments over his fellow countrymen and women (Romans 9:1-3). He even said in that Romans passage that he would swap his place in heaven for them, if that would work! So Paul *would* risk his life to minister to them – even after God had twice told him not to, in this specific city (Jerusalem). *Our* motives for sinning – for disobeying God – can be reasonably good motives at times too. It is not easy to always do what God wants. Sometimes, it means not doing some things that we really want to do.

Paul made a monumental mistake when he went to Jerusalem. We are nearly at that part of the story. Paul will get caught up in a terrible riot and he will nearly be killed in the street. He will be saved by some Roman soldiers, but he also ends up in jail for *years*. His ministry was cut short and a different ministry would happen instead (a jail ministry). He would write various letters that would become part of the New Testament and he would minister to lots of Roman guards and other prisoners. Even though the original will of the Lord was ignored and disobeyed, a second 'will of the Lord' did end up getting done instead.

One last thing: if even Paul can disobey God at times for mixed motives, it is kind of a back-handed encouragement for us to keep persevering. Paul could blur his motives and not listen to God. We do that at times too. We are not total failures because we are not perfect. We don't need to throw in the towel and not be a Christ-follower any more. We can keep going. We can make the most of any situation we find ourselves in, even if it is not God's ideal will for our life, and we can still serve him in that situation.

Don't despair because of imperfection and failing. See it as an area to overcome as you continue to walk the walk!

Reading:
Jesus in John 14:26, and Paul in Ephesians 4:30.

Asking the hard questions:
Was it wrong of Paul to go to Jerusalem in the story above? Or is there a 'blurry area' where just maybe we are given some latitude by God to either follow his leading or not? Or is that just a cop-out, and it is more black and white than that: we either obey or disobey - end of discussion?

Part Four:
Paul in prison

Paul's jail time

We have come to the point in the Book of Acts where Paul was arrested and began his long stint in prison (a few prisons actually). It is easy to lose your way in the last eight chapters of the book. Essentially we need to see it broken down into these critical events:

21:15 - Paul did go to Jerusalem, supposedly for a brief visit, before he went home to Antioch. (It certainly did not end up as a 'short visit' – he would not see his home city of Antioch for over five more years).

21:16-26 – Paul tried hard to 'fit in' and demonstrate to the Jews of Jerusalem that he was in fact a proud Jew (as well as a Christian).

21:27-30 – A riot occurred and angry Jews tried to kill Paul in the street.

21:31-37 – Some Roman soldiers saved Paul from being torn apart.

21:38- 22:21 – Paul was able to address the angry mob but to no avail. Their anger flared up again during his speech to them.

22:22-30 – He was put into custody under Roman guard.

23:1-10 – Paul had a 'trial' (really more of a 'hearing') in front of the Jewish Sanhedrin, but it ended in chaos when Paul successfully divided the forum on a theological issue. He remained under Roman guard.

23:11-35 – A plot to kill Paul was discovered and so the Roman commander sent him to Governor Felix who was in Caesarea. Paul remained in prison there, away from the hot heads in Jerusalem.

24:1-27 – Governor Felix listened to Paul but kept him in jail ('hoping that money would be given to him by Paul' – v. 26). Paul languished there for two years and finally a new governor was appointed: Festus.

25:1-12 – Governor Festus heard Paul, but seemed to want to impress the Jewish leadership. The new governor threatened to send Paul back to Jerusalem for trial there. Paul knew that there would be an ambush to kill him if that happened, so he appealed his case to the Emperor instead.

25:13- 26:32 – Some days later, before he was sent to Rome, King Agrippa and Bernice arrived in Caesarea. Festus invited them to hear Paul. Paul defended himself and his gospel message to the King. The hearing concluded with the Governor and King agreeing that Paul really had not done anything deserving such punishment, but since he appealed to the Emperor he had to be sent to him.

27:1- 28:14 – The journey to Rome took place, including the famous ship wreck.

28:15-31 – Paul arrived in Rome and was in an open imprisonment there for over two years.

The book ends without telling us the outcome of the final trial.

ACTS 22

Read Acts 22 before reflecting on study 52

52) Acts 22. Roman soldiers and governors in Acts

When historians evaluate any document to see if it is trustworthy or not, all kinds of interesting tests are applied. We ask for example:

- Does the author try to make *himself* or *herself* look good? (Like the Jewish historian Josephus does in his autobiography—it is most glowing!)

- Does the writer make his or her *friends* seem terrific? Does the writer 'whitewash' the faults of their *friends* or their *nation*?

- Does the historical data in this material line up with other documents from the same period and offer consistent material? If not, which document seems more credible and why?

- How does the document treat the *enemies* of the writer? Or the enemies of the writer's people? Are they presented in really negative ways or is a balanced perspective offered?

That last question above gets an interesting answer when applied to the gospels and Acts.

The Book of Acts was written at a time when the Romans dominated the world. That included domination over the Jewish people. Rome was an efficient and ruthless power.

It is normal for oppressed people groups, including the Jews, to not particularly like the nation that oppresses them. With that in mind, it is fascinating to read the four gospels and Acts and ask, how do the writers 'view' the Romans who are mentioned? Are they even-handed as they discuss their nation's enemies? Or are they totally one-sided? Are they full of hatred and can't see any positives at all?[39] Or are they full of praises that reveal more an attitude of, 'I have sold out to them and profit from them being here'?

Matthew, Mark and John were all Jews. Luke was a Gentile, and even though he was not personally feeling the Roman oppression of the Jewish people, nevertheless, his dearest friends were Jews. His greatest hero (Paul) was a Jew who would eventually be killed by the Romans.

Luke's treatment of the Romans, whom he mentions in both the gospel and Acts, is rather remarkable. He is not some blindly devoted Roman admirer, I should add. Pilate comes across as weak and easily manipulated by the Jewish crowd (Luke 23:13-25). Commander Lysias' altering of the facts to make himself look good in his letter to the governor is not overlooked (Acts 23:26, 27). Governor Felix' willingness to take bribes is mentioned (Acts 24:26). Nevertheless, Luke's treatment of many other Romans, especially soldiers he comes across, is actually very generous.

We are up to the story of Paul's arrest in Jerusalem in Acts 22. Even before we meet the Roman Commander Lysias here, we have already met other Romans along the way.

In Acts 10 we met Cornelius, a Roman Army commander who lived in Caesarea. He is described as 'devout and God fearing' who 'prayed to God regularly'. He is also described as someone who 'gave generously to those in need' (10:2). Later his servants describe him to Peter, 'He is a righteous and God-fearing man, who is respected by the Jewish people' (10:22). Cornelius certainly comes across that way in the material we have about him from Luke.

During the first missionary journey we are introduced to the proconsul of Cyprus, Sergius Paulus (13:7). He is described as 'an intelligent man' (v. 7) who responded well to the signs and wonders and preaching of Paul.

In Acts 16 Paul ran into trouble in Philippi and was arrested and beaten with rods, and thrown in jail by the officials of the city (that is not downplayed). But the sequel of the story shows us the Roman jailer showing great care and assistance to Paul and Silas.

---

39   I am reminded of that hilarious scene in *The Life of Brian*. From memory, 'What have the Romans ever done for us? *Nothing*!' Then a voice calls out, 'Aqueducts'. 'Sure, we all know they gave us aqueducts, but what else? Nothing!' A voice replied, 'Roads, the end of piracy on the seas, safe travel throughout the empire, law and order, prosperity...' 'Sure sure, but besides all that – what have they done for us? *Nothing*!'

In Corinth, we saw the Proconsul of Achaia, Gallio, come across as an 'indifferent' Roman official, not willing to go along with Jewish plans to hurt Paul. He turned a blind eye to the crowd that beat up one of Paul's enemies. He seemed neither interested in protecting, nor in hurting, the apostle.

By the time we get to chapter 20, we have grown used to seeing imperfect Roman soldiers and officials 'not being too bad' in the way they treated the early Christians.

When Paul was arrested in Jerusalem by the Roman Commander and his troops, the arrest was first and foremost an act to save Paul's life:

> The whole city was aroused, and the people came running from all directions. Seizing Paul, they dragged him from the Temple and immediately the gates were shut. While they were trying to kill him, news reached the commander of the Roman troops that the whole city of Jerusalem was in an uproar. He at once took some officers and soldiers and ran down to the crowd. When the rioters saw the commander and his soldiers they stopped beating Paul.' (Acts 21:30-32)

The Romans were helpful, but still tough. The text goes on to say, 'The commander came up and arrested him, and ordered him to be bound with two chains. Then he asked who he was and what he had done' (21:33). The crowd clearly wanted blood though, and so to get Paul out of there the soldiers had to carry Paul out (21:35). When Paul had tried unsuccessfully to speak to the crowd, the commander had him brought into the barracks, 'He directed that he should be flogged and interrogated to find out why the people were shouting at him like this' (22:24).

Paul waited till they had tied him down with straps, and when they were just about to start whipping him, he asked them, 'Is it legal for you to flog a Roman citizen who has not even been found guilty?' (v.25). The centurion who heard this went to the commander and told him. The commander had to check it out. It is a fascinating short dialogue; 'The commander went to Paul and said: 'Tell me, are you a Roman citizen?' 'Yes I am,' he answered. Then the commander said, 'I had to pay a lot of money for my citizenship.' 'But I was born a citizen,' Paul replied. ... The commander himself was alarmed when he realised that he had put Paul, a Roman citizen, in chains' (vs. 27-29).

This Roman commander (not named yet, but we find out soon his name is Lysias), comes across as sensible, decisive and strong, and yet also quite 'human'. This impression is reinforced as we get more of his story. He organised for Paul to speak at the Sanhedrin the next day (22:30), but that ended in chaos as well (23:1-10) and, 'The commander was afraid Paul would be torn to pieces by them. He ordered the troops to go down and take him away from them by force, and bring him back into the barracks' (23:10).

This Roman commander saved Paul a few times, in fact. When a Jewish conspiracy took place to kill Paul, the commander found out and immediately sent him out of the capital to Caesarea, to protect him from his enemies (23:12-31). The letter that the commander wrote to Governor Felix is rather telling. Listen to part of that letter: 'Claudius Lysias, to his Excellency, Governor Felix... this man was seized by the Jews and they were about to kill him, but I came with my troops and rescued him, for I had learned that he is a Roman citizen' (23:26, 27). Did you notice the way that the facts have been kind of *massaged*? Lysias did not actually know that Paul was a Roman citizen at the time of saving him from the crowd. In fact he had put him in chains, had him stretched out, bound with ropes, and was about to have him whipped before he found out. But that is all conveniently left out of this letter to the Governor.

So we see the strengths and the failings of this particular Roman officer. Overall he saved Paul's life three times: from the crowd, from the Sanhedrin, and from the conspirators.

As you continue to read on, the Romans who meet Paul and who get to spend some time with him, actually grow to quite like him. Governor Felix seemed to like hearing him (but eventually got a bit scared of the message he was hearing - 24:24-25). Felix is certainly corrupt too, and that is mentioned in 24:26. So Luke is not whitewashing these men.

The next governor Festus is a bit of a smart-alec, and not all that likeable (25:9). However, when Paul is finally sent to Rome under the care of another Roman soldier, that particular soldier comes across really well. Paul was, 'handed over to a centurion named Julius, who belonged to the Imperial Regiment' (27:1). Julius would go to great lengths to look after and protect Paul. 'Julius, in kindness to Paul, allowed him to go to his friends so that they might provide for his needs' (27:3). When the shipwreck was happening, the normal course of action would be to kill all prisoners, so that none would escape during the turmoil of the ship wreck. If any escaped, the guards would be held accountable and punished. But when Julius' men planned to do just that, 'the centurion wanted to spare Paul's life and kept them from carrying out their plan' (27:43).

By the end of the Book of Acts, we have met quite a few soldiers and other Roman officials. When all is said and done, they get a pretty good rap. Not perfect by any means but not ruthless and cruel, nor lacking in humanity. This is unusual and not really to be expected of non-Roman writings coming from that period. It all adds a degree of credibility to the whole account. You get a feeling that Luke is trying hard to be impartial and record things accurately. Remember that this book is in all likelihood written to a Christian individual and secondly to the church. It was not a cynical attempt to influence the outcome of any court case. It was not a document for the courts. It was heading to the church via the person it was addressed to. The author is telling us what happened. Part of the story was that there were some decent Roman soldiers who actually helped protect and care for Paul at times, even if Paul would eventually be killed by the Roman system.

We can have confidence that the text is an honest attempt to be accurate. Luke is not hoodwinking us to believe a lot of myths and nonsense. He is not chuckling with some fellow conspirators at the gullibility of his future readers. Like he said in the introduction of the Gospel he wrote, I am writing this after 'carefully investigating everything'(Luke 1:3) 'so that you might know the certainty of the things you have been taught' (Luke 1:4).

Reading:
Revelation 13:1-18.

Asking the hard questions:
Many commentators see the Roman Empire being alluded to in numerous places in the Book of Revelation. The fall of 'Babylon' in Revelation 18 is particularly seen as a prophecy of the fall of Rome (Simon Peter the apostle called Rome 'Babylon' in 1 Peter 5:13). So is Revelation 13, with the beast with seven heads (v. 2). Rome sat on seven hills.

So then, if Revelation 13 actually is about Rome and its persecution of the church (vs. 8-10), how is it still relevant to us today? How can we get something from that message that we can apply to our lives?

ACTS 23

Read Acts 23 before reflecting on study 53

53) Acts 23:12, 13. An oath to commit murder

During the first few days after the arrest of Paul, there is one other thing I would like to highlight.

After Paul had been nearly killed in the street, and after the Sanhedrin had nearly 'torn him apart', there is then a third attempt on Paul's life. A conspiracy is hatched. A plan is devised and a plot is decided on. The plan was to get Paul into a vulnerable situation so he could be killed.

Some very determined men wanted Paul dead. A lot of them, it seems. Forty men decided to fast until they killed Paul, and they sealed that plan with an oath.

The Jews back then had a strong connection between religious zeal and violence. Their not-so-distant history (before Rome dominated Palestine) had been a time of independence where their own people ruled them for about a century. That self-rule had been won only after long and bitter guerrilla warfare. A family of religious Jews (known as 'the Maccabees') led the rebel army to free themselves from their Syrian overlords back then—and they won. The combination of deeply religious fervour with a willingness to use violence to attack a dominating overlord, proved to be a mixed blessing. It would be an inspiration for future generations of Jews who wanted to be rid of Roman domination. But it would ultimately lead to their destruction, as the Romans massacred many, destroyed their precious Temple, and sent them packing from their Holy City for nearly 2,000 years, in 70 A.D.

Put simply, for most of the Jews in Jesus' day and right up to the destruction of Jerusalem in 70 A.D., violence and religion were easy to weave together. There was no complex ethical debate about whether or not a good Jew could use violence for the sake of preserving their faith and culture. Christians would (or at least should) have trouble with that kind of marriage between religion and violence, but not so most Jews of first century Palestine.

One of the things that went hand in hand with acts of violence was 'oath-taking'. Here in this story in Acts, we see forty men seal their commitment to kill Paul (no doubt believing they were doing God a favour) with an oath.

In other ancient writings we see the same kind of thing. Josephus, for example, mentions the fact that early zealots used oaths to crystallise and deepen commitment to their cause. Josephus' *Antiquities* 15. 8.3-4: 'Ten men that were citizens [of Jerusalem] conspired together against Herod and swore to one another to undergo any dangers in the attempt, and took daggers with them under their garments for the purpose of killing Herod. … and this resolution they took, even if they should die for it.'[40]

Oaths were used for many things, but they were often linked to violence.

Oaths were meant to be kept. Paul Minear has explored the importance of oaths in the ancient world. He points out that the oral-aural culture of Palestine considered oaths in a totally different way to people from cultures like our own.[41] Oaths were deeply significant and revealed much about the character of the person making them. To the good Jew of the first century, 'Any dishonest word (even when supported by an oath) discloses an atheistic view of the self and world.'[42] Minear states that speech was 'the test of inner integrity, and every instance of deceitful speech receives condemnation.'[43] The imperatives concerning oaths are imperatives demanding absolute honesty. If you sealed a commitment with an oath, you were not going to back out of it.

As noted above, oaths were used for lots of things. Not *just* acts of violence. But I do wonder if the all too common connection between violence and oaths might have been one of the reasons why both Jesus and James were so hostile to Christians making oaths.

In the Sermon on the Mount, Jesus told us,

> Again you have heard that is was said to the people long ago, 'Do not break your oath but fulfil to the Lord the vows you have made.' But I tell you do not swear an oath at all: either by heaven for it is God's throne; or by the earth for

---

40 Josephus' *Antiquities* 15. 8.3-4. In Josephus *Antiquities* 15.10.4 we also see how binding oaths were.
41 P.S. Minear, 'Yes or No, the Demand for Honesty in the Early Church,' *Novum Testamentum* 13 (1971):12-13.
42 Minear, p. 12.
43 Minear, p. 8.

it is his footstool; or by Jerusalem, for it is the city of the Great King. And do not swear by your head, for you cannot make even one hair white or black. All you need to say is simply 'Yes' or 'No: anything beyond this comes from the evil one. (Matthew 5:33-37).

That teaching is *immediately* followed by a teaching on *non-violence*; no more eye for eye and tooth for tooth any more, but turn the other cheek, and in fact, love your enemies now as well (Matthew 5:38-48).

Likewise, James says something very similar after a letter full of exhortations to abandon the ways of the world, and to abandon the use of violence (e.g.: 1:27; 2:11; 3:13-18; 4:1-10): 'But above all, my brothers and sisters, do not swear – not by heaven or by earth or with anything else. All you need to say is a simple "yes" or "no". Otherwise you will be condemned' (5:12). James is essentially saying, 'Look, I have made a lot of important points so far, but above all, to sum it up and to bring it to a conclusion, don't make oaths!' It seems to me that he is seeing a link between oaths and acts of violence as well. Just as Jesus seemed to in the lining up of his teachings on not taking oaths, with teaching about not being violent, in the Sermon on the Mount.

Oaths are a dumb idea. Christians definitely should not be making them. Even more so if there is any link to acts of violence.

Reading:
Matthew 23:16-22.

Asking the hard questions:
Is it wrong for Christians to make oaths? What about being witnesses in a court case? Or becoming a JP and needing to make an oath of honesty? Or what about wedding vows? Is it *always* wrong to make oaths? In Matthew 23 Jesus seems to allow some kind of oaths, doesn't he? So how does he forbid them in Matthew 5?

Discuss that before weighing the following:

Matthew 23 is the chapter where Jesus is mocking the religious hypocrisy of the scribes and Pharisees. He gets stuck into them big time. He is not teaching his disciples (like he was with the Sermon on the Mount, for example). He is actually talking to people who have chosen *not* to follow him but to stay under the Old Covenant.

> There are eight different 'woe to you scribes and Pharisees, you hypocrites, because… [of some example of their hypocrisy]' (verses 13, 14, 15, 16, 23, 25, 27 and 29.) It is a dialogue that rips into their shallow legalism and utter inability to see their own failings. They think that they are so good at living out the Old Covenant. They think that they are so expert in living the way God wants them to. Jesus tears strips off them, and he does it a number of ways. One of them is highlighting their ridiculous laws and rules about which oaths are essential to keep and which oaths are not essential to keep. He is saying that, 'If you want to follow the law properly, then you should keep your oaths and not try to weasel out of them by some clever little rationale!'

Jesus is *not* actually saying this to his disciples. He is not teaching his followers that we should keep our oaths (He has already told us not to make them at all). Jesus here is talking to people dedicated to living under the Old Covenant and who pride themselves on doing it virtually perfectly. Jesus demonstrates that they do not do it correctly at all. 'If you really want to live under the laws of Moses and the Old Covenant then you would not be rationalising away your 'lesser' oaths. Your logic for such a rationale is pathetic and mistaken anyway! No, if you really want to live under the Old Covenant, keep your oaths!'

Does that explanation above help make sense of the apparent contradiction between what Jesus said in Matthew 5 and what he said in Matthew 23? Or is it unacceptable? Are there other ways to explain the two passages?

ACTS 24

Read Acts 24 before reflecting on study 54

54) Acts 24:27. Paul in prison in Caesarea

The Apostle Paul's prison time and trials get a lot of space in the Book of Acts. It can get a bit hard to follow and difficult to remember where you are if you are only reading a single chapter each time you have a devotion. But keep the big picture in mind. Paul was arrested in Jerusalem, was quickly sent to Caesarea to avoid a plot to kill him; he stayed in the prison there for over two years, and then finally, he was sent to Rome for trial.

Paul finally triggered the trial in Rome because, at the end of the two years of jail time in Caesarea, it looked like the new governor was going to do the Jews a favour at his expense. It looked as if Festus was going to have Paul sent back to Jerusalem to be tried there. Paul knew he had a very good chance of being assassinated if that was to occur. So he appealed his case to Rome.

I sometimes wonder why he did not try to 'speed things up a bit' by appealing to Rome a bit earlier. Why wait two years? Well, there are probably a few reasons for that.

Firstly, Paul hoped to persuade Governor Felix to release him. Initially, at least, this Roman governor seemed to listen to Paul. 'He used to send for Paul often and talk with him' (Acts 24:26). It became apparent to Paul after a while that Felix was actually just waiting for a bribe (24:26). Initially, however, Paul might have believed that despite that flaw in the governor's character, he could bring him around.

Secondly, by the time Paul realised he was not going to be released without paying a bribe, he might have concluded that it would be quicker to wait for a new governor. Under a different governor he might have had better results, rather than go to the lengthy and drawn-out process of appealing for a trial in Rome. Appealing to Rome would have meant travelling to Rome, awaiting the trial and then finding out the outcome. Governors were rotated with some regularity, and it was probably a shorter 'plan' to test the next governor than go the route of a trial in Rome.

Thirdly, once Paul had played his 'I appeal to Rome' card, there was no other option for him. If the trial in Rome went sour and he was found guilty, there were no more appeal options. That was the end of the road. He had to be absolutely desperate to use that final 'trump card' in his hand.

Therefore, he waited for the next governor. Sadly for Paul, that next governor, Festus, seemed less likely to help him than even Felix. He threatened to send him to Jerusalem for trial. Paul saw the reality of an imminent ambush by his enemies. He felt cornered now, so he played the last card in his hand. He appealed to Rome.

Paul had spent over two years in that jail cell in Caesarea, but his ordeal was only about half-way through. He would be off to Rome, and he would spend over two more years there, waiting his turn for a hearing before the Emperor.

Is there any lesson we can learn from this story of Paul's lengthy jail time?

It is interesting that Paul did not just get the church to pay Felix a bribe. The text seems to imply that such an act would have been rewarded with a positive outcome. However these early Christians did not play that game. The church could have called it 'a gift' – giving a gift to the local Roman authority for his good work and good governance. Or something like that! But no, they chose not to and that choice left the Apostle Paul languishing in jail for years.

Should they have paid the bribe? I know some Christians and some church organisations that would pay such 'a gift'. They pay similar gifts all the time in the country they are in, just to get things done. When I arrived in the Philippines many years ago (and lived there for 18 months) I would never have got my home computer out of customs, had I not paid 'a fee' to the people at the airport who handled the luggage. I tried to avoid it and I engaged a local agent to intercede for me. After a month of wrangling he said to me that unless I paid the 'fee', I would soon be charged storage for them holding the carton. I was later told that the local man I engaged to help me was probably working with the luggage handlers and they would have split the fee. Should I have just said 'no', even if it meant them confiscating my computer? I have a feeling Paul might have.

I have friends in Thailand who know that if they are pulled over by police for a so-called traffic offence they have to pay a 'fine' on the spot, in cash, without any paperwork, to be able to 'be on their way'. (Everyone on the roads over there seems to be committing traffic offences all the time, but white faces get pulled over because they are seen to have more cash on them. Indeed, most of them do have more cash on them than locals). If you don't pay the fine, you don't leave the spot until you do, or until the police get tired of waiting. But they don't seem to get tired; and there is always the concern that you might really annoy one of them by waiting, and that they might saddle you with other charges for the heck of it. So you pay the fine. Right? Would Paul have done that? Would Jesus? Maybe they would have. Jesus did say, 'Pay taxes to whom taxes are due', and he did so himself, even though tax collectors charged too much and pocketed much of it. What do you think?

There are some grey areas in all this, aren't there! How do we live a Christ-like life in an imperfect and corrupt world? It is a constant challenge.

Reading:
Exodus 23:8 and Proverbs 15:27.

Asking the hard questions:
Was I failing to live by higher principles by paying the fee to get my computer? Do missionaries in Thailand who pay a fine to the police in cash, with no receipt, fail in their personal walk of integrity? Are we caving in to corrupt structures? Should we make a stand? If so, how, and when? Should I have let my computer be confiscated if it came to that? If we don't resist corrupt structures in small ways when we personally encounter them, are we hypocrites for wanting 'someone to do something about unjust structures' in bigger ways?

On the other hand, is there a place for finding a working compromise in the short term while still working on the big issues in the long term? Consider how Paul told slaves to work hard for their masters, and for masters to treat their slaves well. It is not the ideal way of dealing with slavery (there should be no slavery) but it is a 'working middle path' for a season, perhaps. Discuss how that might or might not be acceptable, regarding unjust structures we are stuck in the middle of.

ACTS 25

Read Acts 25 before reflecting on study 55

55) Acts 25:13ff. A King meets an Apostle

Chapter 25 began with the new Governor Festus being a bit of a smart-alec and toying with Paul, suggesting that he might send him up to Jerusalem to be tried there (25:9). Paul felt cornered and played his final card; he appealed his case to the Emperor.

That took the Governor by surprise, but because Paul had made the appeal and because he was a Roman citizen, he would have to be sent to Rome.

Before Paul was shipped off, however, King Herod Agrippa and his partner Bernice, arrived in Caesarea to welcome the new Governor to his role (25:13).

Some people wonder what a King was doing in a Roman province that has a Governor. Why both? How was power shared? How did they divide the duties? If the Governor was answerable to Rome, who was the King answerable to?

The fact that Palestine had a King as well as a Governor was the result of the history of the area. You might recall in an earlier devotion, I mentioned that before the Romans took over Palestine, the Jews had 'run themselves' for about a century. The Maccabee family that led the original rebellion against the Syrians became a dynasty that ruled over Palestine. They were independent of foreign domination, but they were also quite ruthless.

As Rome grew in power, political intrigues between different descendants of the Maccabee family saw one faction make an alliance with Rome. They saw the growing Roman power over the Mediterranean Sea, and they decided to use it to their advantage. One of the 'players' was a man called Antipas, who had a son called Herod. When the 'game of thrones' finally settled, Herod was made a puppet king to serve Roman interests.

Herod had children, who had children, and the name 'Herod' became a title that each ruler took even though they still had their own names as well.

- The original Herod, 'Herod the Great', was put in his place by Rome, and he was the one who killed the babies in Bethlehem (Matthew 2:16).

- About 30 years later a different Herod, Herod Antipas, was responsible for the arrest and death of John the Baptist (Matthew 14:1-12). He also conducted one of Jesus' trials before sending him back to Pilate (Luke 23:6-11). Antipas was the son of Herod the Great and ruled from his father's death until 39 A.D.

- Still another Herod (Agrippa I) had James Zebedee killed in Acts 12. Agrippa I was the grandson of Herod the Great and the nephew of Antipas. He died in 44 A.D. (Acts 12:23).

- It was yet another Herod who would hear the Apostle Paul in Acts 25. Herod Agrippa II. Agrippa II was the son of Agrippa I. This second Agrippa would be the last of the Herodian Kings over Palestine.

There are other family members mentioned in various parts of the gospels, such as other sons of Herod the Great who shared some of the land of Palestine to rule (Archelaus is mentioned in Matthew 2:22; and Phillip, the first husband of Herodias, in Mark 6:17). The most important four that impacted the early church are noted above.

Marriages were often arranged in those days too. One of Herod Agrippa I's daughters, Drusilla, was married off to the previous governor Felix (Acts 24:24). Another daughter was Bernice, and she was now the 'partner' of her brother Agrippa II (Acts 25:13). All very sordid isn't it? It has a plot that leaves television soap operas for dead!

The Herod family was in power because of Rome. They were there to serve the interests of Rome. When Governors were also appointed, the Herods were expected to work hand in hand with them. They usually had an agreement about which part of Palestine the Governor looked after, and which part of the nation Herod looked after. (Herod Agrippa II, for example, was King over Galilee and some surrounding area.) It was clear that if any of the Kings messed up, Rome would intervene and change the situation. So they tended to be faithful servants of the hated Empire. For that, and other reasons, the Jewish people hated the Herod family.

The first Herod, (the Great), was on the scene for the start of the life of Jesus. A few generations would continue on and finally come to an end, at about the same time as the New Testament comes to an end. The Herod family was a century-long phenomenon—they came and went with the changing tides of history. Their story overlaps the story of the New Testament quite snugly. Indeed, it has been said more than once, that if Jesus had never come and Christianity had never happened, the Herod family would have been forgotten to history, a tiny footnote during the Roman period. The Herods were powerful in their day, in their own small piece of turf, but in the big scheme of things, they were a side show that intersected with Christianity a number of times.

In Acts 25 we see Herod Agrippa II meet the Apostle Paul. Luke devoted a disproportionately large amount of his scroll to Herod arriving, hearing about Paul from the Governor, desiring to listen to him, their actual meeting and Paul's speech to the King (25:13-26:32 – almost two chapters). That indicates how significant Luke saw this incident. Paul had already appealed to Rome. So it was not officially a 'trial', but it was a hearing, and a chance for Paul to witness before the King of the Jewish people. Matthew 10:18 was being fulfilled in this encounter. Jesus had said to his followers, 'You shall even be brought before governors and kings for my sake, as a witness to them and to the Gentiles'.

What is the main emphasis of this speech by Paul? When he had a chance to speak to the King over the Jewish people, what did he highlight? Again, we recognise that Luke is providing us with a summary, but we trust that the main points have been faithfully preserved. That being so, the main part of this speech is Paul's personal testimony. It is Paul retelling the story of his conversion on the road to Damascus. It also gives the reader a bit more of Paul's personal story, both before and after that conversion experience.

Clearly, the one thing this speech is *not* is some in-depth theology in a philosophical vacuum. Paul does talk theology; he begins by talking about belief in a God who raises people from the dead, and belief in a resurrection, and he ends by talking about the Prophets and Moses teaching that the Messiah must suffer. But when he talks theology, he *weaves* his theology *into* his testimony – it becomes a part of his story. This chapter becomes the third time now in the Book of Acts where Luke records the conversion of Paul.[44]

---

44   The first was when it happened on the road to Damascus in Chapter 9; the second was in Jerusalem to the angry crowd that wanted to tear him to pieces in chapter 22; and the third time is here in chapter 26 to Herod Agrippa II.

Even when the intelligent and insightful Apostle Paul got to speak to the King of the Jewish nation, he essentially used his testimony as the hook, to keep the king listening and to challenge him with the truth of the Gospel message. Never underestimate the power of personal testimony. It is the kind of message that convicts and can't be easily dismissed. It is not reasoning in a vacuum. It is real life.

'This happened to me. Let me share it with you!'

Reading:
John 9:1-34 (note especially v. 25).

Asking the hard questions:
Think of a time when you might have felt a bit dwarfed by cynics and other really smart people who could run rings around you with their logic and arguments?

When this man in John 9 is caught like that, what does he end up depending on to see him through? He can't answer their theological questions and their reasoned arguments. He tries a bit, but they are not going to be out-witted and out-reasoned by a man who had never even been to school!

In the end he relies on his encounter with Christ. Verse 25 captures his frustration and his anchor point. He was blind and Jesus made him see. Really, after that, all the clever arguments in the world don't undo the reality of that personal encounter.

How should this story encourage us? How has Jesus 'helped us to see, even though we used to be blind'?

ACTS 26

Read Acts 26 before reflecting on study 56

56) Acts 26:28. Agrippa's famous words

After the Apostle Paul finished sharing his story with the Governor and the King, the reactions of the different people who heard him are telling.

The Roman Governor Festus concluded that Paul had gone mad. 'You are out of your mind Paul! ...Your great learning is driving you insane!' (26:24). Paul immediately replied, 'I am not insane, most excellent Festus...what I am saying is true and reasonable. The king is familiar with these things and I can speak freely to him. I am convinced that none of this has escaped his notice, because it was not done in a corner. King Agrippa, do you believe the Prophets? I know you do!' (26:25-27).

Paul turned the mocking of Festus completely around, and shaped it into a challenge directed at the King. He could safely assume that the King of the Jews knew about the Prophets of Israel (in our Old Testament). The short statement of Paul about the Prophets and Moses teaching about the Christ suffering (26:22-23) was probably unpacked in some detail by Paul (It seems to have led to the comment by Festus that 'your great learning is driving you insane').

Paul's question to the King puts Herod on the spot.

The King gives a most telling reply. The things Paul had said, the testimony, the unpacking of some of the Old Testament material from the Prophets and Moses - it must have made some sense to the King. He replied with a most famous line, 'In a short time, you will persuade me to become a Christian!' (26:28 NASV).

Paul grabbed onto that remark, and replied, 'Short time or long - I pray to God, that not only you, but also all who are listening to me today may become what I am, except for these chains!' (26:29).

The King's reply has been much discussed and debated. It has been reworked and examined under the microscope of careful Greek exegesis. There is considerable debate about the exact wording. Some say the Greek is best translated as I have it above:

1) 'In a short time, you will persuade me to become a Christian!'

Others say it would be best translated as:

2) 'In a short time, you think to make me a Christian!'

Perhaps even as a question:

3) 'Do you think in just a short time, you can make me into a Christian?'

Another option, where the King sums up Paul's intent:

4) 'In short, you think you can make me into a Christian.' (Implication: you have to be kidding!)

If the correct translation is the first option above, it seems that Herod Agrippa II is impressed by Paul's speech and testimony and his use of Scripture and is even warm to his interpretation of things. If the correct translation is any of the other three options, the King is less impressed and a bit incredulous that Paul could even imagine that he might just convert the King with one speech.

Our impression of the King will be affected by the option we choose here.

Nevertheless, at the end of the day, the King (as far as we know) did not embrace the Christian faith. That is the sad reality of human beings, and is often the consequence of free will. We can hear the most wonderful story ever told. We can see a living example of a changed life, from persecuting the faith to being persecuted. We can hear the most convincing arguments from Scripture. However, we still might reject it for all sorts of other reasons: pride, customs, who we will offend, who we might alienate, what we might have to give up, and more. There can be so many things playing on us that stop us from embracing what we suspect might just be true.

Let us never be like the King. Let us not hover around the edges of embracing Jesus but never quite do it. Rather, let us make sure that we are fully committed to the cause. Be a determined Christ-follower. Be someone who will listen to *his* teaching and observe *his* example with the intent of imitating it as much as we can, in our own context today.

Reading:
Luke 9:57-62; 14:15-20.

Asking the hard questions:
What excuses do we make to 'not quite fully follow Jesus'? Surely not us! After all, we are committed Christians, right? We invited Jesus into our hearts years ago. But have we still got pockets of our life carefully guarded and kept from Jesus? Are there areas of pride, personal ambition or other selfish motives driving us? Are we putting off making certain changes to our lifestyle, with the excuse that 'it's not the right time'?

ACTS 27

Read Acts 27 before reflecting on study 57

57) Acts 27. Shipwreck and great danger

Paul was sent to Rome. In Acts 27, we see him being sent off in the custody of a Roman officer. He is under way as a prisoner of Rome. It was therefore an 'all expenses paid' trip for Paul, courtesy of the Empire. He had with him two travelling companions: Aristarchus from Thessalonica, and Luke (27:2). Luke is using the 'we' word again.

It is sometimes asked how a prisoner could have travelling companions. There are a couple of different answers offered to that question:

1. One suggestion is that the church, or the men themselves, paid their way to be on the same boat as Paul. That way they could minister to his needs as the journey proceeded.

2. Another suggestion is that perhaps Luke and Aristarchus made themselves slaves to Paul. Or one or the other might have. Since Paul was a Roman citizen, he would be permitted to take a slave (or two?) along to care for him on such a trip, at the Empire's expense again. Some go further and then add the other speculation that since Luke was a doctor (Colossians 4:14), he might have once been a slave, since often that job fell to a trusted household slave. If he had once been a slave, he might not have minded becoming Paul's slave here.

I tend to think the first suggestion has more credibility than the second. Even though the New Testament does not blatantly state that slavery is evil and should be abolished, it does indicate in many places that slavery is not ideal, and that 'if you gain your freedom, do so' (1 Corinthians 7:21). Paul's little letter to Philemon indicates that Paul expected Philemon to free the previous runaway slave, who was now a Christian brother, and who had returned to his original master (Philemon 21).

I can't see Paul opting to enslave one or two Christian brothers for the sake of saving a few pennies on a one-way sea trip to Rome. It could even be argued to be quite deceitful. I just can't see Paul proposing the following: 'Luke and Aristarchus, let's make you slaves for a while, and when we get to Rome I will free you again. That way we get the government to pay for your tickets to Rome! Clever hey!' It sounds a bit too unethical for the apostle to use that kind of reasoning.

Now it has to be admitted that Paul could and did accommodate imperfect social structures at times. He was born at a particular point in time, and there were some seriously unjust social structures around him. Indeed, it would have been on nobody's radar that one day slavery would be banned around the world. The deeply ingrained and unjust structures that were in existence were not of Paul's making. Paul always wanted people in those structures to live to higher principles than they legally had to (he called on slaves to work hard for their masters, and masters to love their slaves and treat them well, for example).

Working in the unjust system you find yourself in, and trying to improve the lot of people in it, is a long way away from encouraging people to be treated as second-class citizens and to actively support and use the unjust system for short-term financial advantage.

So Paul was on his way to Rome, and the church made sure that at least a couple of his brethren went with him.

What we get next is a detailed description of a shipwreck by someone who was on the boat during it.

Initially, before the big storm, Paul had a bad feeling about the weather. He said to the Roman officer and others, 'Men, I can see that our voyage is going to be disastrous and bring great loss to ship and cargo, and to our own lives also.' (v. 10). This pessimistic outlook was 'revised down' about a week later, after an angel of God visited Paul. After a number of days of darkness from the thick storm clouds, and the growing dismay of all on board because of the beating the ship was taking, Paul spoke again. He said,

> …keep up your courage because not one of you will be lost; only the ship will be destroyed. Last night an angel of the God to whom I belong and whom I serve, stood before me, and said, 'Do not be afraid Paul. You must stand

trial before Caesar; and God has graciously given you the lives of all who sail with you'. So keep up your courage men, for I have faith in God that it will happen just as he told me. Nevertheless, we must run aground on some island. (27:22-26).

I wonder why Paul first said that he could see that this trip would end with loss of life, and then changed it to no loss of life after the visit by the angel? Did he just kind of guess the first prediction? Was it just his gut feeling? The text does not say (of the first prediction) that it was a word from the Spirit, or that God had appeared to him and told him so. Clearly the second prediction was of that more dynamic origin.

Maybe Paul did have a gut feeling that *was* from the Spirit when he gave the first prediction, and it drove him to *prayer*. Perhaps his intercession worked. God responded to the prayers of Paul and agreed to save all the people on board the ship (Abraham had done something many, many centuries earlier when he interceded for Lot and his family in Sodom).

Either way, all 276 persons on board (27:37) survived the shipwreck and scrambled to safely reach the island of Malta (27:43 - 28:1).

One of the biggest lessons that we can learn from this story of the shipwreck is the lesson of staying calm during a crisis. Paul was the only clear-headed and fearless person on the boat. When everyone else was losing hope and falling into despair, Paul gave them leadership, inspiration, and purpose.

Christians who want to be useful in this troubled world need to stay untroubled in their own inner self. Christians who want to tackle the world's big 'storms', need to have a quiet confidence that God is with them during *their* storms, and the certainty of who God is, and his promises, is the anchor of their souls (Hebrews 6:19). They need to be confident that nothing will come their way that God is not permitting. Christians who want to do something meaningful with their lives need to be able to stand tall when all others around them are panicking, like captains on a ship bound for rough weather. They need to be able to offer wise words of advice and a good example in times of despair.

Paul does that in this story. Our stories might require it of us some day too.

Reading:
Isaiah 41:10 and 1 Peter 5:7.

Asking the hard questions:
Are we as calm as Paul was when disasters come our way? When scary things are happening? If our world seems to be crashing in on us? When we have our metaphorical shipwrecks? Or do we fall into a heap and lose our cool? Do we whine to God? Or do we pray expectantly, knowing he is with us?

How can we do this better? How can we really learn to be peaceful and trusting – leaving it with God?

ACTS 28

Read Acts 28 before reflecting on studies 58, 59 and 60

58) Acts 28:1-5. Do bad things only happen to bad people?

There is a lovely short story at the start of chapter 28. The shipwreck survivors had safely reached land—all 276 of them. They had landed in Malta. They were wet and cold. There were groups of people huddled around fires on the beach. Paul was helping collect fire wood. As he laid out the wood he had collected, he was bitten by a poisonous snake (v. 3). The locals superstitiously decided that, 'Undoubtedly he is a murderer, and though he has been saved from the sea, the goddess Justice has not allowed him to live' (v. 4). The text goes on to show just how wrong that simplistic conclusion was; 'But Paul shook the snake off into the fire and suffered no ill effects. The people expected him to swell up or suddenly fall down dead; but after waiting a long time, and seeing nothing unusual happen to him, they changed their minds and said he was a god' (28:5, 6).

You know, when you read a story like that, you would think it really reminds us never to assume that someone's misfortune is caused by their personal sin. Wouldn't you?

Paul had been bitten by a deadly snake. The locals knew their snakes and they knew this one was fatal. They expected Paul to swell up and drop dead. They would have tragically seen it happen to some of their own people at times. So when Paul was bitten, they concluded that he must have done something very bad ('surely he was a murderer!') and justice was now being done to him. In fact the shipwreck was probably designed by the gods to drown such a bad man, but since he managed to survive that – well, now there is a poisonous snake sent to finish him off!

I have known too many Christians over the centuries who have tried to preach this kind of 'karma' message. You know: you get what you deserve, in this life, here and now.

Well, sorry to burst the bubble here, but the reality is that you don't. Some evil people get a pretty good long prosperous life and some really decent loving people have all manner of hardship. In fact, sometimes, the hardships make people more decent and more loving. There is no superstitious karma rule happening to us.

Part of the 'sub-Christian belief' in karma for the here-and-now is linked to verses in other parts of the Bible that are used badly and made to apply to false conclusions. But, to be fair, there are some other verses that lend themselves a bit to the karma idea. The famous 'sowing and reaping' verses are a classic example. In Galatians 6:7-9 we read, 'Do not be deceived, God cannot be mocked. A person reaps what they sow. Whoever sows to please their flesh, from the flesh will reap destruction. Whoever sows to please the Spirit, will from the Spirit reap eternal life. Let us not become weary in doing good, for in the proper time we shall reap a harvest, if we do not give up.'

If you just take out the phrase 'that which you sow, you reap' then you can pretend that it must always be applied to the here-and-now. If however, you read it in its context, it is calling on Christians to continue to sow good deeds in the world, knowing that they will reap 'eternal life'! Our rewards will come mostly *after* this earthly life 'in the proper time'.

Jesus himself made it clear when he said, 'God causes his sun to rise on the evil and the good, and sends rain on the righteous and the unrighteous' (Matthew 5:45). He also said on another occasion (when someone mentioned to him the tragic fact that Pilate had a number of Galileans killed while they were sacrificing),

Do you suppose that these Galileans were greater sinners than all other Galileans, because they suffered this fate? I tell you, no! But, unless you repent, you will all likewise perish. Or do you suppose that those eighteen on whom the tower in Siloam fell, and killed them, were worse culprits than all the others living in Jerusalem? I tell you, no! But unless you repent, you will all likewise perish (Luke 13:1-5).

Jesus uses the questions about fate and 'apparent punishment' to dispel the superstition that bad things only happen to bad people. He is definitely rebutting the idea that you get what you deserve *in this life*. He links that longer discussion into a warning about the impending war with Rome that was still about 35 years off, but in so doing, he reminds people that tragedy and accidents happen. They happen to people who are simply in the 'wrong place at the wrong time'.

When Paul was bitten by a poisonous snake and the locals thought he would die for his sins, they were wrong. Interestingly Paul *had been* 'a murderer' in his earlier days (before his conversion). He *had* helped kill Stephen and many others during the early persecution of Christians, but he was not being bitten by that snake that day because of those past sins. He had been *forgiven*, *restored* and *set on a new path* that would glorify God and bless many others.

There is no 'here-and-now law of karma' for Christ-followers. Our destiny is in God's hands. Good and bad might come our way, but like Paul said on another occasion, 'I know what it is to be in need and I know what it is to have plenty. I have learned the secret of being content in any and every situation, whether well fed or hungry, whether living in plenty or in want. I can do all this through him who gives me strength' (Philippians 4:12, 13).

Reading:

Job 1:1-22 and Matthew 10:16.

Asking the hard questions:

Why are we so easily taken in by sweet-sounding doctrines and teachings like the simplistic sowing and reaping one? Are we 'wired' to look for easy doctrines and self-gratifying beliefs? You know - nonsense like: 'If I am good now, I will get lots of goodies from God. If I am bad now, I will get punished by God!' Clearly this is not Job's story. Nor that of many Christians persecuted all throughout history. What makes so many Christians react in such simplistic and naïve ways? Consider and discuss how Jesus told his followers (in Matthew 10:16) to be as 'wise as a serpent but as innocent as a dove'. What does that *look like*?

Doesn't that teaching of Jesus mean we are meant to be both *'smart* and *godly'*? Why is it that all too often we are about as wise as doves, and as innocent as serpents (dumb and not so godly)?

59) Acts 28:1-9. Miraculous healings and/or medicinal aid?

The story of Paul and the snake-bite continues. After the miracle of Paul surviving the poison, we see a wonderful sequel. The leading man of the island was Publius and he welcomed the stranded company of shipwreck-ees. He seems to have particularly welcomed Paul and his companions, Luke and Aristarchus. 'Publius welcomed us to his home and showed us generous hospitality for three days' (28:7). Luke then adds,

> It came about that the father of Publius was lying in bed afflicted with recurrent fever and dysentery, and Paul went in to see him, and after he had prayed, he laid his hands on him and healed him. And after this had happened, the rest of the people on the island who had diseases were coming to him and getting cured. And they also honoured us with many marks of respect, and when we were setting sail, they supplied us with all we needed. (28:8-10)

Sometimes the above is interpreted as: surviving the poisonous snake – miracle number 1; Publius' father healed from dysentery – miracle number 2; lots of people getting cured – miracles 3, 4, 5, etc.

Actually, there might just be a different way of looking at the curing of lots of islanders.

Don't get me wrong. I believe in a God who can and does do miracles whenever he so chooses. I think the snake-bite and the healing of Publius' father were miracles from God. However, I actually think that the summary statement about lots of folk coming to be cured is about Luke the doctor using his skills and knowledge to assist people with various issues and problems.

The reason I say that is because of the different Greek words used in this paragraph. When Publius' father is *healed*, the word is *iasato*. That word is usually used elsewhere in the New Testament when a healing miracle happens. When the others on the island come to be cured, however, the word used there is *etherapeuonto*. That word is usually used to refer to the application of medical help or rendering assistance.

If you look closely at the longer Greek word, you will even see in the word the letters 'therape'. Later, people decided to adapt that Greek word and make an English word out of it, a word for the application of *therapy*. That does not mean the ancient meaning was exactly our understanding of 'therapy', but it does (in this particular case) remind us that it points in that direction.

So what we have here is actually miracles and medicine happening hand in hand. Paul and Luke are a team. One prays and lays hands and sees miraculous healings at times, and the other uses his training and skills and knowledge to help with healings as well.

There was no conflict in this for Paul. It is not a 'lack of faith' to use medicine as well as pray. The two should go hand in hand for us, just as they did for Paul back then.

The lesson is obvious isn't it? Don't let extremists try to put a guilt trip on you if you use medicine or visit a doctor. Don't be hoodwinked by the naïve and simplistic to think that healing from God and the use of medicine are somehow an 'either/or'. Not so. They can be a 'both/and'.

If it is unspiritual to use medicine (as well as pray and trust God) then Paul was very unspiritual here in Acts 28. For an 'unspiritual man', he sure does get used by God to do some amazing spiritual things!

Reading:
1 Corinthians 12:4-11; 12:28.

Asking the hard questions:
Why is it sometimes so difficult to really accept others who have a different emphasis to ourselves? Who have a different ministry? A different part to play? Do we fall into either of these two extreme positions?

1) Being jealous of someone else's gift

or

2) Thinking that their gift is not really all that important

Paul and Luke seem to have gotten on well. Luke could have thought, 'Paul is used by God to do miracles, and all I do is apply poultices and do basic first aid!' But Luke did not think like that.

How hard is it to actually be happy with the 'part we are in the Body of Christ'?

The ministries of James and Paul had different emphases: James lived and worked with Jewish Christians in Jerusalem, whereas Paul had a ministry to the Gentiles. Would it have been hard for them to accept each other's ministry emphasis?

How gracious and tolerant are you towards others with a different emphasis to your own?

60) Acts 28:30-31. Paul in Rome

The Book of Acts ends with Paul reaching Rome. He is not visiting there as a wandering missionary, doing some tent-making on the side, preaching in the streets. He did not arrive there as a free man able to maintain his own schedule. He arrived as a prisoner of Rome.

Paul had wanted to go to Rome for a long time. He had said as much to the Roman church when he wrote to them from Greece some years earlier (Romans 1:10-13). When he wrote to them he probably had no idea just *how* he would end up in Rome.

Clearly there was no really serious charge against him. Herod Agrippa and Festus had concluded that much back in Caesarea (Acts 26:32). The Roman soldier in charge of Paul had grown to appreciate him and he clearly trusted him enough to allow him some limited freedoms as a prisoner. 'Paul was allowed to live by himself with a soldier to guard him' (28:16). It seems to be some kind of house imprisonment with limited rights of entertaining visitors. He was allowed to call together a meeting of the elders of the Jewish community in his new home there and they came and listened to him (28:17-23).

Paul would stay a prisoner of Rome awaiting trial for over two years. 'He stayed two full years in his own rented quarters, and was welcoming all who came to him, preaching the kingdom of God, and teaching concerning the Lord Jesus Christ with all openness, unhindered' (28:30-31).

With those words, Luke completed his scroll. The Book of Acts comes to an end.

Paul was under house arrest for at least two years, perhaps a bit longer. It must have been both frustrating and a blessing. He could speak to anyone who came to him, but it seems he could not go out and just randomly begin preaching in the streets. He did preach the gospel unhindered, but it does not seem to mean unhindered in movement. It seemed to be more unhindered in message.

The two years or more that Paul spent in Rome are also seen to be the time period when we believe he wrote a number of his smaller letters; in particular Ephesians, Colossians and Philemon.[45] As far as those three letters go, there are some very strong links between the three letters that compel most Bible scholars to see them being

---

45   A lot of scholars add Philippians as well.

written around the same time and sent to the same general location in Asia Minor.

What links both Ephesians and Colossians is the *content*. Some parts are almost word-for-word identical, indicating that he probably completed one of those letters and then used a part of it for the other letter. If you compare especially Ephesians 5:21-6:9 with Colossians 3:18-4:1 you will see what I mean.

What links Philemon to these letters is essentially *the list of names* of who is with Paul at the time of writing. Compare Colossians 4:7-18 with Philemon vs. 1, 10 and 23. You will see how similar the cast is! Ephesians, even though it does not have any personal greetings, mentions Tychicus as being with Paul (Ephesians 6:21). The same Tychicus is with Paul in Colossians 4:7 as well. In both cases, Paul talks about how Tychicus will bring them news when he gets to them. In all probability it was Tychicus who would have carried the letters with him and delivered them for Paul to their respective destinations (That would also explain why Tychicus is not named in Philemon as sending his greeting to Philemon; he would have been there in person with Philemon and so it was not necessary to put that into the letter).

The three little letters of Ephesians, Colossians and Philemon are beautiful treasures from the pen of Paul. Ephesians has sometimes been called the masterpiece that describes the church (Ecclesiology); Colossians the amazing piece that describes Christ (Christology); and Philemon, the small diamond that points to how love conquers social distinctions and man-made human barriers (Ethics). Each letter is not just on these single issues of course, but they do have significant things to contribute in those areas.

You know, there is no excuse to be idle in Christ. Even if you are in *jail* there is still something you can do. Even if you are being hassled and persecuted, there are things you can get done. Who would have thought that the writings of a Jewish Pharisee, who joined a despised sect in the first century, would have become best-sellers and read by millions and millions of people all throughout history?

You never know the impact you will have. You should never underestimate the ripple effect your actions and words and achievements will cause. Whatever your situation, whatever your circumstances – God will still work with you, and through you, and be with you always.

Reading:
1 Corinthians 10:31.

Asking the hard questions:
Is it hard at times to see something worthwhile in the things you are doing? The place where you are working? The job you do day after day? Does it seem so far detached from your faith and your love for God that it is more a waste of time? Do you live for the 'other time slots' in your week? Do you hang out for the church service or the prayer meeting, or the home group or the youth group?

How can you make the most of every moment and every different thing that makes up your life?

Acts has ended, but what did happen to Paul?

Acts has ended, and we still do not know the outcome of Paul's court case. It started back in chapter 21 with his arrest in Jerusalem, and it has travelled about five years since, but we still are not told what actually happened to him.

So what *did* happen to him? To answer that we have to lean on church history and traditions, and try to piece together what evidence we have. That evidence also includes the letters Paul wrote after the end of the Book of Acts, even though there is considerable debate about the authorship of three of them.

When we piece it all together this seems to be the best explanation:

Paul was released from prison after his hearing before the Emperor. Acts 28 ends about 61 or 62 A.D. and at that point, Nero is not particularly interested in hurting the church. Not yet. So, for a number of reasons, we tend to think Paul would have been released. Say, about 62 A.D.

After his release he travelled some more, wrote some more, and ministered some more. He probably wrote 1 Timothy and Titus during the next year or two. There is a lot of debate over whether or not he actually wrote those two letters, or if a later disciple and admirer of Paul wrote them. On the assumption that Paul did write them, then he would have done so during this period of time. Paul might even have travelled as far as Spain, even if he did not stay there long (He had written to the Roman church that he wanted to go to Spain from Rome – see Romans 15:23, 24).

At some point Paul was re-arrested. That should come as no surprise; he often got arrested, but here is where it gets very blurry. The great fire of Rome was in 64, and it seems that in early to mid-65 Nero decided to blame the Christians for the fire and have many of them killed. As far as Paul's final arrest and death are concerned there seem to be three main possibilities:

1) He might have been re-arrested somewhere else in the empire (before Nero began his persecution of Christians in Rome). His plight might have been so serious that he was looking at possible death. So he quite likely appealed to Rome, just as he did the first time. If so, he would have then been transferred to Rome to be held again, until he could be tried. He would have already been in a Roman jail, awaiting trial, when the persecution began (Bad timing!).

2) Or he might have gone to Rome about 64 A.D., before the persecution of Christians, for whatever reasons. He would, therefore, have been in the city when Nero decided to blame the fire of Rome on the church community. That triggered a huge rounding-up of Christians in Rome for execution. He would have been arrested along with many others.

3) Or when Paul heard of the start of the persecution of the Christians in Rome, he felt compelled to visit the afflicted church to try to encourage the brothers and sisters there. Sadly, if that happened, he then found himself getting arrested and killed as well.

Regardless of which of these scenarios is correct about how Paul's second imprisonment came about, the reality is that Paul was in Rome, in prison, under Nero. It was during this final imprisonment that Paul wrote (I would suggest[46]) Philippians, and then a few months later, 2 Timothy (if he wrote that letter— it is highly disputed).

Philippians has a stench of death permeating the pages; the author knows he is going to die; likewise 2 Timothy. Philippians has some other interesting parallels with 2 Timothy as well.

The first parallel is the use of a very unusual metaphor only shared between these two letters: 'But even if I am being poured out as a drink offering upon the sacrifice and service of your faith, I rejoice and share my joy with you all' (Philippians 2:17), and 'For I am already being poured out as a drink offering, and the time of my departure has come' (2 Timothy 4:6).

The second parallel between them is a frustrating disappointment with most of his co-workers: 'I have no one else of kindred spirit who will genuinely be concerned for your welfare. For they all seek their own interests, not those of Jesus Christ' (Philippians 2:20-21), and, 'For Demas, having loved this present world, has deserted me and gone to Thessalonica; Crescens has gone to Galatia, Titus to Dalmatia. Only Luke is with me…At my first defence no one came to my support, but everyone deserted me. May it not be held against them!' (2 Timothy 4:10-11, 16).

Just as we have surviving letters from the pen of Paul from his first Roman imprisonment, so too in this second Roman imprisonment do we have his words. Philippians has in it some of the most wonderful gems to be found in the New Testament. It is a letter that looks death in the face, and is still filled with joy and peace! It has brought those two things (joy and peace) to many a person over the centuries. 2 Timothy gives us a glimpse into the heart of Paul himself. He pines to see his spiritual son again before he dies. It is a heartfelt personal letter to his dear friend Timothy.

---

46 See: Jim Reiher, 'Could Philippians have been written from the *Second* Roman Imprisonment?' *Evangelical Quarterly*. Vol. LXXXIV. No. 3 July 2012. pp.213-233.

So it comes, Paul's death—the close of his earthly ministry. He was not the only Christian killed by Nero, of course. Many church members were slaughtered in cruel ways by that Emperor. The Roman historian Tacitus tells us that Nero delighted in the creative ways he killed these people. Some were wrapped in animal skins and fed to starving animals, others were tied to the tops of poles and set on fire to light up Nero's gardens by night.

During this time both the Apostle Peter and the Apostle Paul were executed. Peter is believed to have been crucified upside down. Paul was said to have been beheaded.

Beheading is a quicker death than crucifixion, of course. Paul was afforded that small blessing because he was a Roman citizen. Depending on how sharp the executioner's sword was, it might take anywhere from one to six blows of the sword to cut the head from the neck.

So ends the story of Paul. What a complex and incredible life. What an impact he had! What an impact he continues to have!

And we have also come to the end of the Book of Acts. The book was more than the life and work of Paul, of course, but that important topic did fill about half the volume. Luke has finished his masterpiece. He was probably finishing off his manuscript during the end of the two years of open imprisonment, since we do not get any mention of what happened after that.

If 2 Timothy is indeed Paul's letter, written from the second Roman imprisonment, then we see that Luke was a faithful and courageous co-worker who stayed with Paul till the very end. His personal story is hardly seen, and his ongoing work as part of Paul's ministry team, is not highlighted. But what a man he must have been! To stay with Paul as Christians were being rounded up and arrested; tried and killed – to not 'desert Paul' like so many others did… Luke is quite the example of encouragement and perseverance. May we be as faithful to God's work, and God's people!

Index of characters in Acts, mentioned in this commentary

The numbers after the name refer to the **devotion** number the person is mentioned in.

Agabus the prophet – 51;

Agrippa I – see Herod Agrippa I;

Agrippa II – see Herod Agrippa II;

Alexander of Ephesus – 46;

Ananias and Sapphira – 11;

Ananias of Damascus – 20;

Apollos – 42;

Aquila, husband of Prisca – see Priscilla and Aquila;

Aristarchus of Ephesus – 46; 57;

Bar-Jesus of Salamis – 29;

Barnabas – 24; 29; 31; 33;

Bernice – Insert after 51; 55;

Cornelius – 22; 23; 52;

Crispus of Corinth – 44;

Demetrius, a silversmith of Ephesus – 46;

Drusilla, daughter of Herod Agrippa I – 55;

Eutychus – 48;

Felix, Governor – Insert after 51; 52; 54; 55;

Festus, Governor – Insert after 51; 52; 54; 55; 56;

Gaius of Ephesus – 46;

Gallio, proconsul of Achaia – 44; 52;

Gamaliel – 13;

Herod Agrippa I – 25; 55;

Herod Agrippa II – Insert after 51; 55; 56;

Jailer (not named) in Philippi – 38; 39;

James the brother of Jesus – 28; 32; 53;

James Zebedee – 25;

John Mark – 26; 27; 29; 33;

John Zebedee – 7; 12;

Julius, Centurion – 52; 57;

Luke – Introduction; 35; 52; 57; 58;

Lydia – 36;

Lysias, army commander in Jerusalem – 52; 53;

Mark – see John Mark;

Mary of Jerusalem, the mother of John Mark – 26; 27;

Paul – Introduction; Inserts after 19; 28; 44; 51; and 60; His writings 47; etc: too many to list;

Peter (see Simon Peter);

Philip the deacon/evangelist - 14; 19; 51;

Priscilla (Prisca) and Aquila – 42; 43;

Publius, leading man of Malta – 59;

Rhoda, the servant of Mary in Jerusalem – 27;

Sapphira and Ananias – 5;

Sergius Paulus, proconsul – 29; 52;

Silas – 29; 34; 38; 39; 43; 52;

Simon Peter – 3; 7; 8; 9; 10; 11; 12; 19; 21; 22; 23; 25; 26; 27; 28; 39; Insert after 60;

Simon of Samaria, the magician – 19;

Simon the Tanner of Joppa – 21;

Sosthenes of Corinth – 44;

Stephen the deacon – 14; 16; 17; 18;

Theophilus – 1;

Timothy – 34; 43;

Tychicus – 60;

Jim Reiher

Since finishing high school in the 1970's, Jim has been an ambulance officer in NSW; a high school teacher; and a Theology lecturer. From 2007 till 2012, Jim worked for Urban Neighbors of Hope (UNOH) based in Springvale, Noble Park and Dandenong. Jim was overseeing the training programs for UNOH. He currently works as a regional support manager for school chaplains in Melbourne.

Jim is an avid writer. In Nov 2005, UNOH published his book *The Eye of the Needle: Discipleship and Wealth*. In 2006, Acorn Press published his *Women, Leadership and the Church*. And in 2009 UNOH Publications put out Jim's social justice commentary on the epistle of James: *James: Peace Activist and Advocate for the Poor*. His first novel *The Sunburnt Circus* came out this year as well.

Jim has a Bachelor of Arts, with a double major in History, a Diploma in Education, and a Masters in Theology with Honors. Jim helped establish a multi-faith network of members of different faith communities in the city of Casey during 2006. That group is now up and running and Jim served as the first President of the Casey Multi-faith Network during 2007 and again more recently. Besides spending time with family (he has 4 adult children and 11 grandchildren), Jim also likes to go to the beach, go bush, get in a game of tenpin bowling, or watch a good movie.

In recent years Jim has been getting some journal articles accepted and published after peer review, including: "Violent Language – a clue to the Historical Occasion of James." Evangelical Quarterly. Vol. LXXXV No. 3. July 2013; "Could Philippians have been written from the Second Roman Imprisonment?" Evangelical Quarterly. Vol. LXXXIV. No. 3 July 2012. pp.213-233; and "Galatians 3:28: liberating for women, or of limited application?" Expository Times. (123.6) pp. 272-277. March 2012.